Vygotskian Perspectives on Literacy Research

The authors in this collection use Vygotsky's cultural-historical theory of human development to frame their analyses of schooling, with particular emphasis on the ways in which literacy practices are mediated by social interaction and cultural artifacts. This volume extends Vygotsky's cultural-historical theoretical framework to embrace nuances of learning and development that are influenced by culture as instantiated through the experiences of race, ethnicity, and language variation. Rather than seeking to provide definitive answers to social questions using Vygotsky's core principles, the authors wrestle with educational problems through the mediation of Vygotsky's theory. In doing so, they both sharpen their focus on the problems and speak back to Vygotsky, helping to extend the foundation of his work to address modern problems. This collection serves as a form of collaborative inquiry that itself will stimulate further consideration of these topics and further learning with Vygotsky about the ways in which individuals and social groups inquire and learn.

Carol D. Lee is Associate Professor of Education and Social Policy at the School of Education and Social Policy, Northwestern University.

Peter Smagorinsky is Associate Professor of English Education at the University of Georgia.

Learning in Doing: Social, Cognitive, and Computational Perspectives

General Editors
ROY PEA, *SRI International, Center for Technology in Learning*
JOHN SEELY BROWN, *Xerox Palo Alto Research Center*

Vygotskian Perspectives on Literacy Research

Constructing Meaning through Collaborative Inquiry

Edited by

CAROL D. LEE
Northwestern University

PETER SMAGORINSKY
University of Georgia

CAMBRIDGE
UNIVERSITY PRESS

PUBLISHED BY THE PRESS SYNDICATE OF THE UNIVERSITY OF CAMBRIDGE
The Pitt Building, Trumpington Street, Cambridge, United Kingdom

CAMBRIDGE UNIVERSITY PRESS
The Edinburgh Building, Cambridge CB2 2RU, UK   http://www.cup.cam.ac.uk
40 West 20th Street, New York, NY 10011-4211, USA   http://www.cup.org
10 Stamford Road, Oakleigh, Melbourne 3166, Australia
Ruiz de Alarcón 13, 28014 Madrid, Spain

First published 2000

Printed in the United States of America

Typeface Janson Text 10.25/13pt   *System* LaTeX 2$_\varepsilon$ [TB]

A catalog record for this book is available from the British Library.

Library of Congress Cataloging-in-Publication Data
Vygotskian perspectives on literacy research : constructing meaning
through collaborative inquiry / edited by Carol D. Lee, Peter
Smagorinsky.
p.   cm. – (Learning in doing)
Chiefly based on papers presented at a conference entitled A
Vygotsky centennial held 1996, Chicago, Ill.
Includes bibliographical references.
ISBN 0-521-63095-9. – ISBN 0-521-63878-X (pbk.)
1. Vygotskiĭ, L. S. (Lev Semenovich), 1896–1934.   2. Learning,
Psychology of – Congresses.   3. Literacy – Social aspects – Congresses.
4. Cognition and culture – Congresses.   5. Sociolinguistics –
Congresses.   I. Lee, Carol D.   II. Smagorinsky, Peter.
III. Series.
LB1060. V95   1999
370. 15'23 – dc21   99-12568
                                                                     CIP

ISBN 0 521 63095 9 hardback
ISBN 0 521 63878 X paperback

NCTE stock number 56290

Contents

In Memoriam

Dr. Jan Hawkins, our Learning in Doing series co-editor, friend, and colleague, died on February 9, 1999, of cancer at the age of 47. We will miss Jan's wisdom, integrity, and leadership in the humanistic study of learning, technology, and education.

Roy Pea
John Seely Brown

Contributors

Arnetha F. Ball Stanford University, School of Education, Stanford, CA 94305

Carol Dixon University of California at Santa Barbara, Graduate School of Education, Department of Education, Teaching and Learning Emphasis, Santa Barbara, CA 93106

Anne Haas Dyson University of California at Berkeley, Graduate School of Education, Berkeley, CA 94720

Richard Durán University of California at Santa Barbara, Graduate School of Education, Department of Education, Teaching and Learning Emphasis, Santa Barbara, CA 93106

Judith Green University of California at Santa Barbara, Graduate School of Education, Department of Education, Teaching and Learning Emphasis, Santa Barbara, CA 93106

Kris D. Gutiérrez University of California, Los Angeles, Graduate School of Education and Information Studies, Division of Urban Schooling: Curriculum, Teaching, and Policy Studies, Los Angeles, CA 90024

Vera P. John-Steiner University of New Mexico, Department of Linguistics and Education, Albuquerque, NM 87131

Carol D. Lee Northwestern University, School of Education and Social Policy, Program in the Learning Sciences, Evanston, IL 60208

Teresa M. Meehan New Mexico State University at Grants, Department of Education and Psychology, Grants, NM 87020

Luis C. Moll University of Arizona, College of Education, Department of Language, Reading and Culture, Tucson, AZ 85721

Cindy O'Donnell-Allen Colorado State University, Department of English, Fort Collins, CO 80523–1773

LeAnn G. Putney University of Nevada at Las Vegas, College of Education, Department of Educational Psychology, Las Vegas, NV 89154-3003

Peter Smagorinsky University of Georgia, College of Education, Athens, GA 30602

Lynda D. Stone California State University at Sacramento, College of Education, Sacramento, CA 95819–0679

Gordon Wells University of Toronto, Ontario Institute for Studies in Education, Department of Curriculum and Center for Teacher Development, Ontario, Canada M5S 1V6

James V. Wertsch Washington University in St. Louis, Department of Education, St. Louis, MO 63130-4899

Beth Yeager McKinley Elementary School, Santa Barbara, CA 93106

1 Introduction

Constructing Meaning through Collaborative Inquiry

Carol D. Lee and Peter Smagorinsky

The work of Lev Vygotsky (1978, 1987) has been appropriated in the last two decades by scholars in diverse fields to account for the processes of thinking, problem solving, interaction, and meaning construction that contribute to the development of human society. Psychologists (Cole, 1996; Lave & Wenger, 1991; Moll, 1990, Rogoff, 1990; Wertsch, 1985, 1991; Wertsch, del Rio, & Alvarez, 1995) turned to Vygotsky as they struggled to understand the influences of history, culture, and context on human development, both individually and in groups. This recognition and adoption of Vygotsky's perspective on development occurred in conjunction with broad paradigmatic shifts in the study of cognition. This shift away from the study of the individual and toward the study of the social group and its cultural history highlights the role of social and material context in understanding how knowledge is both constructed and displayed. As is always the case with intellectual inquiry, these evolving traditions did not merely adopt constructs and propositions articulated by Vygtsky, Leont'ev, Luria, and other progenitors of what has come to be know as *activity theory* (Chaiklin & Lave, 1993; Leont'ev, 1981; Scribner, 1984; Wertsch, 1981) or *cultural-historical activity theory* (Cole, 1996). As these principles have been adopted by researchers beyond the confines of the Marxist Soviet Union of Vygotsky's time, they have been adjusted in relation to the social problems of the diverse cultures they have been called on to help understand. In learning from Vygotsky, we have learned new ways to extend him.

Modern applications of Vygotsky have contributed to research in literacy practices and development, which in turn have contributed to the evolution of Vygotsky's theory of human development. This volume addresses current dialogue in the field of literacy research that is influenced

1

by central tenets of Vygotsky's work. Vygotsky's core assertions include these principles:

1. Learning is mediated first on the interpsychological plane between a person and other people and their cultural artifacts, and then appropriated by individuals on the intrapsychological plane.

2. Learning on the interpsychological plane often involves mentoring provided by more culturally knowledgeable persons, usually elders, who engage in activity with less experienced or knowledgeable persons in a process known as *scaffolding* (Bruner, 1975). Knowledge is not simply handed down from one to the other, however. As Newman, Griffin, and Cole (1989) point out in describing children's instruction by adults, "The appropriation process is reciprocal, and cognitive change occurs within this mutually constructive process. While instructional interactions favor the role associated with the teacher, we cannot lose sight of the continually active role of the child" (p. 58). Meaning is thus constructed through joint activity rather than being transmitted from teacher to learner.

3. The concepts, content knowledge, strategies, and technologies – that is, the mediational tools (Wertsch, 1985, 1991) or artifacts (Cole, 1996) – that are drawn on in the act of meaning construction, are constructed historically and culturally; thus cognition is "distributed" (Pea, 1988; Pea & Gomez, 1992; Salomon, 1993); that is, individuals are connected to cultural history and its manifestation in everyday life. People, tools, and cultural constructions of tool use are thus inseparable (Wertsch, 1991). This construct suggests that learning is inherently social, even when others are not physically present (Bakhtin, 1981, 1986; Perkins, 1993; Smagorinsky, 1995). Because speech is, in the words of Luria (cited in Cole, 1996, p. 108), the "tool of tools," language becomes the primary medium for learning, meaning construction, and cultural transmission and transformation.

4. The capacity to learn is not finite and bounded. Rather, the potential for learning is an ever-shifting range of possibilities that are dependent on what the cultural novice already knows, the nature of the problem to be solved or the task to be learned, the activity structures in which learning takes place, and the quality of this person's interaction with others. In other words, context and capacity are intricately intertwined (Ceci & Ruiz, 1993; Fredericksen, 1986; Gardner, 1991; Lee, 1993; Rogoff, 1990; Rogoff & Lave, 1984; Smagorinsky, 1995). Vygotsky (1978, 1987) argued that because learning takes place in this *zone of proximal development* (ZPD), teaching should extend the student beyond what he or she can do without assistance, but not beyond the links to what the student already knows.

These core tenets of Vygotsky's theory have influenced current debates in literacy research in part because of the centrality of language and the inherently social nature of literacy learning and practice. The following questions are at the heart of such a debate:

- What is the role of language in learning to read and write?
- What is the role of dialogue in literacy learning?
- How do we study the complexity of joint activity in classrooms and other spaces where literacy is learned and practiced?
- How do cultural practices and beliefs contribute to the practices and the learning of literacy?
- What implications do these dilemmas have for the professional development of teachers, both preservice and in-service?

The chapters in this volume extend and explore Vygotsky's core tenets as a way of contributing to this dialogue in literacy research.

These core Vygotskian principles have provided the basis for modern analysis; at the same time, Vygotsky's ideas have been modified through the studies that draw on them. Modern refinements have helped make Vygotskian principles relevant to the framing of diverse social problems not apparent through Vygotsky's primarily laboratory experiments. Wertsch (1991) notes: "one of the major unresolved issues for a socio-cultural approach to mind is how, other than through the influence of decontextualization associated with literacy and 'literacy practice' (Scribner & Cole, 1981), mental functioning changes" (p. 22). For instance, Vygotsky (1987) identified the importance of verbal mediation in learning and problem solving. He emphasized mastery of linguistic systems of decontextualized categorization as evidence of higher mental functioning. Wertsch (1985, 1991) noted that an emphasis on verbal mediation is a decidedly Western value. Wertsch (1991) and Bruner (1990) describe a cultural "tool kit" of mediational means, expanding Vygotsky's conception of mediational means to include goal-directed, tool-mediated action. This framework takes into account mediators (e.g., computers, art, music) that are not necessarily verbally mediated.

Cole (1996) has also critiqued Vygotsky for being insufficiently cultural through his reappraisal of Vygotsky's (1987) claim that biological and cultural lines of development intersect at about the age of 2. Pointing to research on how infants are encouraged to behave, Cole has argued that the cultural line of development is present from the time of a baby's first contact with other people. These examples illustrate how, while providing a foundation for a psychology of human development – one that remains remarkably intact given the passage of time and the crossing of cultural boundaries it has endured – Vygotsky's tenets become salient to subsequent generations through a process of transformation and adaptation. To apply the processes of learning and teaching described by Newman et al. (1989) to how researchers have learned from Vygotsky, the transformation process that takes place when subsequent generations of researchers call on Vygotskian principles is reciprocal and mutually constructive, requiring the active role of the learner (in this case, the researcher) in both adopting cultural knowledge (that is, Vygotsky's published writing) and constructing new meaning from it.

The chapters in this volume seek to draw on Vygotsky and, in the process, transform him to meet new social challenges. They do so by examining literacy practices in diverse sites (e.g., Arnetha F. Ball's study of professional development in American and South African universities; Carol D. Lee's, Kris Gutiérrez & Lynda Stone's, and Anne Haas Dyson's research in urban high schools and primary schools) and by relating Vygotsky's views to those of scholars from a wide spectrum of disciplines (e.g., James V. Wertsch's reexamination of Vygotsky's own development through the historical analysis of Charles Taylor, LeAnn Putney and colleagues' incorporation of Vygotsky's ideas with those of sociolinguists, and Luis C. Moll's union of Vygotsky with the work of Cuban psychologists previously unavailable to Western readers). Through these efforts, we see an affirmation of the dynamic quality of Vygotsky's work and the foundation and stimulus it has provided for understanding the effects of culture on the acquisition and enactment of literacy in societies he never could have envisioned.

In this volume the authors turn their attention to the role of social context in human development. How do the richness and complexity of the setting, the various actors, their goals, and the psychological and cognitive tools available in the setting (Bruner, 1986; Cole, 1996; Wertsch, 1991) all interact to expand the meanings that are constructed and how those meanings are constructed? These are the questions wrestled with by teachers and researchers as well as those in workplace and other settings where learning occurs. In sociocultural studies of literacy and meaning-making, researchers now consider the following issues as central to understanding how people come to learn new knowledge and make new interpretations using the tools of language, written texts, the act of composing, and other symbol systems (such as those used in the arts):

- The importance of speech in relation to learning
- The distinct semiotic potential of different kinds of tools and signs

- The distribution and negotiation of knowledge within social groups working on common tasks
- The ways in which literate practices occur and evolve outside traditional schooling and an appreciation of the complexity of such practices.

To distill these concerns into an overriding objective, the contributors to this volume are fundamentally concerned with the role of joint activity in the construction of meaning in formal learning experiences, primarily those that take place in school. Because of the collective emphasis on the social nature of learning, the authors focus on how people form communities of practice and operate within them. These communities of practice are often problematic, with subgroups forming within them acting in subversive ways. The idea of community, then, does not necessarily refer to a sense of harmony, but rather to a shared set of social practices and goals that become differentiated among subgroups or *idiocultures* (Fine, 1987). The chapters in this volume flesh out the complexity of joint activity, not as a process of one-way appropriation, but rather as a process of multidirectional change over time. In such joint collaborative activity, teachers, students, and even the nature of the task all change over time and are negotiated among interlocutors in complex ways.

Such communities of practice are essentially cultural. Part of the power of the chapters in this volume is in the way they address the cultural issues raised by Vygotsky's writings. Vygotsky argued that cultural artifacts – whether physical or conceptual tools – are historically constructed. He made explicit acknowledgment of the centrality of language as a semiotic tool through which individuals across developmental stages make sense of phenomena and solve problems. His conception of the ZPD includes the use of language between novice and more expert others as a tool for mediating misconceptions and consolidating understandings. In this volume, James V. Wertsch explores the bumpy intellectual territory in which Vygotsky struggled to consolidate his ideas about the functions of language, vacillating between what Taylor (1985) describes as the *expressivist* and *designative* traditions.

This struggle between what appear on the surface as competing traditions and assumptions about the function of language in meaning-making highlights the continued need to grope with the question of the semiotic potential of language. Currently, in the United States as well as in nations in other parts of the world (Saville-Troike, 1989), politically motivated power struggles in institutional settings, especially that of formal schooling, persist over the semiotic potential of symbol systems and, within particular systems, genres. Whole disciplines (arts, home economics, and others) are devalued because they rely on nonlinguistic symbol systems (Gardner, 1983; Smagorinsky, 1995b). Within language-based systems, the modal practice is one in which devalued language varieties are not viewed as intellectual resources (Cazden, 1988; Lee, 1997). Such language varieties may include African American English Vernaclar, Chicano English, Appalachian English, and other national languages such as Spanish and its varieties (Tex Mex, Puerto Rican Spanish).

Gee (1990) argues that Discourse includes more than issues of syntax, phonology, and vocabulary; it also includes certain beliefs, values, and social practices through which members of a speech community constitute their identities. Bakhtin (1981) calls such Discourses *social languages*. Gutiérrez and Stone, Lee, Moll, and Putney and colleagues in this volume make a case for classrooms as speech communities in which Discourse and identity are intertwined. All four authors provide rich examples of how the community languages that students bring to the classroom become cognitive resources, consciously used by teachers to extend student learning. In addition, they argue that the norms for who can talk, about what, with whom, and when offer either opportunities or constraints for how students are able to negotiate their understandings. Dyson adds to this conversation by looking at how issues of ethnic and gender identities, as well as the children's collective participation in media culture, are social and cognitive resources in the classrooms she describes.

These chapters extend and layer our understanding of the centrality of language as a semiotic tool, a perspective fundamental to all of Vygotsky's arguments. Vygotsky's conception of a ZPD implies that more knowledgeable other(s) must understand and attend to the novice's conceptions of the target task and the cognitive resources that the novice brings to it. The interplay between the novice and the more expert other(s) is negotiated through language and use of artifacts. Thus, the expert must consider the semiotic tool of language through which both parties communicate ideas and understandings and in which forms of relevant prior knowledge are couched. The mediation between these parties is a form of collaboration. The historical roots of such collaboration are explored by Wells. Examples of how that collaboration unfolds, particularly in classrooms where diverse languages meet, are fleshed out in the remaining chapters in this book.

The contributors also focus on the notion of *learning as a process of inquiry*, an extension of Vygotsky's (1987) view that meaning is constructed through the process of articulating ideas. This articulation includes both the transformation of inner speech to public speech and the use of public speech in exploratory ways as learners tentatively propose and reflect on ideas in the pursuit of answers to authentic questions. As the contributors to this volume assert, the reconceptualization of school as a site for collaborative inquiry is not unique to Vygotsky but is a central theme in the work of Dewey (1956). The notion of collaborative inquiry, then, is presented here as an overarching goal for the process of education and includes the necessity for teachers to view their work as a means of learning (cf. Sarason, 1990).

To begin the volume, James V. Wertsch points to what he describes as an unresolved conflict in Vygotsky's own work: Vygotsky's (1987) apparently discrepant accounts of the source of meaning construction in human thinking. On the one hand, Vygotsky argues that meaning is constructed through signs, a post hoc attribution of meaning to a communicative artifact, even one as evanescent as the spoken word. Later, however, Vygotsky describes meaning as a function of the process of transforming inner speech into public speech, a constructive process that occurs during, rather than after, the process of articulation. Wertsch finds these two accounts of meaning to be unreconciled in Vygotsky's writing and attributes his seeming inconsistency to his concomitant exposure to two Western philosophical traditions, described by Charles Taylor as the *designative* and *expressivist* traditions. Through his analysis, Wertsch locates Vygotsky as a cultural being whose thinking was mediated by conflicting philosophical heritages, heritages that, Wertsch argues, continue to shape Western thinking. Rather than attempting to resolve the problem of how to escape cultural constraints or resolve ancient disputes, Wertsch offers his analysis of Vygotsky as embodying a tension that any member of Western society needs to acknowledge in order to think about questions of meaning.

Wertsch's identification of the expressivist and designative traditions of thought provides a framework for understanding themes developed in later chapters. All authors in this volume address the question of how meaning is socially constructed through language. Both the expressivist and designative functions of speech are implicated in these accounts. Several authors focus on the importance of encouraging exploratory speech in classrooms, enabling students and teachers to talk through their ideas on their way to constructing meaning. This tentative use of speech falls squarely within the expressivist tradition and includes attention to inquiry through both spoken and written language (e.g., the idea that writing can be a tool for exploring ideas). The designative functions of speech are also critical to communities of inquiry because of the need for intersubjectivity in imputing meaning to words. Wertsch's attention to this paradox in Vygotsky's thinking thus helps frame issues of teaching and learning explored in subsequent chapters.

Vera John-Steiner and Teresa Meehan next identify a second paradox implicit in Vygotsky's account of internalization. How, they ask, do people learn to create new knowledge if thinking is social in origin? If sign-and-tool systems are initially functions of the environment and if learning involves their internalization, how then do people construct new knowledge? John-Steiner and Meehan assume that learning is fundamentally social and cultural and thus collaborative. To understand the paradox of how new learning occurs if learning is tied to internalization, they examine cases of exceptional creativity, including those of Albert Einstein and others involved in integrative collaboration. They argue that creativity involves imagination and thinking in complementary relationships in which social groups are involved in the process of constructing new knowledge by internalizing some aspect of collaborators' knowledge. The creativity or new knowledge constructed may be related to but is ultimately different from the knowledge previously held by any one member of the group or by antecedent members of a culture.

Gordon Wells explicitly describes the need for learning to take place within communities of collaborative inquiry. In Wells's view, Vygotsky's notion of the zone of proximal development suggests that all learning is in some way collaborative, even in cases where immediate human contact is absent. The inherently social nature of learning is a function of the cultural history of mediational tools; that is, tools have historical uses within particular cultures and thus serve to connect members of cultures through shared values. Wells argues that learning takes place through a process of inquiry within a social group, with the inquiry involving the pursuit of authentic questions and learning involving the construction of meaning that comes through exploration. In a community of learners, all participants – including those designated as teachers – engage in inquiry. Wells sees classrooms as sites of two overlapping communities of learners: (1) the students and teacher(s) within particular classroms who identify and explore questions together and (2) a cohort of practicing teachers whose classroom inquiries become part of a professional development quest in a process known as *teacher research*. To Wells, language plays a central role in these inquiries as the primary medium through which learning occurs – that is, through its expressivist function – and through which meaning is shared – that is, through its designative function. He thus sees inquiry as being a dialogic process that, due to its social nature, is necessarily collaborative.

Leann Putney and colleagues provide an ethnographic study of one classroom to identify the ways in which people learn through joint community action, and to show how the group's social practices shape and are shaped by what members learn over time. Like Wells, they see participation in classroom communities of practice as having consequences for each individual and for the group. To illuminate the significance of particular events, Putney and colleagues analyze the history of specific practices in the classroom, investigate the interactions – especially the discourse – that surround those practices, and represent the distribution of those practices and interactions across and among students, teachers, and other persons routinely present in the classroom. Their analysis provides additional support for the importance of dialogic inquiry as a central medium for developing the means of meaning construction.

Anne Haas Dyson looks at collaborative inquiry through her study of a group of second- and third-grade children in an ethnically diverse classroom in California as they interact in the process of co-constructing stories about superheroes. Dyson documents, largely through narrative analysis, the ways that race, gender, and the social relationships among specific students converge not only through the stories the children tell, but also in the processes of co-construction that occur. The children Dyson describes live, as she describes it, in a contested world replete with social tensions. Learning to write, then, is part of learning to participate in these communities of difference; particularly important is the need to develop an understanding of the consequences for textual choices on other inhabitants of the community. The process of writing, then, is simultaneously a process of meaning-making and a process of social interaction. Writing is thus an act of social responsibility through which students need to understand themselves as social agents who contribute to the construction of a community, for good or ill.

Kris Gutiérrez and Lynda Stone approach the challenge of understanding the culture of classrooms by offering an additional analytical framework, the idea of *official scripts* and *counterscripts* in classroom discourse. They do so by endorsing the idea of studying simultaneously occurring social practices in classrooms rather than by focusing on the official script typically following from a teacher's intentions and discourse. Gutiérrez and Stone argue that the official script represents the goals that the teacher has for instruction, while the counterscript represents actions by students that either contradict or resist the teacher's goals. Gutiérrez and Stone argue that the process of learning can be affected by the interactions that occur when these two scripts come face to face in the classroom every day. They argue that researchers should study such counterscripts, their discourse traits, and how they evolve, and should study what these scripts reveal about what students know, what they value, and what meaning they have imputed to the literacy task at hand. This chapter considers the kind of discussion often overlooked in accounts of collaborative inquiry: the discourse of subversion that takes place within the larger social goals of a group. To Gutiérrez and Stone, this resistant discourse often authenticates students' concerns and the ways in which they are not addressed in the teacher's overriding intentions for learning. Not only are the goals of teacher and students at odds here, so are their representations of the task. This chapter reveals the ways in which the assumption of a community may be undermined when instruction does not take into account students' authentic questions.

The problem of subversive discourse is further explored in the chapter by Peter Smagorinsky and Cindy O'Donnell-Allen. The authors provide an analysis of Cindy's high school English class, which she deliberately organized to promote both the development of a respectful, supportive classroom community and the use and appreciation of unconventional tools for interpreting literature. Through the establishment of social practices designed to promote collaboration, personal growth, and practice in multiple interpretive and expressive genres, Cindy strove to create a social context in which students would internalize tenets of social responsibility, methods for literary understanding, and a recognition of multiple pathways for constructing meaning. An analysis of small groups interpreting *Hamlet* through an artistic medium called a *body biography*, however, reveals that students internalized these concepts to different degrees. Smagorinsky and O'Donnell-Allen focus on two small groups that the authors characterize as *idioculturally diverse*; that is, the groups formed subcultures within the overall classroom culture, itself an idioculture within the overall cultures of school and community. Illustrating Vygotsky's principle that appropriation of cultural knowledge is not simply a clear process of transmission but a complex process of reconstruction, these groups operated within Cindy's progressive pedagogy in more and less democratic ways. The less cooperative of these two case study groups illustrates a different kind of subversion from that described by Gutiérrez and Stone, for the resistant group in Cindy's class included students whose counterscript rebelled against the idea of identifying and exploring authentic questions. The authors use Leont'ev's (1981) notion of a setting's overriding *motive* to discuss how and why a class designed according to Wells's dialogic principles can be subverted by students whose goals for schooling do not include personal growth or continuing education. They propose the construct of the *relational framework* as a key factor that affects small group process and the degree of congruence that subgroups achieve with the overall values of the larger group.

Carol D. Lee looks at a form of talk in the African American Vernacular English (AAVE) speech community known as *signifying*. Lee proposes that this genre of talk involves certain heuristics and strategies for interpreting figurative language and literary tropes paralleling the work that more expert-like readers draw on to interpret rich literary texts. Lee classifies the practices involved in participation in signifying talk as kinds of spontaneous concepts that African American adolescents who speak AAVE construct from their everyday experience. Using classroom data, Lee demonstrates how the spontaneous concepts implicit in signifying talk were appropriated as a foundation or scaffold for the evolution of what Vygotsky would have called the *scientific concepts of literary analysis*. At the same time, Lee both expands and critiques more restricted interpretations of scientific and spontaneous concepts. Lee proposes a cultural analysis of the evolution of a zone of proximal development in the classes she describes, documenting the changing forms of participation within this culturally rooted learning activity. Lee's analysis includes both an interpersonal plane of analysis and "the process by which individuals transform their understanding of and responsibility for activities through their own participation" (Rogoff, 1995, p. 150).

Arnetha F. Ball studies questions of meaning construction and concept development through her analysis of student journals in preservice teacher education courses in the United States and South Africa. The courses were designed to help students problematize their conceptions of literacy teaching and learning in preparation for teaching economically and culturally diverse students in urban schools. Ball focuses on the concept development experienced by students she labels *transitional*, that is, ripe for change. The courses she taught included texts featuring cultural accounts of human development, including those of Vygotsky and related authors. Like Vera John-Steiner and Teresa Meehan in this volume, Ball situates her analysis in Vygotsky's account of internalization through community discourse. She then illustrates the preservice teachers' increasingly enriched understandings of literacy and literacy instruction through examples from their course journals. She accounts for these changes by referring to Vygotsky's notions of the ZPD and internalization as a process in which people appropriate ways of thinking by first experiencing them on the interpsychological (social) plane and then reconstructing them as personal tools on the intrapsychological plane. Ball argues that preservice teacher education programs need to provide settings – including appropriate texts and media for thinking and inter-acting – for preparing teachers to work with diverse populations, and through her account of these students, she illustrates what is possible with students who are open to change. She describes the development of the kind of professional community that Wells argues is fundamental to a dynamic teaching force.

Luis C. Moll concludes the volume with his account of professional communities of practice that, like the one Ball strives to create, are knowl-edgeable about and sensitive to the cultural practices and needs of the students they are entrusted to educate. Moll's central theme is that educa-tional practice is culturally mediated. To Moll, culture is a set of practices, leading him to emphasize that the study of culture is the study of how people live culturally rather than the study of presumably static cultural traits. He argues that in order for teachers to structure school so that it acknowledges and builds on students' cultural knowledge, they need to understand the ways in which students live culturally. He accomplishes this by working with a team of teachers who conduct *ethnographic experi-ments* to identify the funds of knowledge that make up the collective and shared knowledge of students' home communities of practice. Through an understanding of the critical cognitive work that takes place in commu-nity problem solving, teachers can better take advantage of students' social or cultural capital to enable schooling to build better on students' home and community literacies. Critical to the success of these ethnographic experiments is the formation and development of mediating structures or study groups through which teachers share their findings and collabora-tively plan classroom strategies for bridging home and school. The ethno-graphic experiments carried out by these groups of teachers illustrate the possibilities outlined by Wells in developing overlapping communities of inquirers: The teachers work together as researchers trying to understand how to use students' community-based knowledge as the foundation for school instruction, and the classrooms center more on students' authentic questions and educational needs. The process is reciprocal, for the class-room processes then become additional data in the teachers' inquiry into how to teach more effectively.

We see the chapters in this collection as a form of collaborative inquiry. Most have been developed from papers presented at the 1996 conference held in Chicago titled "A Vygotsky Centennial: Vygotskian Perspectives on Literacy Research," sponsored by the Assembly for Research of the

National Council of Teachers of English and cochaired by Carol D. Lee and Peter Smagorinsky. Prior to the conference, the 300 or so registrants had the opportunity to participate in a listserve where they discussed issues relevant to their attendance at the conference. The conference itself included breakout sessions and roundtables where the invited talks became the stimulus for further discussion. A plenary session at the end of the 3-day conference enabled the participants to identify issues of special importance and work toward an understanding of them. Following the conference, registrants and speakers had the opportunity to continue with the relationships established through the meeting.

The chapters in this book represent the keystone ideas from the Vygotsky Centennial. Rather than seeking to provide definitive answers to social questions using Vygotsky's core principles, the authors wrestle with educational problems through the mediation of Vygotsky's theory. In doing so, they both sharpen their focus on the problems and speak back to Vygotsky, helping to extend the foundation of his work to address modern problems. To use Bakhtin's (1981) term, the volume is dialogic in many ways: It draws on the history of ideas both influencing and influenced by Vygotsky; it has been mediated by the extensive conversations surrounding the 1996 conference; it is further mediated by our continued studies of classrooms and interactions with other educators through professional media; and it involves a conversation across chapters among the book's contributors. We see this collection as a form of collaborative inquiry that itself will, we hope, stimulate further consideration of these topics. Through this continued discussion, we will continue to learn with Vygotsky about the ways in which individuals and social groups inquire and learn.

References

Bakhtin, M. M. (1981). *The dialogic imagination: Four essays by M. M. Bakhtin* (M. Holquist, Ed.; C. Emerson & M. Holquist, Trans.). Austin: University of Texas Press.

Bakhtin, M. M. (1986). *Speech genres and other late essays* (C. Emerson & M. Holquist, Ed.; V. W. McGee, Trans.). Austin: University of Texas Press.

Bruner, J. (1975). From communication to language: A psychological perspective. *Cognition, 3*, 255–287.

Bruner, J. (1986). *Actual minds, possible worlds.* Cambridge, MA: Harvard University Press.

Bruner, J. (1990). *Acts of meaning.* Cambride, MA: Harvard University Press.

Cazden, C. (1988). *Classroom discourse: The language of teaching and learning.* Portsmouth, NH: Heinemann.

Ceci, S. J., & Ruiz, A. I. (1993). Inserting context into our thinking about thinking: Implications for a theory of everyday intelligent behavior. In M. Rabinowitz (Ed.), *Cognitive science foundatins of instruction* (pp. 173–188). Hillsdale, NJ: Erlbaum.

Chaiklin, S., & Lave, J. (1993). *Understanding practice: Perspectives on activity and context.* New York: Cambridge University Press.

Cole, M. (1996). *Cultural psychology: A once and future discipline.* Cambridge, MA: Harvard University Press.

Dewey, J. (1956). *The child and the curriculum: The school and society.* Chicago: University of Chicago Press.

Fine, G. A. (1987). *With the boys.* Chicago: University of Chicago Press.

Fredericksen, N. (1986). Toward a broader conception of human intelligence. In R. J. Sternberg & R. K. Wagner (Eds.), *Practical intelligence: Nature and origins of competence in the everyday world* (pp. 84–118). New York: Cambridge University Press.

Gardner, H. (1983). *Frames of mind: The theory of multiple intelligences.* New York: Basic Books.

Gardner, H. (1991). *The unschooled mind: How children think and how schools should teach.* New York: Basic Books.

Gee, J. P. (1990). *Social linguistics and literacies: Ideology in discourses.* New York: Falmer Press.

Lave, J., & Wenger, E. (1991). *Situated learning.* New York: Cambridge University Press.

Lee, C. D. (1993). *Signifying as a scaffold for literary interpretation: The pedagogical implications of an African American discourse genre* (NCTE Research Report No. 23). Urbana, IL: National Council of Teachers of English.

Lee, C. D. (1997). Bridging home and school literacies: A model of culturally responsive teaching. In J. Flood, S. B. Heath, & D. Lapp (Eds.), *A handbook for literacy educators: Research on teaching the communicative and visual arts* (pp. 330–341). New York: Macmillan.

Leont'ev, A. N. (1981). *Problems of the development of mind.* Moscow: Progress Publishers.

Moll, L. C. (1990). Introduction. In L. C. Moll (Ed.), *Vygotsky and education: Instructional implications and applications of sociohistorical psychology* (pp. 1–27). New York: Cambridge University Press.

Newman, D., Griffin, P., & Cole, M. (1989). *The construction zone: Working for cognitive change in school.* New York: Cambridge University Press.

Pea, R. D. (1988). *Distributed intelligence and education.* Palo Alto, CA: Institute for Research on Learning.

Pea, R. D., & Gomez, L. (1992). Distributed multimedia learning environments. *Interactive Learning Environments,* 2(2), 73–109.

Perkins, D. N. (1993). Person-plus: A distributed view of thinking and learning. In G. Salomon (Ed.), *Distributed cognitions: Psychological and educational considerations* (pp. 88–110). New York: Cambridge University Press.

Rogoff, B. (1990). *Apprenticeship in thinking: Cognitive development in social context.* New York: Oxford University Press.

Rogoff, B. (1995). Observing sociocultural activity on three planes: Participatory appropriation, guided participation, and apprenticeship. In J. V. Wertsch, P. del

Río, & A. Alvarez (Eds.), *Sociocultural studies of mind* (pp. 139–164). New York: Cambridge University Press.

Rogoff, B., & Lave, J. (Eds.). (1984). *Everyday cognition: Its development in social context*. Cambridge, MA: Harvard University Press.

Salomon, G. (Ed.). (1993). *Distributed cognitions: Psychological and educational considerations*. New York: Cambridge University Press.

Sarason, S. B. (1990). *The predictable failure of educational reform: Can we change course before it's too late?* San Francisco: Jossey-Bass.

Saville-Troike, M. (1989). *The ethnography of communication: An introduction*. New York: Basil Blackwell.

Scribner, S. (1984). Studying working intelligence. In B. Rogoff & J. Lave (Eds.), *Everyday cognition: Its development in social context* (pp. 9–10). Cambridge, MA: Harvard University Press.

Scribner, S., & Cole, M. (1981). *The psychology of literacy*. Cambridge, MA: Harvard University Press.

Smagorinsky, P. (1995). The social construction of data: Methodological problems of investigating learning in the zone of proximal development. *Review of Educational Research, 65*, 191–212.

Taylor, C. (1985). Human agency and Language. *Philosophical papers 1*. New York: Cambridge University Press.

Vygotsky, L. S. (1978). *Mind in society: The development of higher psychological processes* (M. Cole, V. John-Steiner, S. Scribner, & E. Souberman, Eds.). Cambridge, MA: Harvard University Press.

Vygotsky, L. S. (1987). Thinking and speech. In L. S. Vygotsky, *Collected works* (Vol. 1, pp. 39–285) (R. Rieber & A. Carton, Eds; N. Minick, Trans.). New York: Plenum.

Wertsch, J. V. (1981). The concept of activity in Soviet psychology: An introduction. In J. V. Wertsch (Ed. & Trans.), *The concept of activity in Soviet psychology* (pp. 3–36). Armonk, NY: M. E. Sharpe.

Wertsch, J. V. (1985). *Vygotsky and the social formation of mind*. Cambridge, MA: Harvard University Press.

Wertsch, J. V. (1991). *Voices of the mind: A sociocultural approach to mediated action*. Cambridge, MA: Harvard University Press.

Wertsch, J. V., del Río, P., & Alvarez, A. (1995). *Sociocultural studies of mind*. New York: Cambridge University Press.

Part I

Paradoxes in Vygotsky's Account of Development

2   Vygotsky's Two Minds on the Nature of Meaning

James V. Wertsch

Over the three decades that I have been reading Lev Semënovich Vygotsky, I have sometimes encountered what appear to be inconsistencies or even contradictions. Further reflection (conducted on the social as well as the individual plane), coupled with additional reading, usually revealed a kind of coherence that I had not previously appreciated. Upon discovering this, I have often felt like a slow student straining to keep up with a mind that saw order where I had not. On other occasions, however, I have concluded that no such consistency is there to be found. In my experience, this has never meant that Vygotsky simply overlooked something. Instead, it is usually an indication that he was struggling with some of the most difficult as well as the most generative topics he was to broach in his analysis of human consciousness. Indeed, it is precisely these inconsistencies and oppositions that provided the motive for Vygotsky's "quest for synthesis" (van der Veer & Valsiner, 1991).

In this connection, an especially interesting set of issues emerges in Vygotsky's account of the nature of meaning in language. Given that meaning is fundamental to understanding mediation and that mediation is the "central fact" of his psychology (1982, p. 166), these issues take on great importance when trying to understand his approach. In Vygotsky's view, assumptions about meaning provide the foundation for defining human development and its telos (Wertsch, 1996a, 1996b), and hence for defining human nature in general. There are several points in his writings where one can see the unresolved tension I have in mind, but in what follows, I shall focus on a few texts, namely, Chapters 5, 6, and 7 in *Thinking and Speech* (1987). In particular, I shall concentrate on how a view of meaning that Vygotsky developed in Chapters 5 and 6 contrasts with the one he outlined in Chapter 7.

Meaning as Reference and Abstraction

Chapter 5, "An Experimental Study of Concept Development," is primarily concerned with the transitions Vygotsky saw from *heaps* to *complexes* to *pseudoconcepts* to *true concepts*, as manifested in subjects' performances on what came to be known as the *Vygotsky blocks* task. This chapter, which was probably written sometime during the early 1930s, is based on research Vygotsky conducted with Sakharov (1930) in the late 1920s. Chapter 6, "The Development of Scientific Concepts in Childhood," was written for *Thinking and Speech*, which was published in 1934, the year of Vygotsky's death. In this chapter Vygotsky focused on "scientific" concepts and contrasted them with "everyday" or "spontaneous" concepts. As I have noted elsewhere (Wertsch, 1985), there are some important differences between Vygotsky's notions of true or genuine concepts, on the one hand, and scientific concepts, on the other, but for my present purposes, I shall focus on two basic assumptions about meaning that run throughout his account of both. These are the assumptions that (1) language meaning is a matter of referential relationships between signs and objects (both linguistic and nonlinguistic objects) and that (2) the development of meaning is a matter of increasing generalization and abstraction.

With regard to the first of these points, Vygotsky (1987) criticized other accounts of concept formation for overlooking the role of the sign and the associated relationship between sign and object. He argued that in such accounts "The role of the word or sign in the process of concept formation is ignored" (p. 122). In his view it was as if the sign, especially as it plays a role in picking out objects (i.e., reference), does not exist and the development of concepts proceeds along an individual, nonsemiotic path. In a related way he argued in Chapter 6 of *Thinking and Speech* that the relationship between sign and object is fundamental to understanding how children's spontaneous concepts differ from scientific concepts:

The birth of the spontaneous concept is usually associated with the child's immediate encounter with things, things that are often explained by adults but are nonetheless real things.... In contrast, the birth of the scientific concept begins not with an immediate encounter with things, but with a mediated relationship to the object. With the spontaneous concept, the child moves from the thing to the concept. With the scientific concept, he is forced to follow the opposite path – from the concept to the thing. (p. 219)

Underlying all these claims is the assumption that language and meaning are basically concerned with referential relationships between signs and objects.

Vygotsky's (1987) argument about the role of abstraction in the development of word meaning expands upon this basic assumption. It examines the process whereby signs can be used to refer to categories of objects rather than to single items. The key to this process is abstraction, or the "decontextualization of mediational means" (Wertsch, 1985, p. 33), which in turn relies on the existence of systems of interrelationships among sign types. As Vygotsky argued:

> The key difference in the psychological nature of these two kinds of concepts [scientific and everyday] is a function of the presence or absence of a system. Concepts stand in a different relationship to the object when they exist outside a system than when they enter one. The relationship of the word "flower" to the object is completely different for the child who does not yet know the words rose, violet, or lily than it is for the child who does. Outside a system, the only possible connections between concepts are those that exist between the objects themselves, that is, empirical connections. . . . These relationships mediate the concept's relationship to the object through its relationship to other concepts. A different relationship between the concept and the object develops. Supraempirical connections between concepts become possible. (p. 234)

In developing this line of reasoning, Vygotsky stressed the role of systems of signs. It is such systems that provide the key to the conscious awareness, intellectualization, and volition associated with scientific concepts:

> *Only within a system can the concept acquire conscious awareness and a voluntary nature. Conscious awareness and the presence of a system are synonyms when we are speaking of concepts, just as spontaneity, lack of conscious awareness, and the absence of a system are three different words for designating the nature of the child's [everyday or spontaneous] concept.* (pp. 191–192; emphasis in original)

Carried to its logical extreme, this principle of systematicity suggests that mathematics would provide an ideal illustration of abstraction, and indeed Vygotsky (1987) turned to mathematics in the context of a discussion of the claim that "by its very nature, each concept presupposes the presence of a certain system of concepts. Outside such a system, it cannot exist" (p. 224). One of the implications of this systemic property is that concepts can be defined in accordance with the law of concept equivalence, which in principle means that

> *any concept can be represented through other concepts in an infinite number of ways.* . . . Thus, the number one can be expressed as 1,000,000 minus 999,999 or, more generally, as the difference between any two adjacent numbers. It can also be expressed as any number divided by itself or in an infinite number of other ways. This is a pure example of the law of concept equivalence. (pp. 226–227; emphasis in original)

This passage reveals the asymptote of development that Vygotsky envisioned when dealing with abstraction and the decontextualization of mediational means. As such, it also reveals a view of human nature that runs throughout Chapters 5 and 6 of *Thinking and Speech*. In such a view, humans use, or are at least capable of using, systems of decontextualized word meanings and hence of becoming abstract, rational thinkers. From this perspective, meaning is largely a matter of the relationship between semiotic expressions such as words and sentences, on the one hand, and a world of objects, on the other. Furthermore, it is an approach that claims that the semiotic potential of decontextualization is what gives rise to abstraction and what yields increasingly powerful ways to categorize, reflect on, and control this world.

The picture of Vygotsky's account of meaning I have just sketched runs throughout his writings on concept development and related issues of abstract reasoning. In my view, it reflects a side of Vygotsky that was deeply committed to Enlightenment traditions of abstract rationality (Wertsch, 1996a, 1996b). This commitment provided the foundation for the efforts Vygotsky and his colleagues undertook as part of the first grand socialist experiment in the form of the Soviet Union. To be sure, sharp differences emerged among the various parties involved in this effort (Zinchenko, 1995), but the fundamental tenets accepted by all included a belief in some form of universal human rationality and a belief in the possibility of progress toward such rationality.

Meaning as Contextualized, Personal Sense

The view of meaning I have just outlined and the philosophical commitments associated with it stand in striking contrast to some of the ideas and assumptions found elsewhere in Vygotsky's writings. The main text I shall consider in presenting this alternative perspective is Chapter 7 of *Thinking and Speech*, but other texts such as *The Psychology of Art* (1971) are revealing as well. To my knowledge, Vygotsky never explicitly addressed how his account of meaning in Chapter 7 of *Thinking and Speech* differs from that outlined in Chapters 5 and 6. Instead, he simply seems to have shifted gears and moved from one perspective to another.

Vygotsky wrote, or rather largely dictated, Chapter 7 of this volume in the final months of his life. In it he concerned himself with the relationship between "Thought and Word." In actuality, the terms *thought* and *word* in this chapter reflect a more general opposition that Vygotsky saw as operating between two semiotic potentials (Wertsch, 1985). *Word* can be taken as a cover term for the potential that language has for the kind of explicit, expanded, systemic, and decontextualized meaning and form outlined in the previous section. *Thought*, in contrast, can be taken as a sort of cover term for the potential language has for abbreviated form and for contextualized and personal meaning.

Throughout Chapter 7, Vygotsky examined these two general semiotic potentials in terms of several more specific oppositions. For example, he outlined a distinction between the "internal" and "external" forms of the word, a distinction that is prefigured in the ideas of one of his teachers, Gustav Shpet (1927). This opposition is also manifested in the distinctions Vygotsky drew between social and inner speech (with egocentric speech serving as an intermediary), between written speech and inner speech, and between sense (*smysl*) and meaning (*znachenie*).

In all these cases, Vygotsky stressed that the two members of the opposition were quite distinct with regard to form as well as function and meaning. In general, he took *language, social speech, written speech,* the *phonetic* or *auditory* aspect of speech, the *grammatical* categories of subject and predicate, and *meaning* to be associated with explicit, systemically organized, decontextualized, social, expanded form, whereas *thought, inner speech,* the *semantic* aspect of speech, the *psychological* categories of subject and predicate, and *sense* were viewed as being characterized by implicit, condensed, and highly contextualized and abbreviated form and personal sense. In short, he outlined a set of oppositions subsidiary to the general distinction between word and thought.

Explicit, systematically organized form	Implicit, condensed, abbreviated form
Language	Thought
External social speech	Inner speech
Written speech	Inner speech
Phonetic/auditory aspect of speech	Semantic aspect of speech
Grammatical subject and predicate	Psychological subject and predicate
Meaning (*znachenie*)	Sense (*smysl*)

In Vygotsky's (1987) view, the externality associated with the first set of terms is tied to the fact that they are concerned with the social and hence public world, whereas the internality of the second set of terms is tied to the fact that they are concerned with a private psychological world: "Inner speech is for oneself. External speech is speech for others" (p. 257).

Some of Vygotsky's (1987) most interesting comments on the oppositions I have outlined emerge in his discussion of the properties of external and inner speech, and it is in this connection that he presented his distinction between meaning (*znachenie*) and sense (*smysl*). It is perhaps useful to note in this connection that for Vygotsky the Russian *znachenie*, which is related to the verb *znat* (to know) served both as a term standing in opposition to *smysl* and as a sort of unmarked superordinate term incorporating both meaning and sense:

A word's sense is the aggregate of all the psychological facts that arise in our consciousness as a result of the word. Sense is a dynamic, fluid, and complex formation which has several zones that vary in their stability. . . . In different contexts, a word's sense changes. In contrast, meaning is a comparatively fixed and stable point, one that remains constant with all the changes of the word's sense that are associated with its use in various contexts. . . . The actual meaning of a word is inconstant. In one operation the word emerges with one meaning; in another, another is acquired. (p. 276)

In outlining the distinction between meaning and sense in Chapter 7 of *Thinking and Speech*, Vygotsky was not saying that one term reflects reality and the other reflects a mere figment of analysts' imagination or that we should pay attention to one and ignore the other. Furthermore, he clearly was not arguing that the members of these various oppositions could be ranked in terms of some single, unifying hierarchy of development. Although he formulated his account of conceptual functioning in developmental terms, he did not view the highest form of such functioning (i.e., the use of genuine concepts) as either more or less advanced than inner speech functioning (Wertsch, 1996a, 1996b). Instead, he assumed that both members of the various oppositions he outlined in Chapter 7 of *Thinking and Speech* play a role in human action and mental life and hence deserve serious attention. In this respect, his line of reasoning reflects assumptions about heterogeneity in mental functioning (Wertsch, 1991) and runs parallel to what Cassirer (1946) outlined when analyzing how *theoretical* and *mythical* thinking coexist and play essential roles in human consciousness.

The one place where Vygotsky brought his notions of word and thought into contact in such a way as to suggest a genetic hierarchy can be found in his account of speech production in Chapter 7 of *Thinking and Speech*. There he presented speech production as a microgenetic process (Wertsch, 1985) of moving from motive and thought to external speech, and in outlining this process he suggested one way in which some members of the oppositions outlined earlier might be coordinated into a more comprehensive picture. Specifically, he argued that speech production involves a series of genetic transformations from condensed, abbreviated forms of representation involving sense, psychological predicates, and so forth to an explicit form of social speech with all its expanded phonetic and auditory aspects, meaning, and so forth. This microgenetic process has been examined in more detail by Luria (1981) and Akhutina (1975, 1978).

Vygotsky's comments on speech production suggest how poles of an opposition might be related through genetic analysis, but the picture he came up with left some obvious problems unresolved. This lack of resolution is particularly evident with regard to his account of inner speech. In Chapter 7 he wrote extensively about the *semantic* and *syntactic* properties of egocentric and inner speech, and these all had to do with its condensed, abbreviated form and its grounding in sense (i.e., in contrast to meaning). However, even within the confines of this chapter, he seems to have had two different phenomena in mind. On the one hand, he invoked inner speech as one of the phases of the microgenetic process of producing speech utterances; on the other hand, he argued that inner speech serves as an instrument in problem solving and other forms of rational thinking.

Leont'ev (1978) has distinguished these two notions of inner speech as "inner speech in the strict sense" and "inner programming of an utterance" (p. 15). The former involves "the use of an inner-speech code to solve some communicative (usually cognitive) task," whereas the latter concerns "the use of an inner-speech code to plan a speech utterance (or, correspondingly, to retain its content in short-term memory, to remember it as a reference point in translating from one language to another, etc.)" (pp. 15–16). Although Vygotsky never articulated how these two notions of inner speech might be distinct, their difference is obvious for several reasons, the foremost being that inner speech in the strict sense derives from internalizing social speech, but social speech could not exist if it were not for the inner programming of an utterance.

Hence, instead of expecting to find some neat resolution to this inconsistency in Vygotsky's theoretical framework, I believe it must be understood as reflecting an inherent tension, if not opposition, in Vygotsky's writings and, more generally, in the intellectual milieu in which he lived and worked. In particular, I believe it reflects the intellectual heritage of two grand traditions in the history of philosophy that provide the intellectual context in which he, as well as the rest of us, live in the 21st century. I have already mentioned one of these, the Enlightenment. The other is Romanticism.

Designative versus Expressivist Approaches to Meaning

To get some idea of the power that these two philosophical traditions hold over our thinking in the 21st century, it is useful to turn at least momentarily to their history. One very useful review of these issues for my purposes can be found in the writings of Charles Taylor, who has dealt with them as they are played out in the thinking of Hegel and other figures in general (1975) and more particularly as they relate to our understanding of meaning in language (1985a, 1985b, 1995). In this latter connection, Taylor's (1985a) account of *designative* and *expressive* conceptualizations of meaning is particularly relevant:

The battle between expressors and designators is one front in the global war between the heirs of the Enlightenment and the Romantics; such as we see in the struggle between technocracy and the sense of history or community, instrumental reason versus the intrinsic value of certain forms of life, the domination of nature versus the need for the reconciliation with nature. (p. 246)

Taylor (1985a) traces the designative approach to figures such as Augustine, shows how it got a new lease on life with the writings of Hobbes and Locke in the 17th century, and sees it as existing today in the writings of philosophers such as Davidson and Quine. This view of meaning is grounded in the assumption that language functions primarily to represent an independent reality.

[W]e could explain a sign or word having meaning by pointing to what it designates, in a broad sense, that is, what it can be used to refer to in the world, and what it can be used to say about that thing. I say 'The book is on the table'; this is meaningful speech, and it is so because 'book' designates a particular kind of object and 'table' another, 'the' can be used to pick out a particular object in some context of reference, and the whole phrase puts together the two referring expressions in such a way as to assert that the designatum of one is placed on the designatum of the other. On this view, we give the meaning of a sign or a word by pointing to the things or relations that they can be used to refer to or talk about. (p. 218)

The relationship between word and object outlined in the designative approach to meaning is quite consistent with the account of meaning Vygotsky outlined in connection with scientific concepts. For example, Taylor's (1985a) statement that "words have meaning because they stand for things (or perhaps ideas, and thus only mediately for things)" (p. 250) could almost be taken directly from Vygotsky if one simply replaces, the term *idea* with *concept* – both of which are appropriate translations of the

Russian term Vygotsky used (*ponyatie*) in any event. When it comes to abstraction, Vygotsky's notion of meaning in scientific concepts is again quite consistent with a designativist account. As Taylor notes, the designativist approach views words as "indispensable instruments ... for they allow us to deal with whole classes of ideas at a time" (p. 250). Almost identical quotes could be found in Chapters 5 and 6 of Vygotsky's *Thinking and Speech*. (For an understanding of the implications of the designative potential of language and other symbol systems in literacy development, see chapters in this volume by Dyson, Lee, Putney et al., Smagorinsky and O'Donnell-Allen, and Wells.)

Taylor (1985a) traces the expressivist approach to meaning to a quite different set of forces and figures than those that played a role in the designativist tradition. In particular, he sees Herder, Humboldt, and Heidegger as playing a central role, sometimes referring to the resulting view as the *HHH* or *triple-H* approach. A general claim that places these three figures, as well as others such as Wittgenstein, in opposition to the designativist tradition is that they focus on the activity as speaking rather than on "language seen as a lexicon, a system of terms linked to designata, or a quantum of resources now available for the description of things" (p. 256).

Given this general orientation, the issue becomes one of explicating speaking activity. (For further accounts of the need for schooling to promote exploratory thinking by encouraging the expressivist potential of spoken and written language, see other chapters in this volume by Ball, Putney et al., Smagorinsky & O'Donnell-Allen, and Wells.) In this connection, Taylor (1985a) outlines several related proposals. The first of these is most closely tied to the sense of the term *expressivism* and to Herder's original formulation of the HHH approach:

[I]n language we formulate things. Through language we can bring to explicit awareness what we formerly had only an implicit sense of. Through formulating some matter, we bring it to fuller and clearer consciousness.... What happens, for example, when we have something we want to say and cannot, and then find the words for? What does formulation bring off? What is it to be able to say something, to make it explicit? Let us say I am trying to formulate how I feel, or how something looks, or how she behaved. I struggle to find an adequate expression, and then I get it. What have I achieved?

To start with, I can now focus properly on the matter in question. When I still do not know how to describe how I feel, or how it looks, and so on, the objects concerned lack definite contours; I do not quite know what to focus on in focussing on them. Finding an adequate articulation for what I want to say about these matters brings them in focus. To find a description in this case is to identify a feature of the matter at hand and thereby to grasp its contour, to get a proper view of it. (p. 257)

The kinds of processes involved in formulating something or bringing it into focus are strikingly similar to what is involved in the microgenesis of speech production as outlined by Vygotsky. Like Taylor's account of the process of bringing something into explicit awareness, Vygotsky's (1987) account of speech production moves from abbreviated, undifferentiated, contextualized form and sense to expanded, explicit meaning.

Thought does not consist of individual words like speech. I may want to express the thought that I saw a barefoot boy in a blue shirt running down the street today. I do not, however, see separately the boy, the shirt, the fact that the shirt was blue, the fact that the boy ran, and the fact that the boy was without shoes. I see all this together in a unified act of thought. In speech, however, the thought is partitioned into separate words. Thought is always something whole, something with significantly greater extent and volume than the individual word. Over the course of several minutes, an orator frequently develops the same thought. This thought is contained in his mind as a whole. It does not arise step by step through separate units in the way that his speech develops. What is contained simultaneously in thought unfolds sequentially in speech. Thought can be compared to a hovering cloud which gushes a shower of words. . . . the transition from thought to speech is an extremely complex process which involves the partitioning of the thought and its recreation in words. (p. 281)

In short, the distinction between meaning as reference and abstraction and meaning as contextualized, personal sense in Vygotsky's writings bears some striking parallels with the distinction Taylor has outlined between designative and expressivist approaches of meaning. This should come as no great surprise since Vygotsky was quite aware of, and quite immersed in, the two general philosophical traditions outlined by Taylor, and he often struggled with the differences between them. It was this struggle that led him to suggest two different images of what it is to be human.

Conclusion

If we take Vygotsky's account of the mediation, especially the semiotic mediation, of human action to heart, we are led to recognize that, like anyone else, he employed an existing set of cultural tools in his thinking and speaking. Indeed, in Vygotsky's view, there is no other possibility for carrying out human action, including mental action. The result of following this line of reasoning is that we must recognize how Vygtosky's views were fundamentally shaped by the mediational means he employed, mediational means that in this case take the form of theoretical traditions.

What Taylor's analysis highlights is that the various cultural tools employed by Vygotsky in this connection were by no means consistent with one another. Instead, the mediational means included in the cultural *tool kit* (Wertsch, 1991) he was using sent contradictory signals, and as a result, Vygotsky was a child of multiple competing philosophical heritages. In Taylor's (1985a) view, such a picture of competing voices characterizes the situation in which we all find ourselves: "there are very few of us who do not feel the force of both these [designative and expressivist traditions]" (p. 246). In this view, it is practically impossible to formulate a position on meaning and human nature in 21st-century intellectual discourse without drawing on these two contradictory traditions, and the outcome is likely to be unsatisfying in one way or another. As Taylor puts it: "however effective this compromise may be politically, it is a rotten one intellectually; it combines . . . scientism (objectivism) with . . . subjectivist forms of expression" (p. 247).

My point in outlining this set of issues for Vygotsky and the rest of us is not to lead up to the claim that I know how to escape or transcend this quandary. Indeed, it has only been by watching Vygotsky struggle with it that I have become aware of what the quandary is in the first place. Instead, my point is that when reading Vygotsky, it is essential to recognize some of the intellectual compromises he had to make in order to outline his account of human consciousness. If Taylor is right, these are compromises with which all of us must struggle in contemporary discussions in the human sciences. Perhaps the most we can reasonably do at this point is become more aware of how and why the cultural tools we employ constrain as well as empower us. It is my hope that what I have said here can help us move toward this modest goal.

References

Akhutina, T. V. (1975). *Neirolingvisticheskii analiz dinamicheskoi afazii [The neurolinguistic analysis of dynamic aphasia].* Moscow: Izdatel'stvo Moskovskogo Gosudarstvennogo Universiteta.

Akhutina, T. V. (1978). The role of inner speech in the construction of an utterance. *Soviet Psychology, 16*(3), 3–30.

Cassirer, E. (1946). *Language and myth* (S. K. Langer, Trans.). New York: Dover.

Leont'ev, A. A. (1978). Some new trends in Soviet psycholinguistics. In J. V. Wertsch (Ed.), *Recent trends in Soviet psycholinguistics* (pp. 10–20). White Plains, NY: Sharpe.

Luria, A. R. (1981). *Language and cognition* (J. V. Wertsch, Ed. & Trans.). New York: Wiley.

Shpet, G. (1927). *Vnutrennyaya forma slova [The internal form of the word].* Moscow: Gosudarstvennaya Akademiya Khudozhestvennykh Nauk.

Taylor, C. (1975). *Hegel*. New York: Cambridge University Press.

Taylor, C. (1985a). *Human agency and language: Philosophical papers 1*. New York: Cambridge University Press.

Taylor, C. (1985b). *Philosophy and the human sciences: Philosophical papers 2*. New York: Cambridge University Press.

Taylor, C. (1995). *Philosophical arguments*. Cambridge, MA: Harvard University Press.

van der Veer, R., & Valsiner, J. (1991). *Understanding Vygotsky: A quest for synthesis*. Oxford: Basil Blackwell.

Vygotsky, L. S. (1971) *The psychology of art*. Cambridge, MA: MIT Press.

Vygotsky, L. S. (1982). *Sobranie sochinenii. Tom pervyi: Problemy teorii i istorii psikhologii [Collected works, vol. 1: Problems in the theory and history of general psychology]*. Moscow: Izdatel'stvo Pedagogika.

Vygotsky, L. S. (1987). Thinking and speech. In L. S. Vygotsky, *Collected works* (Vol. 1, pp. 39–285) (R. Rieber & A. Carton, Eds.; N. Minick, Trans.). New York: Plenum.

Wertsch, J. V. (1985). *Vygotsky and the social formation of mind*. Cambridge, MA: Harvard University Press.

Wertsch, J. V. (1991) *Voices of the mind: A sociocultural approach to mediated action*. Cambridge, MA: Harvard University Press.

Wertsch, J. V. (1996a). *Vygotsky: The ambivalent Enlightenment rationalist*. Volume 21, Heinz Werner Lecture Series (pp. 39–62). Worcester, MA: Clark University Press.

Wertsch, J. V. (1996b). The role of abstract rationality in Vygotsky's image of mind. In A. Tryphon & J. Vonèche (Eds.), *Piaget-Vygotsky: The social genesis of thought* (pp. 25–43). East Sussex, UK: Psychology Press.

Zinchenko, V. P. (1995) Cultural-historical psychology and the psychological theory of activity: Retrospect and prospect. In J. V. Wertsch, P. del Río, & A. Alvarez (Eds.), *Sociocultural studies of mind* (pp. 37–55). New York: Cambridge University Press.

3 Creativity and Collaboration in Knowledge Construction

Vera P. John-Steiner and Teresa M. Meehan

As we enter the 21st century, the exploration of creativity has become a more vigorous endeavor in the human sciences. During periods of rapid industrialization, scientists and educators have addressed primarily the transmission of knowledge and skills rather than the transformation of knowledge and skills. As natural resources are being depleted, new ways of organizing, renewing, and adapting to a changed world picture are needed. Thus, a new focus on creative and innovative thinking is taking place. Most contemporary students of creativity (Amabile, 1983; Csikszentmihalyi, 1996; Feldman, 1994; Gardner, 1993; Wallace & Gruber, 1989) have relied on Piagetian and psychodynamic theories for studying the construction of the new. We will argue in this chapter that sociocultural theory has an important contribution to make in this domain. This argument will be made in spite of the fact that the word *creativity* does not occur in most of the publications grounded in Vygotskian and activity theory. The lack of focus on this area is particularly striking, as Vygotsky's first major work was on *The Psychology of Art [Psikhologiya iskusstva]* (1925/1971).

In order to present a theory of creativity as informed by a sociocultural perspective, we will rely on the Vygotskian notions of *synthesis* and human *interdependence*. In addition, we will consider the roles of multiple perspectives, complementarity, and the social construction of knowledge – themes that have emerged in the study of creative lives.

Human Interdependence and Semiotic Mediation

Scholars identified with Vygotsky's legacy share a basic recognition of the social sources of development. Life begins with the infant totally dependent on caregivers. Cole and Engeström (1993) write of "the special importance of the social world in human development, since

31

only other human beings can create the special conditions needed for that development to occur" (p. 9). Interdependence is essential to the survival of the youngest. It is also central to the construction of our humanity.

Interdependence takes many forms throughout life. Vygotsky (1978) postulated a transformation of interpersonal (or intermental) processes into intraindividual processes. He wrote that "an operation that initially represents an external activity is reconstructed and begins to occur internally.... [T]he transformation of an interpersonal process into an intrapersonal one is the result of a long series of developmental events" (pp. 56–57). The way this transformation is conceptualized varies among contemporary interpreters of Vygotsky's work (see Ball, this volume, for an extended discussion of *internalization*). The debates about the nature of this transformation, namely, the role of human interdependence and the construction of the new in sociocultural theory, are relevant to this chapter. We will first describe two different interpretations of the social sources of development and issues of internalization that are linked to them.

In this framework, the move from shared activity to internalization depends on *semiotic mediation*. By this we mean the use of *psychological tools* – signs and symbol systems such as language, mathematical symbols, and scientific diagrams (see Smagorinsky & O'Donnell-Allen, Wells, this volume). Psychological tools are constructed socially. We have access to them by participating in the social world where they are made and shared. So, for example, when adults say to young children, "The stool is next to the refrigerator," they are helping them to organize their spatial orientation with linguistic symbols. The crucial role of mediation in human action is agreed on by the sociocultural community. According to Smagorinsky (1995): "These cultural or psychological tools ... are central to human thought and development; they are the means through which children internalize cultural knowledge and exercise their own mentation" (p. 107).

Some of the examples of psychological tools mentioned by Smagorinsky (1995) are the brush and the computer. These tools may vary in technological complexity, but they have in common the way in which they modify and enrich cognitive activity. Kozulin (1990) offers a clock as an example of a psychological tool. Before technology developed, people told time by the sun's position. Later, people used sand flowing through an hourglass. With the invention of mechanical and now electronic clocks, the measurement of time became dependent on the symbol system of digits. The most extensive discussion of psychological tools as part of semiotic mediation is given by Wertsch (1994), who refers to them as the "carriers of sociocultural patterns and knowledge" (p. 204).

A natural question arises about the way individuals use psychological tools. Is their use internalized? What do we mean by that notion? Wertsch and Stone (1985) proposed that Vygotsky's notion of internalization was not a simple transfer from the external to the internal: "Vygotsky argued that there is an inherent relationship between external and internal activity, but that it is a *genetic* or *developmental* relationship in which the major issue is how external processes are *transformed* to *create* internal processes" (p. 163; emphasis in original). The notion of internalization, then, refers to a "much more subtle semiotic process, one that might be called 'appropriation of meaning,' or 'semiotic uptake'" (Packer, 1993, p. 257).

In spite of these elaborations, there are critics of internalization within the sociocultural community. Packer (1993) sees a Cartesian dualism at work when what we posit moves from the social plane to the individual one. He claims that "the processes and mechanisms being examined keep creeping back inside the head" (p. 263). He further argues that "there is a temptation to interpret the internalization that results from learning in the zone of proximal development as a movement directed toward autonomy and independence. . . . In such an account, the person is indeed social in origin, but the outcome is an autonomous, solitary individual" (p. 264). A number of participants in the sociocultural community are uncomfortable with models of internalization that emphasize autonomy. In a similar vein, Lemke (1995) comments that models of development that include internalization are part of a Western concept of humans as autonomous agents. He sees the problem of the subject "as how to have an active, creative human subject which constructs social meanings, at the same time that this subject itself must be a social construction" (p. 80).

Constructivist critics of the Vygotskian framework make a different objection to a sociocultural model of internalization. For instance, Cobb and Yackel (1996) view it as a transmission model in which "students inherit the cultural meanings that constitute their intellectual bequest from prior generations" (p. 186). In this interpretation the mutuality of learning – its interpersonal and intergenerational dynamics – is reduced to one-way transfer. These critics see the emphasis on the social sources of development as minimizing the active role of the individual. Although their emergent approach has many commonalities with sociocultural theory, they view the latter as unidirectional, focusing on the influence of social practice on individual thought.

Historically, Vygotsky and his followers participated in the challenging task of promoting the development of literacy and scientific concepts in a country with millions of illiterate people at the time of the Russian Revolution. The rapid industrialization and social transformation of the Soviet Union during the 1920s provided a sense of urgency to accomplish this goal. This emphasis overshadowed other aspects of his theoretical framework relevant to novelty and creative endeavors. It may have contributed to the limited interpretation of his ideas by critics such as Cobb and Yackel (1996).

Both of these criticisms – of Cartesianism and of mechanism – are simplifications of social–individual interactions. The former critics of internalization view the process as it has developed in sociocultural writings as but one more example of a cranial storage approach. They fail to acknowledge the emphasis of interpersonal and intrapersonal cognitive activity as basic to a Vygotskian approach. Critics who see sociocultural approaches as mechanistic fail to recognize that in Vygotskian theory, representational activity occurs simultaneously at the social, individual, and physiological levels. A neurophysiological explanation of representational activity is provided by Damasio (1994), who writes:

[I]mages are *not* stored as facsimile pictures of things or events or words or sentences. The brain does not file Polaroid pictures of people, objects, landscapes; nor does it store audio tapes of music and speech; it does not store films of scenes in our lives; nor does it hold the type of cue cards and TelePrompTer transparencies that help politicians earn their daily bread. In brief, there seem to be no permanently held pictures of anything, even miniaturized, no microfiches or microfilms, no hard copies. . . . Mental images are momentary constructions, *attempts at replication* of patterns that were once experienced, in which the probability of exact replication is low but the probability of substantial replication can be higher or lower, depending on the circumstances in which the images were learned and are being recalled. (pp. 100–101; emphasis in original)

This conception from neuroscience corresponds to the socioculturalists' notion of internalization as a *representational activity*. We think of that activity both as embedded in social practice and as instantiated in constructions of the human brain/mind.

Rogoff's (1990) participation model of learning is relevant to the developmental aspect of representational activity. She rejects the notion that internalization is "bringing something across a barrier . . . individuals are constantly involved in exchanges that blend 'internal' and 'external' – exchanges characterized by the sharing of meaning" (p. 195). Penuel and Wertsch (1995) further elaborate. Rather than giving primacy to the social or the individual, they show that sociocultural processes and individual functioning exist in an irreducible dynamic tension. According to this conceptualization, neither the social nor the individual process can explain its dynamic opposite. The tension between them and the activity engendered by them contribute to the construction of the new. An example comes from an exchange John-Steiner recently had with a colleague: "While discussing dialectical concepts with one of my collaborators, her questions and my responses to her questions created an environment for joint understanding. At the same time, the interaction contributed to clarification and reorganization in my own thinking." Knowledge, therefore, is both reconstructed and co-constructed in the course of dialogic interaction. It involves agentive individuals who do not simply internalize and appropriate the consequences of activities on the social plane. They actively restructure their knowledge both with each other and within themselves. Such reconstruction can occur as the outcome of positive shared dialogue and joint activities. It is also a consequence of criticism, rejection, and resistance to events that occur on the social level (see Dyson, Gutierrez & Stone, this volume). The dialectic, constructive processes form the basis for Penuel and Wertsch's (1995) rejection of dualistic approaches to human development. Rather, they see the dynamic tension between the social and the individual as contributing to learning, internalization, and the construction of the new. This formulation is especially important in discussions of creative work, to which we turn shortly.

The controversy about internalization freezes the debate and restricts it to the issue of transmission. By focusing on *transformation* and the communication of transformed ideas, the discussion is broadened to include new forms of classroom activities (see Ball, Dyson, Wells, this volume). These activities include cooperative learning and imaginative uses of technology such as the Internet and dialogue journals. This emphasis on transformation also raises issues of creative activities. It suggests a view of internalization as part of a sustained endeavor, a sufficiently deep familiarity with what is already known to be a constituent part of the dynamics of its transformation. Shallow internalization leads to a facile combination of ideas. In contrast, working with, through, and beyond what one has internalized and appropriated is part of the dialectic of creative synthesis. It also highlights the importance of multiple sources for internalization. Participation, construction, and transformation are well documented in the classroom. They are also documented in studies of creative apprenticeships. To illustrate some of these processes, we will draw on the creativity literature. It is a particularly interesting domain, highlighting the dynamic tension between social connectedness and individual engagement.

Creativity and the Zone of Proximal Development

When we first studied creative apprenticeships, few of Vygotsky's notions were being applied to creativity. Extending his theory was a complex task. Part of the challenge came from our participation in two groups who traditionally ignored each other: creativity researchers and sociocultural scholars.

In John-Steiner's (1997) *Notebooks of the Mind*, Vygotskian notions were influential but not made explicit. Creative endeavors were documented, but they were not linked carefully to the transformative nature of knowledge construction from a Vygotskian viewpoint. Creative lives, however, offer many examples of technologies, psychological tools, and scientific and artistic symbols being appropriated and transformed. And as many of them have been studied in detail, they lend themselves to this discussion of representational activities and the concept of internalization.

In the 1990s, Vygotsky's three essays on creativity and imagination in childhood and adolescence became available in English (Smolucha, 1992; van der Veer & Valsiner, 1994; Vygotsky, 1930/1967). These essays and a reliance on Vygotsky's better known concepts can help us apply his notions to creativity more systematically. One of the best examples of the zone of proximal development (ZPD) in creative apprenticeships is illustrated in the lives of composers. During Stravinsky's 6-year apprenticeship with Rimsky-Korsakov, the older composer had the young man orchestrate his own pieces. Then they compared the novice's efforts with the mentor's work on the same passage:

Once a week I took my work to him and he criticized and corrected it, giving me all the necessary explanations, and at the same time he made me analyze the form and structure of classical works. A year and a half later I began the composition of a symphony. As soon as I finished one part of a movement I used to show it to him, so that my whole work, including the instrumentation, was under his control. (John-Steiner, 1997, p. 137)

Shostakovich also learned orchestration this way, reorchestrating some of Mussorgsky's works. These accounts tell of mastering the psychological tools of music and transforming apprenticeship experiences into the novice's own efforts. This mode of appropriation illustrates a dual process, that of strengthening the novice's knowledge of orchestration while also finding the young composer's own voice. This view of internalization is an active process of co-construction that can lead to creative contributions.

Smolucha and Smolucha (1992), who first translated into English and interpreted Vygotsky's essays on creativity and imagination, discuss some useful aspects of creative apprenticeships, especially the beginner's access to the way an experienced person thinks. They write: "In order for students to learn the creative process by collaborating with teachers in making art, the teachers would have to feel comfortable verbalizing and sharing their inner thoughts with their students" (p. 8). When interactions across generations are successful and the mentor conveys his or her style of thought to the learner, their joint activity is meaningful to both parties. It provides renewal for the mentor and shared knowledge for the novice.

Long-continued collaboration between a more and a less experienced partner may lead to the beginner's becoming imitative as a result of too much internalization. The novice can resist that danger by remaining exposed to more than one mentor or distant teacher. For many of us, Vygotsky is a *distant teacher*, a scholar whose work evokes a special resonance in us, whose writings we try again and again to understand and interpret. And although his work has had a major influence on our thinking, it may not be the only one. Some in the sociocultural community (e.g., Ball, Lee, Wells, this volume; Wertsch, 1991, 1997) have combined his work with that of Bakhtin. Others have looked at connections with the American pragmatists. In analyzing the impact of multiple mentors, Howard Gruber (1986) used Mozart as an example. He wrote:

Recently, one of my students analyzed two series of string quartets composed by Mozart, the first in 1773 when he was 17 years old and the second, begun after a lapse of 9 years, from 1782 to 1785. . . . Both series were immediately preceded by the appearance of string quartets by Haydn, and both owed much musically to him. The first series are imitative, well schooled, formal and a little dull. The second series – richer, more subtle and more flowing – were begun shortly after Mozart made his personal discovery of Bach whose music he studied with ardor. Mozart dedicated the 1782–85 quartets to Haydn and wrote to his friend and master a letter openly acknowledging his debt. . . . [W]hen Mozart had grown musically independent of his older model, and had time to assimilate other influences into forms that were more and more "Mozartish," then he could acknowledge his origins with gratitude. (p. 251)

Constructing the new requires the mastery of varied psychological tools (including different musical traditions). It is also sustained by the lengthy and complex transformations of knowledge appropriated from mentors and distant teachers. Central to this process is synthesis; Vygotsky consistently synthesized perspectives, opposing ideas, and disciplinary traditions (see Wertsch, this volume). Van der Veer and Valsiner (1991) write: "Throughout his life Vygotsky persistently tried to create novel ideas by way of dialectical synthesis" (p. 390). He integrated the ideas of his contemporaries, his collaborators, and his distant teachers as part of his ongoing construction of new ideas. These authors describe his dialectical method: "For Vygotsky any two opposing directions of thought served as opposites united with one another in the continuous whole – the discourse on ideas.... [F]or Vygotsky it was the reasoning against other viewpoints that could lead his ideas to reach a breakpoint for a novel synthesis" (p. 393). It was his willingness to explore other systems of thought, by moving inside them, as it were. We think of this immersion as going through a tunnel. When you emerge at the other end, you are able to stand up again.

Van der Veer and Valsiner (1991) claim that an essential part of the dialectic of creativity is intellectual interdependence. Vygotsky's own modes of work are examples of such interdependence, both the dialogic interaction with coworkers and the more dialectical exchange of ideas with others. These differing but connected modes led him to new syntheses. In thinking about Vygotsky's methods of theory construction, the discussion of internalization is recast into a new understanding. Internalization in this framework is simultaneously a social and an individual process. In Wertsch's (1991) sense, there is an irreducible tension between the mediational means, as provided by the sociocultural setting, and their unique instantiation. In van der Veer and Valsiner's (1991) words, "messages located in the cultural environment" are not merely accepted as they are "by the creative individual, but, rather, they are analyzed and reassembled in novel ways. Hence the individual is a co-constructor of culture, rather than a mere follower of the enculturation efforts of the others" (p. 395).

Intellectual and artistic interdependence occur at many stages in creative lives. Just as interdependence with mentors is crucial during formative years, sustained interaction with one's peers is essential thereafter. Hersh and John-Steiner (1993) wrote of some Hungarian mathematicians who made a profound impact on world mathematics. They were individuals who were deeply influenced by their teachers. They also stimulated and supported each other later, during the difficult Depression years of the early 1930s. Most of these young men and women could not get employment in mathematics until many years later. They met weekly to share interesting mathematics problems and to sustain their passion for their field. This emotional support was no less essential than the intellectual stimulation.

These young mathematicians were an example of a *thought community* (Fleck, 1979) – a group of thinkers, usually experienced thinkers, who carry on intense interaction with each other and promote significant change in their discipline. Vygotsky's thought community was formed at the Institute of Psychology in Moscow in 1924. It included Luria, Leontiev, Levina, Zaporozhec, and Shif, among others. Members of this group often traveled together. They helped to establish new laboratories. They talked and argued; they co-constructed their ideas through sustained, intense interaction. Other examples of thought communities include the group of writers who founded the *Harlem Renaissance* (Driskell, Lewis, & Ryan, 1987), the young architects who joined Frank Lloyd Wright at Taliesin, and the physicists led by Niels Bohr who created quantum mechanics in the 1920s (Holton, 1973).

Increasingly, students of creativity are recognizing intellectual interdependence and the social dynamics of knowledge construction. Psychologists Mihaly Csikszentmihalyi, Howard Gardner, and David Feldman have recently written of a shift in psychology from an individual-centered approach to a more social conception of human thinking. After years of longitudinal research focusing on individual art students, Csikszentmihalyi and his collaborators have found limited predictive power using a complex scoring system to assess creative potential. That is, although their measures had high validity at the time of their original research, the art students who were identified as most promising in this study were not the ones who became most successful. They interpreted these results by highlighting the shifting requirements of the artistic domain. Subsequently, Csikszentmihalyi developed a systems approach that includes a set of social institutions he calls the *field*, a stable cultural or disciplinary *domain*, and the *individual* (Csikszentmihalyi & Robinson, 1986).

In *Creating Minds*, Gardner (1993) identified an unanticipated theme in his case studies: "The time of creative breakthrough is highly charged, both affectively and cognitively. Support is needed at this time, more so than at any other time in life since early infancy. The kind of communication that takes place is unique and uniquely important. . . . The often inarticulate and still struggling conversation also represents a way for the creator to test that he or she is still sane, still understandable by a sympathetic member of the species" (p. 386).

The work of Feldman (1994) is particularly interesting in a sociocultural context. After decades of work on child prodigies, he has come to rely strongly on Vygotskian ideas. He proposes the notion of *cultural organism*, "a cooperative structure that is formed and reformed in order to enhance the possibilities for discovery, development, and (occasionally) optimal expression of human talent in various domains" (p. 169). Although Feldman does not use the term *psychological tools*, he writes of cultural organisms as "constructed with humanly crafted tools, technologies, symbol systems, traditions, rules, customs and beliefs, organized around a particular human collective enterprise" (p. 169).

The work of these researchers has challenged the image of the lonely creative genius that has been part of the Western mindscape for generations. Instead, they recognize the centrality of social interaction and mutual support in creative lives; they see creativity as a dynamic system rather than a collection of individual traits and abilities. Within a Vygotskian perspective, the social construction of development is a fundamental assumption of the theoretical framework. In this chapter, we are expanding the assumption of social construction as it applies to creative works. This assumption is manifested through intellectual interdependence and creative synthesis. One aspect of interdependence in studies of collaboration is that of complementarity in discipline and training. Another is close collaboration among participants in a thought community trying to construct a new paradigm. These are among the ways that creative synthesis is achieved.

Complementarity in Discipline and Training

Physicists and their collaborators from other disciplines provide intriguing illustrations of complementarity in modes of thought as well as disciplinary knowledge (John-Steiner, in press). While a student at Zurich's Polytechnic Institute, Albert Einstein made friends with the future mathematician Marcel Grossmann. Their friendship sustained Einstein while he was at school. Later, Grossmann's father helped Einstein get a job in the patent office in Berne. That position left time for physics; it was during his years in Berne (1902–1909) that he wrote his papers on special relativity. This work was not done in total isolation; Einstein was helped by his friend Michele Besso, who also worked in the patent office; by his first wife, Mileva Maric; and by his correspondence with Grossmann.

Einstein's mode of thinking was visual and kinesthetic. He relied on thought experiments and understood space "by being sympathetically in touch with experience." In describing his mode of thought, he said,

"My power, my particular ability, lies in *visualizing the effects, consequences, and possibilities*, and the bearings on present thought of the discoveries of others. I grasp things in a broad way easily. I cannot do mathematical calculations easily. I do them not willingly and not readily" (Holton, 1973, p. 380).

As a child, Einstein built complicated structures out of blocks and cards. His uncle Jacob, an engineer, stimulated his interest in science and geometry. He enjoyed popular science books given him by a medical student, Max Talmey. His memory for words was limited, so it is likely that he visualized what he read about. His ability to solve scientific and engineering problems was recognized early by his uncle Jacob (Hoffman, 1972).

Holton (1973) quotes Einstein's sister Maja as saying that her brother was slow to start speaking and that the family was concerned about this. But Holton says that this lack was accompanied "by an extraordinary visual imagery that penetrated Einstein's very thought processes" (p. 367). In his *Autobiographical Notes* Einstein evoked the play of patterned pictures/images, which to him were basic in concept construction. Holton (1973) comments: "The objects of the imagination were to him evidently persuasively real, visual materials, which he voluntarily and playfully could reproduce and combine, analogous perhaps to the play with shapes in a jigsaw puzzle" (p. 368). Maja recalled how as a young man Einstein "loved to observe the smoke clouds' wonderful shapes, and to study the motions of the individual particles of smoke and the relationships among them" (Hoffman, 1972, p. 57).

One of Einstein's earliest visual thought experiments occurred as a student. He recalled that when he read Maxwell's writings about light waves, he had imagined himself riding through space astride a light wave and looking back at the wave next to him (Einstein, 1972). Einstein visualized the jostling agitation of gas molecules and the interaction between a light beam and an electromagnetic field. In imagination he could reverse physical relationship – for instance, between a magnet and a stationary conductor. He could synthesize physical concepts by posing and eventually overcoming conceptual polarities.

These characteristics of his thinking played a particularly important role in general relativity. His insights were linked to "a tactile coexistence with natural phenomena," writes Pais (1982, p. 201). "Another element may be ... the simplicity and ingenuity of his *Gedankenexperimente* – experiments carried out in thought in just the idealized milieu that turns out to be needed (Holton, 1973, p. 380). In 1907, while working on a comprehensive paper on special relativity, Einstein wrote:

[T]hen there occurred to me the happiest thought of my life, in the following form . . . *for an observer falling freely from the roof of the house there exists* – at least in his immediate surrounding – *no gravitational field* . . . and if a person falls freely he will not feel his own weight. (Quoted in Pais, 1982, p. 179; emphasis in original)

This insight provided the bridge between Einstein's special and general theories of relativity. The power of visual and kinesthetic experiences is striking in these thought experiments, but they provide only the beginning of a long process of physical and mathematical problem solving. Between 1905 and 1912 Einstein published a number of papers, some of them more tentative than his earlier work. He had "embarked on one of the hardest problems of the century: to find the new gravitational dynamics" (Pais, 1982, p. 201). This period of searching required new concepts, including a nonlinear theory of the gravitational field and the use of mathematical tools that were new to him. Einstein's relationship with mathematics is crucial to this discussion of disciplinary complementarity.

In a conversation with Abraham Pais, Einstein recalled how he turned to Marcel Grossmann for help in choosing mathematical models for his emergent understanding of general relativity. Grossmann suggested the non-Euclidean geometry of Bernhard Riemann. The collaboration with Grossmann, resulting in two coauthored papers in 1913 and 1915, gave Einstein the tools he needed for general relativity (Pais, 1982). With Grossmann's help, Einstein had appropriated a new mode of mathematical thought. To go beyond his or her earliest successes, a thinker frequently needs to absorb new and different ways of thinking. Differences in modalities and the elaboration of one's thoughts in diverse notational forms contribute to creative syntheses.

Complementarity in knowledge and in modes of thinking is not a static division of labor. The appropriation of new styles and modes of thought is critical to many creative endeavors in science and art. An example of this process can be found in the collaboration between the highly visual physicist Richard Feynman and the mathematician-turned-physicist Freeman Dyson. Feynman's notebooks are full of diagrams. These diagrams are visual representations of the "lines and vertices floating in his mind" (Gleick, 1993, p. 131). Feynman's diagrams of space–time paths were at first foreign to physicists used to verbal and mathematical presentations of physical concepts. In the course of long discussions, Dyson made Feynman's visual language mathematically precise and thus accessible to other physicists (Dyson, 1979). This collaboration too resulted in a mutual appropriation of different modes of thought.

In John-Steiner's (in press) interviews with collaborators from a variety of disciplinary backgrounds, she found a similar pattern. The authors of *Rescuers: Portraits of Moral Courage in the Holocaust* – Gay Block, a photographer, and Malka Drucker, a writer of children's stories – build well on their complementarity in training and temperament. Their joint project consists of narratives and photographs of people who rescued Jews during World War II. It was a large project that was originally initiated by Drucker. She recalled: "The project took place in so many stages that each of us pushed the other one through."

When interviewing people who have undergone difficult experiences, it is important to be sensitive and available to them. At the same time, one needs to record enough to be able to go back and fully absorb and analyze the material. By taking different roles during the interviews, Block and Drucker met both objectives. Drucker developed the personal connection. She said: "If I am asking people, especially in the case of this subject, to open their hearts to me, the only way I know how to do that is to do the same to them . . . to make a very powerful connection." While she was talking, her partner was videotaping. "I just get it down," says Gay Block, "get everything they say and what they look like and then I can deal with it in my own time."

When Block and Drucker first submitted the interviews and photographs to publishers, they received many rejections. Not wanting to abandon the project, Block started to exhibit pictures of the rescuers. "It was by working on the exhibition that the form of the book came about." The visual format of the resulting highly praised book combines the past and the present. The authors needed a form of narrative that captured the same immediacy as the pictures. The book required many reworkings, a process that would have overwhelmed either person working alone. The power of their collaboration is in the complementarity of their disciplinary training and vision. It is also in their mutual support during this long project. It let them share risks and take artistic and emotional chances.

Increasingly, we view collaboration as central to learning, to knowledge construction and transformation. It is also a crucial methodological resource for gaining information about ongoing thought processes. As Engeström (1994) wrote:

When thinking is defined as a private, individual phenomenon only indirect data is accessible. Thinking embedded in collaborative practical activity must to a significant degree take the form of talk, gesture, use of artifacts, or some other publicly accessible instrumentality; otherwise mutual formation of ideas would be rendered impossible. Collaborative thinking opens up access to direct data on thought processes. (pp. 44–45)

Synthesis

The themes of transformation, complementarity, and synthesis are central to a sociocultural approach to the construction of the new. Vygotsky wrote of synthesis in two senses: as the result of interpersonal interaction but also of intrapersonal interaction. The latter is the interlacing of different psychological functions such as thought and imagination. These themes are described in Vygotsky's recently translated papers on imagination and quoted by Smolucha (1992):

The analysis of the activity of imagination in its various forms and the analysis of activity of thought shows that only by approaching these forms of activity as systems do we find it possible to describe the most important changes which happen to them (p. 56). . . . A true understanding of reality is not possible without a certain element of imagination, without a departure from reality, from those immediate concrete holistic impressions by means of which reality is presented in the elementary acts of our consciousness. Let us take for example the problem of invention, the problem of artistic creativity. Here you see that the solution of a problem in large measure demands the participation of realistic thinking in the process of imagination, that they act in unity. (p. 65)

The painter Ben Shahn (1957) described this process as "the long tug of war between idea and image" (p. 29). He wrote of how the report of a tragic fire in Chicago served as the beginning of a painting that he named *Allegory*. Shahn wanted to capture on canvas an immense idea that "asks for the full orchestration of color, depth, texture and form." He wrote about the unity of abstract thought and imagination that Vygotsky presents as crucial to creativity:

From the moment at which a painter begins to strike figures of color upon a surface he must become acutely sensitive to the feel, the textures, the light, the relationships which arise before him. At one point he will mold the material according to an intention. At another he may yield intention – perhaps his whole concept – to emerging forms, to new implications within the painted surface. . . . Thus an idea rises to the surface, grows and changes as the painting grows and develops. (p. 49)

Throughout this chapter, we have been building on Vygotsky's notions of unification and synthesis. Ben Shahn's description illustrates the unification of imagination and thinking. The accounts of complementary relationships highlight the syntheses made possible by building on our diversity, what we have come to call *cognitive pluralism* (John-Steiner, 1995). Complementarity implies mutual internalization, a making into one's own some aspect of one's partner's knowledge. When internalization is interpreted as a single influence, a unitary process, an acceptance of conventionalized knowledge, then indeed it can be thought of as limiting, as argued by the diverse critics of this concept.

Internalization is not the opposite of creativity. Depending on the way in which it takes place, it is an essential part of creativity. We have tried to illustrate some of the ways in which through complementarity, through opposition of other points of view, through combining different human processes, we move from internalization to novel construction. William James's metaphor of the alternation of flight and perchings captures the notion we have been presenting in this chapter, namely, that what appears to be a temporarily stable system of understanding is but a momentary perching within which the dynamics of transformation are situated.

The last example of this process we will present is the emergence of a unified voice of what we have called *integrative collaboration*: the collaborative trajectory of the four women who wrote *Women's Ways of Knowing* (Belenky, Clinchy, Goldberger, & Tarule, 1986). They are interesting in that they chose to practice interdependence consciously in their way of work, and they have been successful in creating a small thought community within the larger, frequently impersonal world of academia. During our interviews with them, they described how they began by immersing themselves in a variety of theoretical positions in adult development current at the time when they started working together (Perry, Levinger, and others). They also defined their own approach in emerging opposition to these positions. They collected interviews with women drawn from different social settings and spent years together listening to the interviews. They attempted to apply these existing frameworks to the interviews they collected. By listening to and reading repeatedly their own interviews, and in their sustained dialogue with each other, they emerged with a new framework. One of them used the metaphor of finding the right stone to fit into a niche of a wall that they were building together. "We were and are very good at building on each other's ideas." In the preface of their book, they describe their interaction as follows:

In collaborating on writing this book we searched for a single voice – a way of submerging our individual perspectives for the sake of the collective "we." Not that we denied our individual convictions or squelched our objections to one another's point of view – we argued, tried to pursuade, even cried at times when we reached an impasse of understanding – but we learned to listen to each other, to build on each other's insights, and eventually to arrive at a way of communicating as a collective what we believe. (p. ix)

Language plays a crucial role in the transformation of knowledge and the development of interdependence (see Wells, this volume). In a recent study of the verbal interaction patterns of collaborative partners (John-Steiner, Meehan, & Kennedy, 1996), we asked: (1) What can an analysis of the discourse between collaborative pairs tell us about how topics are negotiated? and (2) Are there differences across collaborative models in the frequency with which participants speak simultaneously or finish each other's sentences?

Using discourse analytic methods, we found instances of the practice of synthesis even at the sentence level. The collaborators most deeply engaged in joint thinking produced the largest percentage of co-constructed utterances. In contrast, those in complementary relationships managed their interaction somewhat differently, taking longer turns to produce their ideas and having fewer co-constructed utterances.

In sum, Vygotskian sociocultural theory has an important contribution to make in the study of human creativity. The notions of intellectual interdependence and synthesis are crucial to our understanding of the construction of the new. Because Vygotsky's approach is a historical theory, it richly demands, indeed requires, changes and modifications in diverse contexts. As Vygotskian scholars, we embrace the opportunity to jointly experience this diversity.

References

Amabile, T. M. (1983). *The social psychology of creativity*. New York: Springer-Verlag.

Belenky, M. F., Clinchy, B. M., Goldberger, N. R., & Tarule, J. M. (1986). *Women's ways of knowing: The development of self, voice, and mind*. New York: BasicBooks.

Block, G., & Drucker, M. (1992). *Rescuers: Portraits of moral courage in the Holocaust*. New York: Holmes and Meyer.

Cobb, P., & Yackel, E. (1996). Constructivist, emergent, and sociocultural perspectives in the context of developmental research. *Educational Psychologist, 31*, 175–190.

Cole, M., & Engeström, Y. (1993). A cultural-historical approach to distributed cognition. In G. Salomon (Ed.), *Distributed cognitions: Psychological and educational considerations* (pp. 1–46). New York: Cambridge University Press.

Csikszentmihalyi, M. (1996). *Creativity: Flow and the psychology of discovery and invention*. New York: HarperCollins.

Csikszentmihalyi, M., & Robinson, R. E. (1986). Culture, time and the development of talent. In R. J. Sternberg & J. E. Davidson (Eds.), *Conceptions of giftedness* (pp. 264–284). New York: Cambridge University Press.

Damasio, A. R. (1994). *Descartes' error: Emotion, reason, and the human brain.* New York: G. P. Putnam's Sons.

Driskell, D. G., Lewis, D. L., & Ryan, D. W. (1987). *Harlem renaissance: Art of Black America.* New York: Harry N. Abrams.

Dyson, F. (1979). *Disturbing the universe.* New York: Harper and Row.

Einstein, A. (1972, March 27). Unpublished papers. *New York Times,* p. 26.

Engeström, Y. (1994). Teachers as collaborative thinkers: Activity-theoretical study of an innovative teacher team. In I. Carlgren, G. Handal, & S. Vaage (Eds.), *Teachers' minds and actions: Research on teachers' thinking and practice* (pp. 43–61). Briston, PA: Falmer.

Feldman, D. (1994). *Beyond universals in cognitive development* (2nd ed.). Norwood, NJ: Ablex.

Fleck, L. (1979). *Genesis and development of a scientific fact.* Chicago: University of Chicago Press.

Gardner, H. (1993). *Creating minds: An anatomy of creativity seen through the lives of Freud, Einstein, Picasso, Stravinsky, Eliot, Graham, and Gandhi.* New York: Basic Books.

Gleick, J. (1993). *Genius: The life and science of Richard Feynman.* New York. Vintage Books.

Gruber, H. (1986). *Self-construction of the extraordinary in conceptions of giftedness.* (R. Sternberg & J. Davidson, Eds.) New York: Cambridge University Press. (pp. 247–263).

Hersh, R., & John-Steiner, V. (1993). A visit to Hungarian mathematics. *The Mathematical Intelligencer, 15,* 13–26.

Hoffman, B. (1972). *Albert Einstein: Creator and rebel.* New York: Plume.

Holton, G. (1973). *Thematic origins of scientific thought: Kepler to Einstein.* Cambridge, MA: Harvard University Press.

John-Steiner, V. (1995). Cognitive pluralism: A sociocultural approach. *Mind, Culture, and Activity, 2,* 2–11.

John-Steiner, V. (1997). *Notebooks of the mind: Explorations of thinking* (Rev.). New York: Oxford University Press.

John-Steiner, V. (in press). *Thought communities: Dynamics of collaboration.* New York: Oxford University Press.

John-Steiner, V., Meehan, T. M., & Kennedy, C. (1996, March). *Collaborators' joint reconstruction of shared experience.* Paper presented at the annual meeting of the American Association of Applied Linguistics, Chicago.

Kozulin, A. (1990). *Vygotsky's psychology: A biography of ideas.* Cambridge, MA: Harvard University Press.

Lemke, J. (1995). *Textual politics: Discourse and social dynamics.* London: Taylor & Francis.

Packer, M. J. (1993). Commentary: Away from internalization. In E. A. Forman, N. Minick, & C. A. Stone (Eds.), *Contexts for learning: Sociocultural dynamics in children's development* (pp. 254–265). New York: Oxford University Press.

Pais, A. (1982). *Subtle is the Lord: The science and the life of Albert Einstein.* New York: Oxford University Press.

Penuel, W. R., & Wertsch, J. V. (1995). Vygotsky and identity formation: A sociocultural approach. *Educational Psychologist, 30,* 83–92.

Rogoff, B. (1990). *Apprenticeship in thinking: Cognitive development in social context.* New York: Oxford University Press.

Shahn, B. (1957). *The shape of content.* Cambridge, MA: Harvard University Press.

Smagorinsky, P. (1995). The social construction of data: Methodological problems of investigating learning in the zone of proximal development. *Review of Educational Research, 65,* 191–216.

Smolucha, F. (1992). A reconstruction of Vygotsky's theory of creativity. *Creativity Research Journal, 5,* 49–68.

Smolucha, L., & Smolucha, F. (1992). Vygotskian theory: The emergent paradigm with implications for a synergistic psychology. *Creativity Research Journal, 5,* 87–98.

van der Veer, R., & Valsiner, J. (1991). *Understanding Vygotsky: A quest for synthesis.* Oxford: Blackwell.

van der Veer, R., & Valsiner, J. (1994). *The Vygotsky reader.* Oxford: Blackwell.

Vygotsky, L. S. (1930/1967). *Voabraszeniye I tvorchestvo v destkom vosraste. [Imagination and creativity in childhood].* Moscow: Prosvescheniye.

Vygotsky, L. S. (1978). *Mind in society: The development of higher psychological processes.* (M. Cole, V. John-Steiner, S. Scribner, & E. Souberman, Eds.). Cambridge, MA: Harvard University Press.

Wallace, D. B., & Gruber, H. E. (Eds.). (1989). *Creative people at work.* New York: Oxford University Press.

Wertsch, J. V. (1991). *Voices of the mind: A sociocultural approach to mediated action.* Cambridge, MA: Harvard University Press.

Wertsch, J. V. (1994). The primacy of mediated action in sociocultural studies. *Mind, Culture, and Activity, 1,* 202–208.

Wertsch, J. V. (1998). *Mind as action.* New York: Oxford University Press.

Wertsch, J. V., & Stone, C. A. (1985). The concept of internalization in Vygotsky's account of the genesis of high mental functions. In J. V. Wertsch (Ed.), *Culture, communication, and cognition: Vygotskian perspectives* (pp. 162–179). New York: Cambridge University Press.

Part II

Studies of Collaborative Inquiry

4   Dialogic Inquiry in Education

Building on the Legacy of Vygotsky

Gordon Wells

The last twenty-five years have seen a number of changes of great significance in our thinking about learning and teaching. Thanks, in large measure, to the work of James Moffett in the United States and of James Britton and the Royal Commission in England and Wales (HMSO, 1975), there is now a greater recognition of the central role of language in education, not only as a subject in the curriculum, but also as the medium in which the learning and teaching of all subjects is actually carried out. Arguments similar to those advanced by the Royal Commission have also underpinned the Whole Language movement worldwide (Goodman, 1987) and the emphasis on Writing Across the Curriculum, both in schools and in first-year university courses in the United States (Russell, 1991). During the same period, starting in the disciplines of science and mathematics, there has been a growing recognition of the constructive nature of learning (Bruner, 1990; von Glasersfeld, 1989), which, as one of its outcomes, has led to a renewed emphasis on the inquiry approach that Dewey advocated nearly a century ago (Dewey, 1900/1990). And from a quite different direction has come strong support for cooperative learning and the importance of tasks carried out in small groups (Johnson, Johnson, & Holubec, 1993; Sharan & Sharan, 1992; Slavin, 1983).

However, this is not to say that the practices associated with these new conceptualizations of learning and teaching have been wholeheartedly

The preparation of this chapter, which is based on an invited presentation at the Annual Conference of the National Council of Teachers of English, Detroit, November 1997, was supported, in part, by a grant from the Spencer Foundation to the Ontario Institute for Studies in Education of the University of Toronto. In thanking the Foundation for their encouragement and support, I wish to make it clear that the views I have expressed are not necessarily those of the Foundation. I should also like to thank the teachers and students whose work I have quoted and from whom I have learned so much.

51

adopted in the majority of classrooms, as large-scale studies carried out in the United States (e.g., Nystrand & Gamoran, 1991) and in Britain (e.g., Galton, Simon, & Croll, 1980) have shown. A number of reasons can be suggested for teachers' reluctance to abandon traditional whole-class instructional methods that rely on individual seatwork and what Tharp and Gallimore (1988) dubbed the *recitation script*. Without doubt, a major influencing factor is the increasing pressure of accountability for delivering a centrally determined curriculum and for increasing students' scores on standardized tests of "basic" skills and memorized items of information. As Edwards and Mercer (1987) have argued, when there is a conflict between espoused beliefs and perceived external requirements, teachers' actual practices are likely to be swayed by the latter. It is difficult for them to adopt innovative practices when these practices are not supported by educational administrators and by the wider community of parents and other interested stakeholders.

But equally important, I believe, is that the majority of teachers see these innovations as quite independent of each other, each being a fad that will, in turn, be superseded by another. If these new ideas about learning and teaching are to take hold in schools, therefore, a major effort will be required to explain them, not only to teachers and teacher educators, but also to the wider public, in order to win their informed support. This will certainly be no easy task given the deep-rooted conservatism that pervades thinking about education by professionals and policy makers alike. However, the contention of this chapter is that the various insights about learning and teaching that were briefly listed earlier are not at all unrelated. On the contrary, I shall argue that they each take on additional significance by being seen as essential components of a coherent overarching theory of human development and behavior that, if generally adopted and put into practice, could significantly improve the contribution that schooling makes to the well-being both of society as a whole and of its individual members.

The theory to which I refer is that first outlined by Lev Vygotsky, who, during the years immediately following the Russian Revolution, set himself the task of reconstructing the human sciences, and in particular psychology, so that they would serve more effectively to guide attempts to make sense of, and create practical solutions to, the social and educational problems of his time (Wertsch, 1985). From the start, his intention was to create a theory that would not only help us to better understand what it is to be human, but also help us to act effectively to improve our human situation. Unfortunately, because of his untimely death, Vygotsky was unable to complete this ambitious program. However, he did succeed in sketching out its overall framework as well as in filling in much of the detail, particularly in the area of early intellectual development. From this it can be seen, as Bruner (1962) wrote in his introduction to the first of Vygotsky's works to be translated into English, that "Vygotsky's conception of development is at the same time a theory of education" (p. v).

The translation into English of *Thought and Language* in 1962 began the continuation and enlargement of Vygotsky's endeavor, as his ideas were taken up and extended, not only by his colleagues and followers in the Soviet Union, but in Europe and subsequently in North America and the rest of the world. Today, under the descriptors *sociocultural* and *social constructivist*, the theory that he originated is coming to have a growing influence on those who are trying to envision and enact a form of education better suited to the increasingly diverse and changing world in which we live compared to the one that we inherited from the Industrial Age of the 19th and early 20th centuries.

In this chapter I shall be able to do no more than provide an outline of a social constructivist theory of education. However, my aim will be to show how the various innovative practices that I listed at the beginning of this chapter belong together in a conception of education that is indeed revolutionary in its implications.

Vygotsky's Theory of Human Development

The puzzle that most preoccupied Vygotsky concerned the scope and rapidity of human development: How do humans, in their short life trajectories, advance so far beyond their initial biological endowment and in such diverse directions? To an educator, this is likely to be interpreted as a question about the development of individual human beings and about the role that formal education plays in the process. This was the focus of much of Vygotsky's thinking and experimentation. However, from the very beginning he saw that in order to arrive at an adequate answer, it would be necessary to look not only at individuals but also at the social and material environment with which they interacted in the course of their development. He saw, furthermore, that this environment was itself constantly changing, and that the history of an individual's development could therefore not be understood without also considering the history of the social group or groups of which the individual was becoming a member, on the one hand, and of the actual unfolding over time of the particular social events in which he or she successively took part, on the other. In other words, understanding the development of an individual human being requires that ontogenetic development be seen not as an isolated trajectory, but in relation to historical change on a number of other levels: that of the particular formative events in which the individual is involved (microgenesis); that of the institutions – family, school, workplace – in which those events take place and of the wider culture in which those institutions are embedded (cultural history); and finally, that of the species as a whole (phylogenesis). (See Wertsch, this volume, for an account of how Vygotsky's own thinking was mediated by his immersion in Western intellectual culture.)

However, in order to understand why Vygotsky placed so much emphasis on adopting a historical perspective – a *genetic approach* as he called it – it is necessary to consider a second fundamental feature of his theory, that of the mediating role of artifacts in activity. Human beings are not limited to their biological inheritance, as other species are, but are born into an environment that is shaped by the activities of previous generations. In this environment they are surrounded by artifacts that carry the past into the present (Cole, 1996), and by mastering the use of these artifacts and the practices in which they are employed, they are able to "assimilate the experiences of humankind" (Leont'ev, 1981, p. 55). In other words, to the biological inheritance carried in the genes is added the cultural inheritance carried in the meanings of artifacts and practices in the individual's environment. Human development is thus not simply a matter of biological maturation; it is immeasurably enriched and extended through the individual's appropriation and mastery of the cultural inheritance as this is encountered in activity and interaction with others. As Vygotsky (1981) put it, the intellectual abilities that make us distinctively human "are a copy from social interaction; all higher mental functions are internalized social relationships" (p. 164).

This point brings us to the third key feature of Vygotsky's theory: the mutually constitutive relationship between individuals and the society of which they are members. This feature can best be understood by considering two interdependent perspectives. First, a society can be thought of as a set of overlapping activity systems with their associated communities of practice that, taken together, are the culture-specific means of producing and reproducing the conditions of human existence (Wartofsky, 1979). In contemporary developed societies these involve activity systems of education, health care, the arts, law, and so on, as well as the multifarious activity systems concerned with the exploitation of material resources for the production and distribution of the products required to support the society's way of life. Although they change over time, these activity systems have a continuity that is independent of the particular individuals who participate in them; nevertheless, their continued existence depends on the expert contributions of current participants and on continual recruitment and apprenticeship of new members who will eventually take their place. From this perspective, therefore, a society is maintained and developed by the particular individuals who contribute to its activity systems at any particular point in time.

From the complementary perspective, the formation of individual persons – their identities, values, and knowledgeable skills – occurs through their participation in some subset of these activity systems, starting with activities in which they are involved with family members, then in school and on into activity systems of work, leisure, and so on. From this perspective, who a person becomes depends critically on which activity systems he or she participates in and on the support and assistance he or she receives from other members of the relevant communities in appropriating the specific values, knowledge, and skills that are enacted in participation (Lave & Wenger, 1991).

Thus, in specific situated activities involving particular concrete individuals, both individuals and society are mutually produced and reproduced. Here, too, the four levels of history interact, because the way in which an activity is played out on a particular occasion depends on the affordances of the situation, including the cultural tools available, the way in which the participants construe it, and the resources of knowledge and skills they can bring to solving the problems they encounter. However, both the way in which they construe the situation and the resources that they bring to bear depend, in turn, on the manner and extent to which, from their past experiences of participation in similar situations with others, they have appropriated the practices, tools, motives, and values in terms of which the activity is organized within the larger society. These resources, in turn, have their own developmental trajectories, which are both constitutive of and shaped by the historical development of the culture; and this itself is conditioned by the stage reached in the phylogenetic development of the human species. When activities are viewed in this way, the continuity and reproduction of society are highlighted – the past living on and informing the present.

However, it is equally important to see these same situated activities as the site of potential change and renewal. Every situation is to some degree unique, posing challenges that in some respects require the participants jointly to construct solutions that go beyond their past experiences. Each instance of joint activity is thus also an occasion of transformation: transformation of the individual participants and of their potential for future participation; of the tools and practices or of the ways in which they are deployed; and of the situation itself, opening up possibilities for certain kinds of further action and closing down others. Although usually only to an imperceptible degree, it is also through the novel solutions constructed on particular occasions of joint activity that transformations in society are brought about and, on an even slower time scale, the transformations that constitute biological-cultural evolution (Donald, 1991). From this perspective, particular occasions of situated joint activity are the crucible of change and development, as well as the means whereby society is perpetuated. Here, history extends in both directions.

This latter perspective also allows us to gain a better understanding of learning. For when people's participation in a society's ongoing activity systems is seen to be the basis of the mutually constitutive relationship between individuals and society, learning no longer seems so mysterious. It is simply a way of referring to the transformation that continuously takes place in an individual's identity and ways of participating through his or her engagement in particular instances of social activities with others. Change may not always be in a direction that is either socially acceptable or empowering for the learner. Negative experience with others can also be identity forming in the sense of disposing the individual to withdraw from involvement and to resist rather than welcome the assistance of others. However as Litowitz (1993) points out, resistance can also be an important means of development (see Gutiérrez & Stone, this volume).

As Lave and Wenger (1991) insist, learning is not a separate and independent activity, but an integral aspect of participation in any "community of practice." All participants thus continue to learn throughout their lives, as each new situation makes new demands and provides opportunities for further development. Nor is learning dependent on teaching if teaching is construed as deliberate instruction according to a set of preformulated objectives. In joint activity, participants contribute to the solution of emergent problems and difficulties according to their current ability to do so; at the same time, they provide support and assistance for each other in the interests of achieving the goals of the activity as these emerge in the situation. In this way newcomers are progressively inducted into the activity, its motivations, values, and goals, and provided with models to imitate and assistance in playing their parts. Oldtimers, too, continue to learn, both from new situations and from their changing responsibilities within the community. Furthermore, it is not necessarily the most expert member(s) of the group who are most helpful in inducting newcomers; participants with relatively little expertise can learn with and from each other, as well as from those with greater experience. Indeed, in many situations, there *is* no expert; in the case of the invention of radically new tools and practices, this is self-evidently so.

I believe that it is in the context of this broader conceptualization of learning that we should interpret Vygotsky's construct of the *zone of proximal development* (ZPD) – the zone in which an individual is able to achieve more with assistance than he or she can manage alone. As I have noted elsewhere (Wells, 1999), this construct was relatively late to appear in Vygotsky's writings, and his thinking about it seems to have been still in the process of development at the time of his death. The two expositions of the ZPD in his published work arose from two different immediate concerns: the assessment and placement of children who were "learning disabled" (Vygotsky, 1978, Chapter 6) and the role of instruction in the development of scientific concepts (Vygotsky, 1987, Chapter 6). It is only in the section of the former chapter – in which he sketches the applicability of the ZPD to the child's learning of the mother tongue – that one can see how Vygotsky might have developed a more expanded account of the role of the ZPD in human development. Since his death, however, others have taken up this task, and the ZPD is now seen as providing a way of conceptualizing the many ways in which an individual's development may be assisted by other members of the culture, both in face-to-face interaction and through the legacy of the artifacts that they have created. Also emphasized in recent work is the identity-forming effect of assistance in the ZPD, since the whole person is involved in joint activity, not merely an artificially segregated component called *cognition* (Penuel & Wertsch, 1995).

About one feature of the ZPD, however, there is probably complete agreement. That concerns the central role of language – and, more generally, of all modes of shared meaning-making – in the coordination and interpretation of joint activity. For, in addition to its function of facilitating the negotiation of joint action and interpersonal relations, language also provides a conventional means for construing and reflecting on present, past, and potential future actions, on the persons and artifacts involved, and on the relationships between them. Thus, as Halliday (1993) puts it, "language is the essential condition of knowing, the process by which experience *becomes* knowledge" (p. 94; emphasis in original).

In *Thinking and Speech* Vygotsky (1987) devoted several chapters to the question of how social speech comes to function as the medium for individual as well as interindividual thinking (see Wertsch, this volume). As is well known, he proposed – in opposition to Piaget – that the phenomenon of egocentric speech, which appears at about the age of 3 to 4 years and "disappears" a few years later, provides the key to this puzzle. Initially, speech is learned as an integral part of interaction with caregivers and other members of the child's immediate community, and is almost entirely other-oriented and embedded in social activity. In learning to talk through talking with others, the child takes over the culture's historically developed theory of experience as this is encoded in and through the language in which they construe their shared activity. Egocentric speech, or "speech for oneself," originates as part of the gradual differentiation of the self from the collective and the transition from other-control to self-control. In function, speech for self is "inner" directed; it serves as a means that "facilitates intellectual orientation, conscious awareness, the overcoming of difficulties and impediments, and imagination and thinking" (p. 259). As the child's control of these intramental functions strengthens, the structural differentiation of egocentric speech from social speech increases; it also becomes internalized as inner speech – the means for individual thinking and problem solving – and is no longer directly observable. But it needs to be emphasized that although Vygotsky refers to "inner speech," the mediational means of mental activity are not limited to those derived from speech but include all the semiotic systems that are used in intramental meaning-making (John-Steiner, 1987).

However, this seeming disappearance does not mean that, from then on, social speech ceases to be important as a resource for intellectual development. On the contrary, with the differentiation of speech for self from speech for others, there opens up the possibility of dialogue, that is to say, a form of collaborative meaning-making in which both individual and collective understandings are enhanced through the successive contributions of individuals that are both responsive to the contributions of others and oriented to their further responses. As I shall explain in more detail later, it is by attempting to make sense with and for others that we make sense for ourselves. Before developing that theme, though, I want to consider the more general implications of Vygotsky's ideas for the organization of formal education.

Some Implications of Vygotsky's Ideas for the Organization of Education

Socialization or enculturation of each new generation has always been an integral aspect of human activity, but the creation of a separate activity system devoted to the provision of systematic instruction is, in the history of the species, a fairly modern invention. Almost certainly, it owes its origin to the invention of writing and the need to train people with the scribal skills required in the administration of states, whether lay or religious. But at least from the beginnings of the Greek academy, education has also been intimately concerned with the creation of knowledge as well as with the formation of personal identity. Until very recently, however, only a small minority of each generation was educated through attendance at schools and universities; most young people learned what they needed to know and be able to do through participation in the activities of community life and through various forms of apprenticeship (Lave & Wenger, 1991).

Against this background, universal public education through mandatory attendance at a separate, encapsulated institution called *school* can be seen as a temporary aberration – a historically and culturally localized activity system that owes more to models of industrial mass production than to that of development through assisted participation in social activity that was just sketched. As was emphasized there, learning is not dependent on teaching; still less is it dependent on participation in the activity system found in most contemporary schools. Indeed, as is increasingly being recognized, with their emphasis on transmitting cultural knowledge and skills through the delivery of curricula designed independently of the needs and aspirations of the recipients, these institutions often impede rather than facilitate learning by mistakenly conceptualizing and evaluating learning as the product, or outcome, of instruction. (See Ball, Dyson, Gutiérrez & Stone, Lee, Moll, & Putney et al., this volume, for accounts of schooling that build on students' cultural experiences.) Moreover, in this transmissional process, schools have a strong tendency to cultivate conforming, risk-avoiding identities in those who are successful in fitting the rules and expectations of the activity system while simultaneously cultivating alienated and either self-doubting or rebellious identities in those who are unsuccessful. Furthermore, because the proportion of students who can be successful is systematically reduced at successive stages by the pyramidal structure of opportunity, this activity system called *formal education* can hardly be defended as either just to individuals or even effective in enriching and transforming society.

At the same time, it is clear that the educational practices that served well in preindustial societies are no longer appropriate for ours. On the one hand, local communities are no longer organized in ways that easily afford opportunities for apprenticeship; on the other hand, prior to entering the activity systems in which they hope to make their careers, many young people will need to master ways of acting and thinking that are not transparently evident in the behavior of experts but are nevertheless prerequisite for full participation. In addition, given the increasing scale on which societies are organized and the increasing diversity within them, it is important for young people to develop an understanding of the complexity of contemporary life, of how it came to be as it is, and of the ethical as well as the practical issues that we need collectively to grapple with. In other words, provision needs to be made for young people to develop the understanding and dispositions that enable them to participate fully and democratically as informed, critical, and responsible members of the many overlapping communities and interest groups that constitute contemporary society. Last, and by no means least, they need the opportunity to explore alternative possibilities for the development of fulfilling personal identities in settings that are supportive and relatively free of serious risk.

Increasingly, efforts are being made to envision alternative forms of education in which these requirements might be better met, in many cases through greater use of the technologies that allow virtual as opposed to face-to-face communication. Valuable though these efforts are, however, they are unlikely to be successful unless they take full account of the history of the societies and institutions they are intended to transform and of the individuals – their identities, dispositions, and aspirations – whose participation will necessarily be involved in bringing about the desired changes. In other words, because change necessarily starts within the activity systems currently in place – in particular classrooms, schools, and school districts – it is just as important to encourage the participants in these local communities to become agents of change by trying to improve the activity systems in which their development takes place.

Here, I believe, Vygotsky's legacy can be of greatest value in suggesting directions in which to proceed. Central to his theory, as I have already emphasized, is the concept of artifact-mediated joint activity, which involves change and transformation of participants and settings over time. From this concept follow a number of important implications for the way in which we think about learning and teaching:

- *The Classroom is seen as a collaborative community.* Joint activity, by definition, requires us to think of the participants not simply as a collection of individuals but also as a community that works toward shared goals, the achievement of which depends on collaboration.

- *Purposeful activities involve whole persons.* Transformation of the participants occurs as a function of participation in activities that have real meaning and purpose; learning is not simply the acquisition of isolated skills or items of information, but involves the whole person and contributes to the formation of individual identity.
- *Activities are situated and unique.* Any activity is situated in place and time; although there may be common features across activities and settings, each activity is unique, because it involves the coming together of particular individuals in a particular setting with particular artifacts, all of which have their own histories, which, in turn, affect the way in which the activity is actually played out.
- *Curriculum is a means, not an end.* If the aim is to engage with particular students in productive activities that are personally as well as socially significant, covering the curriculum should not be thought of as the ultimate goal of education. Instead, the specified knowledge and skills that make up the prescribed curriculum should be seen as items in the cultural tool kit that are to be used as means of carrying out activities of personal and social significance.
- *Outcomes are both aimed for and emergent.* Outcomes of activity cannot be completely known or prescribed in advance; although there may be prior agreement about the goal to be aimed for, the route that is taken depends on emergent properties of the situation – the problems encountered and the human and material resources available for the making of solutions.
- *Activities must allow diversity and originality.* Development involves "rising above oneself," both for individuals and for communities. Solving new problems requires diversity and originality of possible solutions. Without novelty, there would be no development; both individuals and societies would be trapped in an endless recycling of current activities, with all their limitations.

Vygotskian theory, or *social constructivism*, as we might call its application to education, thus calls for an approach to learning and teaching that is both exploratory and collaborative (see Smagorinsky & O'Donnell-Allen, this volume). It also calls for a reconceptualization of curriculum in terms of the negotiated selection of activities that challenge students to go beyond themselves toward goals that have personal significance for them (Dyson, Gutiérrez & Stone, this volume; Vygotsky, 1978, Chapter 8). These activities should also be organized in ways that enable participants to draw on multiple sources of assistance in achieving their goals and in mastering the means needed in the process (Lee, Moll, Putney et al., this volume). As I have suggested elsewhere (Wells, 1994, 1995, 1999), this means reconstituting classrooms and schools as communities of inquiry.

It may be argued that the values of inquiry, dialogue, and community are relevant only to the Western cultural tradition. However, I would contend that they are a necessary prerequisite, in any culture, for educational change to be truly inclusive of all the interests involved. While proposing a general approach to education, the values themselves do not prejudge what topics should be focused on in particular situations of learning and teaching, nor how they should be approached, since these are properly the subject of inquiries in the relevant communities. It is to be expected, therefore, that where these values are espoused, the particular classroom practices through which they are realized will vary both between and within cultures.

Inquiry as the Organizing Principle of Curricular Activity

As I have already argued, learning is not an end in itself, but an integral aspect of participating in a community's activities and mastering the tools, knowledge, and practices that enable one to do so effectively. The questions that need to be considered, then, are: What should be the nature of classroom activities? and To what object should they be directed?

As a start to answering these questions, it would be difficult to improve on the ideas propounded by Dewey (1938) in *Experience and Education*. Dewey proposed starting with "ordinary experience," emphasizing the importance of involving students in "the formation of the purposes which direct [their] activities" (p. 67) and in selecting "the kind of present experiences that live fruitfully and creatively in future experiences" (p. 28). One of the clearest examples of what he envisaged is found in *The School and Society* (Dewey, 1900/1990), where, having described a group of upper elementary students making a practical comparison of working with cloth made from different types of fiber – cotton, flax, and wool – he wrote:

I need not speak of the science involved in this – the study of the fibers, of geographical features, the conditions under which raw materials are grown, the great centers of manufacture and distribution, the physics involved in the machinery of production; nor, again, of the historical side – the influence which these inventions have had upon humanity. You can concentrate the history of all mankind into the evolution of the flax, cotton and wool fibers into clothing. (pp. 21–22)

The significance of investigations that start with firsthand exploration of familiar aspects of the students' experience is that, as Dewey (1900) emphasizes:

[T]he occupation supplies the child with a genuine motive; it gives him experience at first hand; it brings him into contact with realities. It does all this, but in addition it is liberalized throughout by its translation into its historic and social values and scientific equivalencies. With the growth of the child's mind in power and knowledge it ceases to be a pleasant occupation merely and becomes more and more a medium, an instrument, an organ of understanding – and is thereby transformed. (p. 22)

In our age of high technology, Dewey's panegyric on natural fibers may seem somewhat dated. However, it would not be difficult to find contemporary examples, such as film production, air travel, or waste recycling, that would afford the same sorts of opportunities for a broad range of significant inquiries (see Gallas, 1994; John-Steiner & Meehan, this volume). As more recent writers in this tradition have made clear, the key characteristic of investigatory activities of this kind is that they take as object the influential and often problematic features of the students' experience and environment and have as their intended outcome the growth of the students' understanding, that is, not simply factual knowledge but knowledge growing out of, and oriented to, socially relevant and productive action (Cohen, McLaughlin, & Talbert, 1993).

It is not only Dewey who places inquiry at the heart of the curriculum, however. The same emphasis on firsthand investigation, both through hands-on experimentation and through the use of reference material, is found in the school-based projects of such cognitive scientists as Brown and Campione (1994), Gardner (1989), Palincsar, Magnusson, Marano, Ford, and Brown (1998), and Scardamalia, Bereiter, and Lamon (1994). In each case, a major purpose of the activities in their classroom communities is to cultivate a general stance with respect to the world of experience that might be characterized as a disposition to engage in systematic inquiry about the questions or topics in which one is interested. From this perspective, then, inquiry is as much about being open to wondering and puzzlement, and trying to construct and test explanations of the phenomena that evoked those feelings, as it is about mastering any particular body of information, although the two facets of inquiry are ultimately interdependent.

As I have argued, the choice of experiences that provide the topics for investigation is critical. They must be such as to arouse students' interest, engaging their feelings and values as well as their cognition. In addition, they must be sufficiently open-ended to allow alternative possibilities for consideration, thus providing challenges appropriate to individual students' current abilities while at the same time encouraging them to collaborate with others in constructing shared understanding that is both practical and theoretical. In other words, they need to be experiences that generate real questions. What I mean by *real* questions is captured by Bettencourt (1991):

Understanding starts with a question; not any question, but a *real* question. Said in another way, a real question expresses a desire to understand. This desire is what moves the questioner to pursue the question until an answer has been made. Desiring to understand opens ourselves to experiencing what is new as new, and the already known under new aspects. (p. 3)

One particularly memorable example of the energizing power of a real question occurred in a presentation to classmates, in a sixth-grade unit in which I participated, on the theme of time (Wells, 1993). Nir had struggled hard to understand the principles on which the international time clock is based, and had made use of adult assistance as well as of works of reference. In order to explain what he had finally understood, he made two small sundials, which he placed on a large globe at the locations of Greenwich, England, and Toronto, Canada. Taking a powerful flashlight to represent the sun, he held it above the "equator" in a position due south of Greenwich. As everybody could see, the sundial at Greenwich registered 12 noon, whereas that at Toronto showed 7 A.M. Then, when he rotated the globe until the sun was due south of Toronto, the time shown on the sundial at Toronto became 12 noon, whereas at Greenwich it was 5 P.M. As he explained, the time in Toronto is 5 hours behind that at Greenwich because it takes 5 hours for the Earth to make that part of its daily rotation corresponding to the distance between Greenwich and Toronto.

The key feature of activities of this kind, I would contend, is that for the students the goal of inquiry is making, not learning. When they are motivated and challenged by real questions, their attention is focused on making answers. Under these conditions, learning is an outcome that occurs because the making requires the student to extend his or her understanding in action – whether the artifact constructed is a material object, an explanatory demonstration, or a theoretical formulation. However, in arguing for an approach to curriculum that is organized in terms of questions for inquiry, I must make two further points. First, although for a question to be real the student must really care about making an answer to it, it does not follow that the only real questions are ones that are first asked by students. Teachers' questions or questions suggested in books that students are reading can become equally real if they correspond to or awaken a wondering on the part of the student. What is at issue here is the student's attitude to the question rather than where it originated; for it to motivate genuine inquiry, the question must be taken over and "owned" by the student. The second point is that inquiry does not have to start with a clearly formulated question. In fact, some of the most absorbing questions arise only after some preliminary work on the topic has been carried out or as a by-product of trying to answer some other question. Questions may also occur quite spontaneously and unexpectedly in the course of reviewing work carried out to date.

The more general point, then, is that inquiry is not a "method" of doing science, history, or any other subject, in which the obligatory first stage in a fixed, linear sequence is that of students each formulating questions to investigate. Rather, it is an approach to the chosen themes and topics in which the posing of real questions is positively encouraged, whenever they occur and by whomever they are asked. An equally important hallmark of an inquiry approach is that all tentative answers are taken seriously and are investigated as rigorously as the circumstances permit.

However, inquiry should not only be the principle in terms of which students' activity is organized. It should also characterize the teacher's mode of participation in the classroom community (see Moll, this volume). Here we need to distinguish two levels at which the teacher needs to be involved (Wells, 1995). First, the teacher should be involved as a coinquirer with the students in the topics that they have chosen to investigate. To be able honestly to say, in response to a student's question, "I don't know. How could we find out?" is probably more important, in creating an ethos of collaborative inquiry in the classroom, than always being able to supply a ready-made answer. Even for the most well-informed teacher there are almost certain to be aspects of the topic that she or he does not fully understand. To be able to wonder aloud about these issues and to take action to understand them better not only provides an excellent model for the students to emulate, it also demonstrates the authenticity of the teacher's commitment to inquiry.

The second level concerns the teacher's role as leader and organizer of the community's activities. Although the responsibility for deciding on the topics to be investigated, and on the manner in which the investigations should proceed, should be shared as far as possible with the students, the teacher cannot avoid the ultimate responsibility for the selection of activities to be undertaken and for ensuring that, in the process, time and resources are used both productively and safely. Quite apart from the teacher's accountability to parents and administrators in this respect, providing the best possible opportunities for both individual and community development is one of the moral imperatives of teaching.

What I am suggesting is that this responsibility should also be approached in a spirit of inquiry, with increased understanding and improved practice as the intended outcomes. As with the students, however, these outcomes cannot be separated from engagement in particular purposeful activities undertaken with others. One aspect of this engagement has already been touched on: consideration of the teacher as a coparticipant with the students in investigating the chosen curricular topic. I now want to propose a second mode of participation, namely, that of the teacher researcher who not only reflects on his or her practice (Schön, 1983, 1987) but also systematically makes changes and collects and critically evaluates evidence about the consequences (Carr & Kemmis, 1983). In this context, Vygotskian theory can serve as a tool for action research by providing a framework within which to make sense of the current situation, to identify contradictions, and to consider ways of making improvements (Engeström, 1991). Here teacher colleagues constitute the coparticipants in the community of inquiry, both teachers in the same school and kindred spirits in other institutions, both school and university (see Moll, Putney et al., this volume). In such professional communities of inquiry, some of the most productive transformations of schooling are being carried out, often using a social constructivist framework to assist them. In a later section of this chapter, I shall describe some specific examples.

On Knowledge and Knowing

As I hope I have made clear in the previous section, inquiry is not to be thought of in terms of isolated projects undertaken occasionally by individual students as part of a traditional transmissionary pedagogy. Nor is it a method to be implemented according to a preformulated script. On the contrary, it is the stance that pervades all aspects of the life of a classroom community that is based on the social constructivist belief that understanding is constructed in the process of people working together to solve the problems that arise in the course of shared activity. Organization of classroom resources, resolution of interpersonal disputes, planning of field trips, and curriculum-based activity are all approached in the same open-ended and exploratory way in an inquiry-oriented classroom. Equally important is the dialogic mode of interaction that is pervasive in the life of such a community. Dialogue necessarily plays a central mediating role because it is the principal means of arriving at a common understanding of whatever question is at issue (see Ball, Dyson, Gutiérrez & Stone, Putney et al., and Smagorinsky & O'Donnell-Allen, this volume).

Unfortunately, however, in most classrooms dialogic interaction is not evident. As several studies have noted (Galton et al., 1980; Lemke, 1990; Nystrand & Gamoran, 1991), there is a dearth of dialogue throughout the years of schooling. One of the principal reasons for this, I believe, is to be found in the misconceptions that exist about the nature of knowledge that can be seen in many state and district policy statements. There the prevailing view is that knowledge is a commodity that is stored either in individual minds or in texts and other artifacts. Like other commodities, it can be transmitted from one person to another; it can also be itemized, quantified, and measured. In this transmissionary view, classroom dialogue is, not surprisingly, seen as an unnecessary waste of time; all that students need to do is to read and listen attentively to the knowledge conveyed through authoritative texts and lectures, and absorb and remember it for subsequent reproduction.

However, there are several reasons for rejecting this *banking* conception of knowledge (Freire, 1970), not least being the evidence from classrooms that what students understand does not have a straightforward correspondence to what they have been told or have read. As has been cogently argued, minds are not containers of knowledge propositions (Bereiter & Scardamalia, 1996); nor can knowledge be directly transmitted through talk or text (Reddy, 1979), because it must be constructed by each individual knower (von Glasersfeld, 1989).

But in my view, the most serious problem with the prevailing view is that, in treating knowledge as a *thing* that people possess, it loses sight of the relationship between knowing and acting and of the essentially collaborative nature of these processes. Knowledge is created and re-created between people as they bring their personal experience and information derived from other sources to bear on solving some particular problem. What we refer to as knowledge is thus both the enhanced understanding of the problem situation gained by the participants, on the one hand, and the representation of the understanding that is produced in the process, on the other. Furthermore, neither the participants' understanding nor the knowledge representation can be appropriated by others unless they too engage in some comparable problem solving. This point is made very clearly by Popper and Eccles (1977) when discussing theoretical knowledge:

We can grasp a theory only by trying to reinvent it or to reconstruct it, and by trying out, with the help of our imagination, all the consequences of the theory which seem to us to be interesting and important.... One could say that the process of understanding and the process of the actual production or discovery [of theories] are very much alike. (p. 461)

Not all knowing is theoretical, however, even though, in our highly literate and technologically oriented society, there is a strong tendency to privilege theoretical knowing over those modes of knowing that are more typically involved in the practical activities of everyday living. As Wartofsky (1979) has argued, different modes of knowing have emerged over the course of human history as a result of the increasing range of types of activity in which people engaged and of the types of artifacts that entered into those activities.

The most fundamental mode is the *instrumental* knowing involved in transforming the material world for the purposes of survival; such knowing is inherently involved in making and using the primary artifacts that are involved in these activities. However, joint activity in which instrumental knowing needs to be shared and coordinated with others requires a further mode, that of *procedural* knowing, which, in turn, depends on the use of communicative representations or secondary artifacts. Initially, these were probably mimetic in form and involved demonstrative action, gesture, and facial expression (Donald, 1991). Then, with the invention of language, with its potential for representing not just objects and actions, but also the relationships into which they enter and the conditions under which these relationships are observed, there emerged the third, *substantive*, mode of knowing. In this mode joint planning and reflecting became possible, as well as the consideration of alternative, hypothetical actions and states of affairs.

However, it was with the creation of aesthetic artifacts in the form of myths, rituals, and visual art that humans first attempted to construct overarching explanations of human existence in the world as experienced. This *aesthetic* knowing, as we might call it, can thus be thought of as the first mode in which knowing became self-conscious and deliberate, with myth serving as the prototypical integrative tool. As Donald (1991) argues, "The importance of myth is that it signaled the first attempts at symbolic models of the human universe, and the first attempts at coherent historical reconstruction of the past" (p. 267).

These four modes of knowing mediated all the activities of early human societies, and although the artifacts and technologies we now use are vastly more complex and diverse, they still underpin the majority of activities in which we habitually engage. It is against this large-scale historical background that we need to consider *theoretical* knowing, the last – and, as some would have it, the most powerful – mode of knowing to emerge.

In fact, theoretical knowing, as we currently understand it, was not to emerge for many millennia. It seems to have required, first, the availability of visuographic means of giving a permanent representation to the meanings expressed in speech (Olson, 1994) and, second, an ideological shift toward the scientific objectification of the material world. Thus it was only from the time of the European Renaissance, with the conjunction of three inventions – the controlled experiment (Hacking, 1990), the register of scientific writing (Halliday, 1988), and the technology of printing (Ong, 1982) – that theoretical knowing, with its attendant artifacts in the form of scientific reports, theories, and models, began to achieve its current supremacy.

Nevertheless, although very different in important respects, myths and theoretical models are both examples of what Wartofsky (1979) calls *tertiary artifacts*. In describing them, he writes that they "can come to constitute a relatively autonomous 'world', in which the rules, conventions and outcomes no longer appear directly practical" (p. 208). However, although they are, in that sense, bracketed from practical activity, they are not cut off from it. They provide possible ways of seeing and understanding and so "can come to color and change our perception of the 'actual' world, as envisioning possibilities in it not presently recognized" (p. 209).

There are several important points to be made about the historical sequence I have just sketched. First, it is developmental in the sense that each mode of knowing builds on those that went before, although without displacing them. Thus, theoretical knowing, the latest to emerge, should not for that reason be treated as superior in all situations (Wertsch, 1991). Second, this developmental trajectory is also relevant at the ontogenetic level. Of course, this is not a matter of simple recapitulation, because the conditions in which children grow up are always relative to the stage reached in the development of the culture to which they belong. In contemporary developed cultures, all the modes of knowing distinguished earlier are involved, to varying degrees, in most if not all of the activities that make up everyday living. They are therefore available to be appropriated and do not have to be invented anew in each generation, as Vygotsky was well aware (Scribner, 1985). Nevertheless, there are strong grounds for treating the historical sequence itself as ontogenetically accurate, with theoretical knowing emerging only in the school years, along with mastery of the genres of written language and the other modes of representation by which it is mediated.

One obvious implication of this argument is that the development of theoretical knowing should be given high priority in the middle years of schooling and beyond, once basic literacy and numeracy are well established. However, there is a second implication that is equally important. Just as, in human history, theoretical knowing arose on the basis of knowledge derived from a broad base of practical activity, so the same sequence should hold in school. In one sense it might be argued that this, too, is already the case: The early years of schooling provide ample opportunities for practical experiences of many kinds. However, what I am proposing is that this should be the pattern for each new area of study: There should, wherever possible, be opportunities for gaining firsthand, practical experience of tackling problems in the relevant domain so that there will be a perceived need for the theoretical constructs that provide a principled basis for understanding those problems and making solutions to them. By the same token, because theoretical knowing should not be treated as an end in itself, there should also be opportunities to put the knowledge constructed to use in some situation of significance to the students so that, through bringing it to bear on some further problem, they may deepen their understanding. In Vygotsky's (1987) terms, there should, wherever possible, be an opportunity to establish a firm basis of *everyday* concepts with which the learning of *scientific* concepts can connect (see Gutiérrez & Stone, Lee, Moll, and Putney et al., this volume). It is this interplay between theory and practice, involving different and complementary modes of knowing, that is one of the key features of the inquiry approach to classroom activities that I have proposed.

The final point I wish to make about the development of the modes of knowing concerns the different kinds of artifact by which these modes are mediated and the different roles that language plays. Following Wartofsky, we can distinguish three categories of artifact: material tools and the social practices in which they are employed; representations of these tools and practices by means of which activities are organized and their motives, goals, and knowledgeable skills passed on to new participants; and the imaginative representational structures in terms of which humans attempt to understand the world and their existence in it.

Viewed from different perspectives, language figures in all of them. In the form of spoken and written words and utterances, language is a primary artifact that is materially produced, together with gestural and other nonverbal behaviors, as a means of interacting with others. As secondary, representational artifacts, utterances enable people to coordinate their perceptions, beliefs, and intentions with respect to their shared situations;

here it is the referential function of language that is most salient (see Wertsch, this volume, for an explanation of Vygotsky's attention to the *designative* potential of language). Finally, as a shared system of interrelated meanings, or *meaning potential* (Halliday, 1978), language provides a resource for the construction of the tertiary artifacts that mediate knowing in the aesthetic and theoretical modes.

Whichever perspective we take, however, it is discourse – the situated, purposeful use of the phonological/graphological and meaning potential of language – that needs to be focused on if we wish to understand how knowledge can be created and appropriated in and through participation in joint activity. This is the question to which I now turn in the remaining sections of this chapter.

Dialogue and the Construction of Knowledge

An important clue in my own search for an answer to this question came during a recent conference in Toronto on the "Ecology of Mind," which was chaired by Ursula Franklin (1966), a doyenne of Canadian science. In introducing one of the speakers, she proposed that knowledge is created and re-created "in the discourse between people doing things together." In these words she brought together three important features of knowledge building:

- It is an intrinsic part of "doing things,"
- It is created between people.
- It occurs in their collaborative meaning-making through discourse.

Another way of putting the first point would be to say that knowledge is situated: It is (re)created in a specific activity setting, involving particular individuals who have a common goal, or at least a set of overlapping goals, to which they are all orienting. This goal we might call the *object* of their activity, with a quite deliberate play on the dual meaning: the object to which their actions are directed as well as the intended outcome – the transformation of that object by means of those actions. Scardamalia, Bereiter, and Lamon (1994) nicely capture this in their work on knowledge building when they speak of the need for an "improvable object" as the focus of the activity.

The situation also contains other potential participants in the form of artifacts of various kinds that can be used as the mediators of the activity. These include material tools ranging from hammers and saws to chalkboards and computers; they also include intellectual tools, such as scripts for constituent tasks, mathematical operations, or principles of experimental design, to the extent that one or more of the participants can bring them to bear on the object (see Gutiérrez & Stone, this volume, for an extended discussion of scripts). In this sense, the most important mediational means is the participants' current understanding of the object and of possible artifacts to use in effecting the desired transformation.

The second feature of knowledge building is that it takes place *between* people. This is related to the joint nature of the activity to which it is related. It is sometimes objected that significant advances are often achieved by individual "knowledge workers" as they experiment with a machine in their garage, for example, or ponder on an intellectual problem in solitary silence. Certainly, advances in most of the different modes of knowing can occur when people are working alone. However, the critical issue is not whether they are alone or in the physical presence of coparticipants at the time, but that the project on which they are working is one that is shared with others.

In one sense, collaboration always occurs because these people are linked to the wider community, past and present, through the artifacts that they use. The problem that preoccupies them, too, is likely to be one that arises out of a broader sphere of activity in which many other people are involved and to whom the solution will ultimately be addressed. Knowledge building, whether conducted alone or in company, is thus always situated in a discourse in which each contribution both responds to what has preceded it and anticipates a further response.

This principle of *responsivity* is one of the defining characteristics of the dialogue of knowledge building, the mode of discourse in which a structure of meaning is built up collaboratively over successive turns. To some extent, as Bakhtin (1986) pointed out, all discourse is dialogic. Not only are the meanings of words and expressions "borrowed" from the speech of others, but each "utterance is a link in a very complexly organized chain of other utterances" (p. 69); in both of these ways, it is "filled with *dialogic overtones*" (p. 92; emphasis in original). Not all discourse is concerned with knowledge building, however, nor is there any reason why it should be. There are many other important functions that discourse serves in any activity system, even in one devoted to knowledge building. Nevertheless, as I shall try to show, the dialogic principle is a necessary feature of any discourse that aims to be "progressive" (Bereiter, 1994; Nystrand, 1997; Smagorinsky & O'Donnell-Allen, this volume).

Bereiter (1994) proposed the term *progressive discourse* to describe the process by which the sharing, questioning, and revising of opinions leads to "a new understanding that everyone involved agrees is superior to their own previous understanding" (p. 6). Such discourse, he says, is based on four commitments that all participants make:

- To work toward common understanding satisfactory to all;
- To frame questions and propositions in ways that allow evidence to be brought to bear on them;
- To expand the body of collectively valid propositions;
- To allow any belief to be subjected to criticism if it will advance the discourse.

Although intended to characterize the discourse practices of, for example, a scientific community, similar commitments can apply, in principle, to any setting in which knowledge building is intentionally made part of the activity. These commitments are therefore equally relevant in the classroom. As Bereiter argues:

[C]lassroom discussions may be thought of as part of the larger ongoing discourse, not as preparation for it or as after-the-fact examination of the results of the larger discourse. The fact that classroom discourse is unlikely to come up with ideas that advance the larger discourse in no way disqualifies it.... The important thing is that the local discourses be progressive in the sense that understandings are being generated that are new to the local participants and that the participants recognize as superior to their previous understandings. (p. 9)

With the twin notions of progressive discourse and improvable objects, we now have a partial explanation of how knowledge is co-constructed in dialogue. But it might still reasonably be asked how exactly participation in this sort of dialogue leads to a growth in the understanding of indivdual participants. In an attempt to answer this question, I should like to recall an earlier quotation from Halliday (1993): "language is the essential condition of knowing, the process by which experience *becomes* knowledge" (p. 94; emphasis in original).

One of the characteristics of an utterance, whether spoken or written, is that it can be looked at as simultaneously process and product: as "saying" and as "what is said." In uttering, the speakers' efforts are directed to the saying – to producing meaning for others. To do this, speakers have to interpret the preceding contribution(s) in terms of the information it introduces, as well as their own stance toward that information; compare that interpretation with their own current understanding of the issue under discussion, based on their experience and any other relevant information of which they are aware; and then formulate a contribution that will, in some relevant way, add to the common understanding achieved in the discourse so far by extending, questioning, or qualifying what someone else has said. It is frequently in this effort to make their understanding meaningful for others that speakers have the feeling of reaching a fuller and clearer understanding for themselves. (See Wertsch, this volume, for an account of Vygotsky's realization of the *expressive* functions of speech.)

But in uttering, speakers are also producing "what is said," a material utterance to which they can respond in much the same way as those to whom it is addressed: by interrogating the meaning of what is said, evaluating its coherence and relevance, and beginning to formulate a further response. This is the second way in which speaking can enhance understanding. It was partly this function of uttering that Wertsch and Stone (1985) had in mind when they wrote that young language learners "can say more than they realize and [that] it is through coming to understand what is meant by what is said that their cognitive skills develop" (p. 167).

In contributing to a knowledge-building dialogue, then, a speaker is simultaneously adding to the structure of meaning created jointly with others and advancing his or her own understanding through the constructive and creative effort involved in saying and in responding to what was said. And, since a similar constructive effort is required to listen responsively and critically to the contributions of others, that too provides an opportunity to advance understanding. I should emphasize, though, that it is the joint attempt to construct common understandings "that the participants recognize as superior to their previous understandings," as Bereiter (1994) puts it, that makes dialogue such an effective means for participants to enhance their individual understandings. Certainly, dialogue of this kind involves both the internalization of the meanings created in the intermental forum of discussion and the externalization of those intramental meanings that are constructed in response; it also constitutes a particularly clear instance of Vygotsky's (1981) insight that "the individual develops into what he/she is through what he/she produces for others" (p. 162).

The Spiral of Knowing

I have tried to bring together the preceding ideas about the central role that dialogue plays in the construction of knowledge and the development of understanding in an inquiry-oriented curriculum with the construct of the "spiral of knowing" that is represented in Figure 4.1 (Wells, 1999). Here I want to draw attention to some of the key features that I have attempted to capture in this diagram.

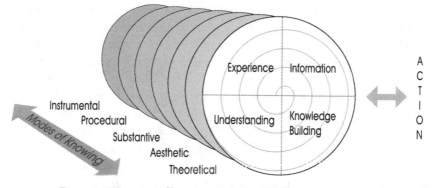

Figure 4.1 The spiral of knowing. From Wells (1999).

Following Dewey, I shall start with the segment labeled "experience," meaning by this an individual's firsthand engagement in activity, whether undertaken solo or in collaboration with others. The second segment represents the addition of "information" from others, either gained through observation or speech or through the medium of print and other visuographic artifacts. However, for this information to contribute to a growth in "understanding," which is the goal of knowing and the fourth segment in the diagram, it must be transformed through the process of "knowledge building," that is, through the sort of dialogue that I have been calling *progressive discourse*. This is dialogue that is focused on the object of the activity and aimed at making an answer to a question or a solution to a problem to which the activity has given rise.

The term *dialogue* typically refers to face-to-face interaction using the resources of spoken language. This is certainly the mode in which dialogue is first experienced, and it remains the most ubiquitous and versatile. However, the means for knowledge building are not limited to speech. On the one hand, solving practical problems often depends as much on the coordination of skillful action as on speech; on the other hand, theoretical knowledge building may be carried on across time and space through a dialogue that uses writing and other visuographic modes of representation. Across all these modes, however, two features of the dialogue that support knowledge building are paramount: responsivity and the attempt to achieve enhanced understanding. It then becomes clear – as Vygotsky argued – that a similar sort of dialogue can take place when one is alone, using the resources appropriated from engaging in dialogue with others.

So far, the focus has been on a single cycle. However, the understanding attained through knowledge-building dialogue at the end of one cycle provides the basis for making sense of further experience and information in the next cycle. This is one of the senses in which there is a spiral of knowing over successive engagements with the object of the activity, with the knowing serving to mediate these engagements. I have used a two-headed arrow to represent this dynamic interaction between the cycle of knowing and "action" with respect to the object/outcome of the activity. Such action may take a variety of forms, not all of them overt. In many situations the action may be restricted to discourse, and in some cycles it may be in the discourse that Vygotsky referred to as *inner speech*.

However, there is a second kind of spiral that the diagram attempts to represent. This spiral represents the relationship between the different modes of knowing distinguished previously. There is a sense in which each individual's ontogenetic trajectory recapitulates the emergence of the different modes of knowing in the history of the species, as understanding gained in one mode provides the basis for appropriating those modes to be mastered later.

Stated in these schematic terms, the spiral of knowing is undoubtedly simplistic. In particular, the form of the representation seems to imply that theoretical knowing is the endpoint to which all engagement in the spiral of knowing should aspire. However, it is sufficient to look closely at any complex activity, whether inside or outside the classroom, to dispel this misapprehension. As quickly becomes clear, most activities are mediated by more than one of the modes of knowing, so that, in practice, there is a convoluted spiraling backward and forward between them as attention is focused on the different kinds of objects involved in the component actions through which the goals of the activity are realized. Thus, although formal education may provide the setting in which most young people first systematically engage in theoretical knowing, as Vygotsky (1987) argued, it is important that theoretical knowing does not become an end in itself, but that the understandings gained be directed to effective and responsible action in the world of practical activity.

Knowledge Building through Dialogue about Texts

As I have just pointed out in discussing the spiral of knowing, dialogue is not restricted to the spoken mode. Indeed, powerful though it is as a means of engaging participants in a joint activity, dialogue in the oral mode has one serious disadvantage as a medium for knowledge building: It leaves no record of what has been jointly constructed. For this reason, the rise of theoretical knowing had to wait for the invention of technological means that made knowledge representations independent of oral memory in the form of writing or such other visuographic forms of representation as maps, diagrams, and graphs. The particular advantage of such relatively permanent representations of meaning is that they can be responded to by readers who are not present in the same time or place; they can also be critically re-viewed and revised by both writer and readers, and, in this way, deliberately improved and developed. For this reason, as Lotman (1988) argues, a text can serve a dialogic function, becoming what he calls "a thinking device" and "a generator of meaning" (p. 40)

On the basis of arguments of this kind, much has been made in recent years of the potential of writing as a means of learning, and certainly *expert* writers will attest to the fact that, for them, writing shapes thinking (Langer & Applebee, 1987; Murray, 1982). However, few students, even at the undergraduate level, seem to have discovered that writing can function as a thinking device. Because many assignments emphasize the accurate reproduction of information from a textbook, many student writers habitually adopt a strategy of "knowledge telling" (Bereiter & Scardamalia, 1987). This strategy corresponds to the assumption that texts serve only a transmissional function, and it often involves no more than the transfer of information from memory or the source text to the assignment, without any constructive or critical engagement with it. Expert writers, by contrast, typically treat each writing assignment as an occasion for "knowledge transformation" as they try to organize the information at their disposal in a rhetorical structure appropriate both to their purpose and to the audience in view. In terms of my argument, writing approached in this manner is an occasion for knowledge building as the writer both tries to anticipate the likely response of the envisaged audience and carries on a dialogue with the text being composed.

Not surprisingly, sophisticated strategies of this kind are not developed simply through carrying out individually undertaken writing assignments, particularly those that require no more than a restatement of what is known or remembered. As Vygotsky's concept of the ZPD makes clear, such strategies are most readily appropriated from situations in which they are demonstrated and collaboratively deployed in the joint construction of written texts. This is the principle underlying such initiatives in literature-based reading and writing programs as Book Clubs (McMahon & Raphael, 1997) and Literature Circles, in which students meet to discuss the books they have been reading and on that basis go on to create further texts in response. Writing conferences, in which writers are able to discuss their developing texts with their peers or teacher, provide another setting in which such strategies may be made overt and so available for appropriation.

However, it is not only by focusing on texts as end products that the dialogic potential of written texts can be realized, as can be seen in the work of The Developing Inquiring Communities in Education Project (DICEP; http://www.oise.on.ca/~ctd/DICEP/), a collaborative action research group made up of school-based and university-based educators to which I belong. In our project, which aims to promote an inquiry-oriented approach to learning and teaching with the goal of undertanding and improving the role of both spoken and written discourse in this process, teacher members have been exploring a number of ways of enabling their students to use writing as a tool for making sense of information or for problem solving in the course of some other activity, and in every case these inquiries have involved spoken dialogue about texts of various kinds.

Mary Ann Van Tassell asked the parents of her Grade 1 and Grade 2 students to engage in shared book reading with their children, and to write down the children's responses to the stories on Post-It notes and to affix them to the relevant pages. These written notes then became the "seeds" for a discussion between the teacher and all those who had read a particular story in which, together, they created a web diagram on which the Post-It notes were arranged to represent the similarities and differences between their responses. In this way, the teacher used the brief written texts scribed by the parents as the basis for a group exploration of the aspects of the story that the children had found particularly significant. In this process, one of their most important discoveries was that, like the Post-It notes, ideas could be combined and arranged in different ways, depending on the writer's purpose.

Extending the scope of "text" to the domain of mathematical problem solving, Gen Ling Chang posed a problem to her Grade 6 and Grade 7 students in the context of preparing for a simulated landing on Mars as part of an international project in which they were involved. The forthcoming task, on the day of the landing, would be to construct a habitat from clear plastic sheeting in the shape of a rectangular prism measuring $3.5 \times 3.5 \times 2.5$ meters. In preparation, the teacher had bought a roll of thin plastic sheeting, 4 meters long and 3 meters wide, folded in four so that the width of the roll was 75 centimeters, so that each group of three students could make a scale model of the habitat 1/10th of the eventual size. The problem was to find a way of cutting the roll of plastic so that each of the 10 groups received enough material to make its own model habitat. After 20 minutes or so, in which each group worked at the problem, the teacher asked the representatives of each group to write or draw their proposed solutions on the blackboard. Then, one by one, the representatives explained their proposals, each of which was critically discussed by the rest of the class.

One group in particular was fascinating to watch. While the designated group member was writing on the blackboard, the remaining pair was scanning the various alternatives proposed by other groups when one of them suddenly saw the flaw in her own group's proposal. She quickly did some further calculations and, satisfied that the new proposal would work, she discussed it with her partner and then went to the blackboard to substitute it for the solution they had originally proposed. In due course, the group representative explained the annotated diagram in which the new proposal was presented, and it was eventually accepted as one possible way of solving the problem. In this example, proposed solutions inscribed on the blackboard served as thinking devices for other students and then as the basis for a consideration of alternative ways in which the problem could be solved.

The third example is taken from an investigation of light carried out by a class of gifted students in Grades 6 and 7. Following a period in which the students explored a range of relevant materials that had been provided, the teacher, Karen Hume, invited the students to propose questions for further study both by means of experimentation and through the use of reference materials. Of the many questions that were proposed, the 30 or so that were judged worthy of investigation were then posted on the "knowledge wall" – a large notice board occupying almost one entire wall of the classroom – and students were encouraged to continue the dialogue started by each question by posting further notes on the knowledge wall. After 2 or 3 days, when the wall was almost covered with notes, the teacher asked those students most interested in each question to prepare a summary of the written dialogue on that topic to date. The following is an extract from the discussion focusing on preparation of the summary of the discussion on the question: Why does light travel at the speed of 300,000 kilometers per second?

Ian: I have a thought. I don't know if it's true. Maybe light would go slower if it were underwater, or faster, or maybe –

Eren: But Ian, no. Do you know how light travels? It goes through the molecules of the water

Ray: But what about in outer space? Maybe the molecular structure is different. Maybe it's just one big molecule

Eren: It goes through a vacuum, I know that

Steve: Eren, I think it was Nikki said up there [on the wall] that if you shine light through a glass it slows down

Eren: Yeah, I know (thoughtfully)

Ian: Maybe light would go faster in a black hole because there's nothing in it...Maybe if there's something in it then that's not good

Eren: I'm not really sure

Ian: Maybe there was this alien planet and a black hole, and we're on the other side of the black hole...
Well I don't know (in response to quizzical glances from Eren and Steve)

Eren: That would be very impossible to trace, and even if it were –

Steve: So are you saying that on the other side of black holes, there's an alien planet?

Ray: Okay, this is my theory (He says something, mostly inaudible, about the density of molecules in other galaxies)

Steve: You said that light goes through the molecules
If we can prove that glass affects the speed of light...

Eren: It does

Steve: So glass does affect the speed of light?

Eren: Yes

Ray: So then the molecules must –

Steve: The molecules must affect it

Eren: No I don't think so

Ray: You're contradicting yourself

Steve: But Eren, something in the glass affects it. And if there's nothing inside of the glass, then it must be the molecules of the glass

Ray: I'm thinking of the density of the molecules

Steve: I know, that's what I think too

Ray   Okay, light can go (draws a diagram showing light refracting through glass and slowing down)

Eren   Okay, it says here (referring to a book he got from the public library) "In a glass light travels only two thirds as fast as through air. Why?" Oh nooooo, it leaves out the why. We have to figure out the why

Here the discussion of the topic already carried on through the medium of the written notes posted on the knowledge wall pushes the four boys to reconsider their question. Prompted by the quotation Eren reads from the book, they go on to reformulate it in terms of the effect of the medium through which light passes on the speed at which it travels.

In presenting these three vignettes, my first intention has been to illustrate different ways in which texts of different kinds can provide objects to be interrogated and improved through dialogic knowledge building, thereby enabling participants to increase their individual as well as their collective understanding of the topics investigated. At the same time, my intention in presenting these three examples has been to show how teachers can, through inquiries focusing on their own practice, significantly extend the scope and depth of the opportunities that they provide for their students to appropriate these cultural tools for knowledge building and simultaneously increase their own understanding of the critical features of classroom activities that make this development possible. What we have found is that, just as our students benefit from participation in a dialogic community of inquiry, so too do we, their teachers. Whether through opportunities for discussion and analysis of data at our regular meetings or through our ongoing e-mail conversation, it is the opportunity to engage in collaborative knowledge building with fellow educators that is the key to the gains we have each made in our own understandings. And it is the sense of empowerment that we gain as whole persons, and not just as professionals, that provides the motivation to continue to engage in these inquiries (Chang-Wells & Wells, 1997). Finally, these vignettes and those cited earlier make it clear that this is no utopian vision that I have been proposing, but a reality that is already being created in DICEP classrooms and others like them, where teachers are exploring the possibilities for practice of a social constructivist theory of education.

Conclusion

In this chapter I have tried to show how Vygotsky's theory of learning and development, with its core concept of artifact-mediated joint activity, can integrate some of the most important insights that have been gained in recent years from research in education. Building on his ideas, I have proposed that, by conceptualizing the classroom as a Community of Inquiry, we can see how collaborative group work, dialogic knowledge building, and an inquiry-oriented curriculum are essential and interdependent components of a vision of education that, rising above the age-old conflict between traditional attempts to transmit basic knowledge and skills on the one hand, and progressive emphases on individual discovery on the other, recognizes that both convention and invention are necessary for the development of society as well as for its individual members.

Of course, communities of inquiry do not exist in a vacuum; what happens within classrooms is both facilitated and constrained by institutional and societal values and expectations, as well as by the material surroundings and the availability of appropriate resources. To realize the vision that I have proposed will require more than a change in the practices through which education is enacted within the classroom. Nevertheless, because individuals and society are mutually constitutive of each other, though on different time scales, it is on the nature and quality of the particular activities in which teachers and students participate together, and through which learning occurs, that I believe our attention now needs to be focused. For it is in the formation of individuals' identities and dispositions through their collaborative engagement with others in worthwhile and intrinsically motivating activities, carried out thoughtfully and with commitment to the quality of the artifacts that are produced and used, that we can most effectively make these the values of the wider society. It is this understanding that I believe to be Vygotsky's most important legacy to us and the means for transforming the institution of schooling so that it better serves both society and its individual members.

References

Bakhtin, M. M. (1986). *Speech genres and other late essays* (C. Emerson & M. Holquist, Eds; Y. McGee, Trans.). Austin: University of Texas Press.

Bereiter, C. (1994). Implications of postmodernism for science, or, science as progressive discourse. *Educational Psychologist, 29*(1), 3–12.

Bereiter, C., & Scardamalia, M. (1987). *The psychology of written composition*. Hillsdale, NJ: Erlbaum.

Bereiter, C., & Scardamalia, M. (1996). Rethinking learning. In D. R. Olson & N. Torrance (Eds.), *The handbook of education and human development* (pp. 485–513). Cambridge, MA: Blackwell.

Bettencourt, A. (1991). *On understanding science*. Unpublished paper, Michigan State University.

Brown, A. L., & Campione, J. C. (1994). Guided discovery in a community of learners. In K. McGilly (Ed.), *Integrating cognitive theory and classroom practice: Classroom lessons* (pp. 229–270). Cambridge, MA: MIT Press/Bradford Books.

Bruner, J. S. (1962). Introduction. In L. S. Vygotsky, *Thought and language* (pp. v–x). Cambridge, MA: MIT Press.

Bruner, J. S. (1990). *Acts of meaning*. Cambridge, MA: Harvard University Press.

Carr, W., & Kemmis, S. (1983). *Becoming critical: Knowing through action research.* Geelong, Victoria, Australia: Deakin University Press.

Chang-Wells, G. L., & Wells, G. (1997). Modes of discourse for living, learning and teaching. In S. Hollingsworth (Ed.), *International action research and educational reform* (pp. 147–156). Philadelphia: Falmer Press.

Cohen, D. K., McLaughlin, M. W., & Talbert, J. E. (Eds.). (1993). *Teaching for understanding: Challenges for policy and practice.* San Francisco: Jossey-Bass.

Cole, M. (1996). *Cultural psychology: A once and future discipline.* Cambridge, MA: Harvard University Press.

Dewey, J. (1900/1990). *The school and society.* Chicago: University of Chicago Press.

Dewey, J. (1938). *Experience and education.* New York: Collier Macmillan.

Donald, M. (1991). *Origins of the modern mind: Three stages in the evolution of culture and cognition.* Cambridge, MA: Harvard University Press.

Edwards, D., & Mercer, N. (1987). *Common knowledge.* London: Methuen/Routledge.

Engeström, Y. (1991). Activity theory and individual and social transformation. *Activity Theory, 7/8,* 6–17.

Franklin, U. (1996). Introduction to the symposium *Towards an ecology of knowledge.* Toronto: University of Toronto.

Freire, P. (1970). *Pedagogy of the oppressed.* New York: Herder and Herder.

Gallas, K. (1994). *The languages of learning: How children talk, write, dance, draw, and sing their understanding of the world.* New York: Teachers College Press.

Galton, M., Simon, B., & Croll, P. (1980). *Inside primary schools.* London: Routledge.

Gardner, H. (1989). *Art, mind, and education: Research from Project Zero.* Urbana: University of Illinois Press.

Goodman, K. (1987). *What's whole in Whole Language.* Portsmouth, NH: Heinemann.

Hacking, I. (1990). *The taming of chance.* New York: Cambridge University Press.

Halliday, M. A. K. (1978). *Language as social semiotic: The social interpretation of language and meaning.* London: Arnold.

Halliday, M. A. K. (1988). On the language of physical science. In M. Ghadessy (Ed.), *Registers of written English: Situational factors and linguistic features* (pp. 162–178). London: Frances Pinter.

Halliday, M. A. K. (1993). Towards a language-based theory of learning. *Linguistics and Education, 5,* 93–116.

Her Majesty's Stationery Office. (1975). *A language for life.* London: Author.

Johnson, D., Johnson, R., & Holubec, E. (1993). *Circles of learning: Cooperation in the classroom* (4th ed.). Minneapolis: Interaction Book Co.

John-Steiner, V. (1987). *Notebooks of the mind: Explorations of thinking.* New York: Harper and Row.

Langer, J. A., & Applebee, A. N. (1987). *How writing shapes thinking: A study of teaching and learning.* (NCTE Research Report No. 22). Urbana, IL: National Council of Teachers of English.

Lave, J., & Wenger, E. (1991). *Situated learning: Legitimate peripheral participation.* New York: Cambridge University Press.

Lemke, J. L. (1990). *Talking science: Language, learning, and values.* Norwood, NJ: Ablex.

Leont'ev, A. N. (1981). The problem of activity in psychology. In J. V. Wertsch (Ed.), *The concept of activity in Soviet psychology* (pp. 37–71). Armonk, NY: M. E. Sharpe.

Litowitz, B. (1993). Deconstruction in the zone of proximal development. In E. Forman, N. Minick, & A. Stone (Eds.), *Contexts for learning: Sociocultural dynamics in children's development* (pp. 184–196). New York: Oxford University Press.

Lotman, Y. M. (1988). Text within a text. *Soviet Psychology, 26*(3), 32–51.

McMahon, S. I., & Raphael, T. E., with Goatley, V. J., & Pardo, L. S. (Eds.). (1997). *The Book Club connection: Literacy learning and classroom talk*. New York: Teachers College Press.

Murray, D. (1982). *Learning by teaching*. Portsmouth, NH: Heinemann.

Nystrand, M. (1997). *Opening dialogue: Understanding the dynamics of language and learning in the English classroom*. New York: Teachers College Press.

Nystrand, M., & Gamoran, A. (1991). Student engagement: When recitation becomes conversation. In H. C. Waxman & H. J. Walberg (Eds.), *Effective teaching: Current research* (pp. 257–276). Berkeley, CA: McCutchan.

Olson, D. R. (1994). *The world on paper*. New York: Cambridge University Press.

Ong, W. (1982). *Orality and literacy*. New York: Methuen.

Palincsar, A. S., Magnusson, S. J., Marano, N., Ford, D., & Brown, N. (1998). Designing a community of practice: Principles and practices of the GIsML Community. *Teaching and Teacher Education, 14*(1), 5–20.

Penuel, W., & Wertsch, J. V. (1995). Vygotsky and identity formation: A sociocultural approach. *Educational Psychologist, 30*(2), 83–92.

Popper, K. R., & Eccles, J. C. (1977). *The self and its brain*. Berlin: Springer-Verlag.

Reddy, M. (1979). The conduit metaphor – a case of frame conflict in our language about language. In A. Ortony (Ed.), *Metaphor and thought* (pp. 284–324). New York: Cambridge University Press.

Russell, D. R. (1991). *Writing in the academic disciplines, 1870–1990: A curricular history*. Carbondale: Southern Illinois University Press.

Scardamalia, M., Bereiter, C., & Lamon, M. (1994). The CSILE project: Trying to bring the classroom into World 3. In K. McGilley (Ed.), *Classroom lessons: Integrating cognitive theory and classroom practice* (pp. 201–228). Cambridge, MA: MIT Press.

Schön, D. (1983). *The reflective practitioner*. New York: Basic Books.

Schön, D. (1987). *Educating the reflective practitioner*. San Francisco: Jossey-Bass.

Scribner, S. (1985). Vygotsky's uses of history. In J. V. Wertsch (Ed.), *Culture, communication and cognition: Vygotskian perspectives* (pp. 119–145). New York: Cambridge University Press.

Sharan, S., & Sharan, Y. (1992). *Expanding cooperative learning through group investigation*. New York: Teachers College Press.

Slavin, R. E. (1983). When does cooperative learning increase student achievement? *Psychological Bulletin, 94*, 429–445.

Tharp, R., & Gallimore, R. (1988). *Rousing minds to life*. New York: Cambridge University Press.

von Glasersfeld, E. (1989). Cognition, construction of knowledge, and teaching. *Synthese, 80*, 121–140.

Vygotsky, L. S. (1978). *Mind in society: The development of higher psychological processes* (M. Cole, V. John-Steiner, S. Scribner, & E. Souberman, Eds.). Cambridge, MA: Harvard University Press.

Vygotsky, L. S. (1981). The genesis of higher mental functions. In J. V. Wertsch (Ed. & Trans.), *The concept of activity in Soviet psychology* (pp. 144–188). Armonk, NY: M. E. Sharpe.

Vygotsky, L. S. (1987). Thinking and speech. In L. S. Vygotsky, *Collected works* (Vol. 1, pp. 39–285) (R. Rieber & A. Carton, Eds.; N. Minick, Trans.). New York: Plenum.

Wartofsky, M. (1979). *Models, representation and scientific understanding*. Boston: Reidel.

Wells, G. (1993). Working with a teacher in the zone of proximal development: Action research on the learning and teaching of science. *Journal of the Society for Accelerative Learning and Teaching, 18*, 127–222.

Wells, G. (Ed.) (1994). *Changing schools from within: Creating communities of inquiry*. Toronto, Canada, and Portsmouth, NH: OISE Press and Heinemann.

Wells, G. (1995). Language and the inquiry-oriented curriculum. *Curriculum Inquiry, 25, 233–269.*

Wells, G. (1999). *Dialogic inquiry: Towards a sociocultural practice and theory of education*. New York: Cambridge University Press.

Wertsch, J. V. (1985). *Vygotsky and the social formation of mind*. Cambridge, MA: Harvard University Press.

Wertsch, J. V. (1991). *Voices of the mind: A sociocultural approach to mediated action*. Cambridge, MA: Harvard University Press.

Wertsch, J. V., & Stone, C. A. (1985). The concept of internalization in Vygotsky's account of the genesis of higher mental functions. In J. V. Wertsch (Ed.), *Culture, communication and cognition: Vygotskian perspectives* (pp. 162–179). New York: Cambridge University Press.

5   Consequential Progressions

Exploring Collective-Individual Development in a Bilingual Classroom

LeAnn G. Putney, Judith Green, Carol Dixon,
Richard Durán, and Beth Yeager

Recently, neo-Vygotskian and sociocultural researchers have written about communities of practice that teachers and students construct in their classrooms (e.g., Dyson, this volume; John-Steiner, Panofsky, & Smith, 1994; Lave & Wenger, 1991; Rogoff, 1995; Smagorinsky & O'Donnell-Allen, this volume; Wells, this volume; Wells & Chang-Wells, 1992; Wertsch, 1995). Converging with this work is research drawing on ethnographic and sociolinguistic perspectives focusing on classrooms as cultures (e.g., Cochran, 1997; Collins & Green, 1990, 1992; Floriani, 1993; Gutierrez & Stone, this volume; Lin, 1993; Putney, 1996; Santa Barbara Classroom Discourse Group, 1992a, 1992b). Although these perspectives have different disciplinary and theoretical roots, they share an overlapping set of goals: to identify ways in which students and others learn with, and through, interactions among members in particular communities; and to understand how community practices shape and are shaped by what members learn in and across time. One way of understanding this body of work is to see these researchers as concerned with social and academic consequences for members of living in a particular collective or community of practice (e.g., a reading group, a class, a school, a family, etc.).

The purpose of this chapter is twofold. First, we present an argument for ways of studying how communities of practice are constructed and how practices within these developing communities become cultural resources for members. Second, we examine how members' use of these developing resources is consequential for both the individual and the collective.

Support for this chapter come from grants from the California Writing Project, The Spencer Foundation, and the Linguistic Minority Research Institute. The authors would like to thank Ana Floriani (Illinois Wesleyan University) for her contributions to the data presented.

Specifically, we explore social and academic consequences of participating in a particular developing collective in a fifth-grade bilingual classroom.

To identify the consequential nature of life in this bilingual classroom for both the collective and individuals, we drew on two bodies of work: sociocultural-historical (Vygotskian and neo-Vygotskian) perspectives on the nature of learning and ethnographic-sociolinguistic perspectives (interactional ethnography) on the social construction of everyday life within and across groups. We argue that combining these mutually informing perspectives creates a new expressive potential (Strike, 1974) for studying learning as a social process by providing an enhanced theoretical language for studying the dialogic, constructed, and consequential nature of individual-collective activity. We present the mutually informing potential of these perspectives using a three-part structure. In the first part, we examine particular interpretations of Vygotsky's (1978, 1981, 1986) theory of learning and discuss how this theoretical perspective implicates a particular approach to studying learning in social groups. In the second part, we describe our approach, *interactional ethnography*, and discuss how it provides a systematic way of studying learning as culturally and socially constructed. In the third part, we present data analyses that illustrate the consequential nature of collective-individual development and the enhanced expressive potential formed by integrating these perspectives.

Using a *telling case* approach (Mitchell, 1984), we explore how actions and interactions of the teacher with one student in a particular discursive event were shaped by what was constructed in previous events, and how conceptual understandings shaped in and across these events became resources for this student in subsequent events. The choice of the telling case approach was purposeful. A telling case is not a representative case, but one that allows in-depth exploration of theoretical issues not previously visible. Our telling case, *Jared developing point of view as a cultural resource across time and events*, provides a way of exploring the relationship between individual and collective development across time and events, which is often overlooked when research focuses solely on individual student learning.

Understanding Learning as Constructed: A Sociohistorical-Sociocultural Process

In the last two decades a number of educational researchers have explored Vygotsky's theory of cultural-historical human development. Each brings a particular interpretation or dimension of Vygotsky's theory to the fore, often resulting from a specific focus or question. Collectively, the theorists reviewed in this section provide insights into aspects of Vygotsky's conceptualization of the relationship between individual and collective development and learning.

Moll (1990) described the dialogic nature of learning proposed by Vygotsky, stating that "the intellectual skills children acquire are directly related to how they interact with others in specific problem-solving environments. He [Vygotsky] posited that children internalize and transform the help they receive from others and eventually use these same means of guidance to direct their subsequent problem-solving behaviors. Therefore, the nature of social transactions is central to a zone of proximal development analysis" (p. 1; see Ball, this volume, for an extended discussion of Vygotsky's notion of internalization). Learning, viewed in this way, occurs both in the moment and over time, and involves individual–collective relationships and interactions. This perspective implies a two-step process of analysis: one focusing on the developing collective and the other on the individual within the collective.

Wertsch (1981) contributes further to our understanding of Vygotsky's view of the dialogic nature of learning and development by focusing on the individual within a social interaction. He describes how interactions provide particular opportunities for students and how the child's interpretation and take-up of the sociocultural resources constructed in and through the social interactions are consequential. He argues that Vygotsky is saying that "the very means (especially speech) used in social interaction are taken over by the individual child and internalized" (p. 146). For Vygotsky, then, speech and other means (e.g., nonverbal actions, graphic representations; see Smagorinsky & O'Donnell-Allen, this volume) are not merely vehicles for learning; they are also the focus of learning. Thus, as students interact with others, they are acquiring knowledge of how to learn (i.e., the processes and practices of the group) as well as what to know. By foregrounding the issue of speech, Wertsch also draws attention to the role of discourse in the social construction of opportunities for learning (see Wells, this volume).

Souza Lima (1995) proposes how individual–collective relationships shape the development of both the individual and the collective. Drawing on sociohistorical perspectives (e.g., that of Freire), she argues that "We have two dimensions of development: one that resides in the individual and the other in the collectivity. Both are interdependent and create each other. Historically created possibilities of cultural development are themselves transformed by the processes through which individuals acquire the cultural tools that are or become available in their context" (pp. 447–448). This view of development presumes that the course of development is not linear, nor is it totally predictable; rather, it is cultural, historical, dynamic, and interactive for both the individual and the collective. The individual and the collective are in a reflexive relationship, one that is recursive, transformational, and socially produced. The individual does not merely acquire cultural knowledge but also contributes to the shape and resources of the collective (see also Gaskins, Miller, & Corsaro, 1992). These interpretations suggest that a focus on individuals, or on small strips of social interactions alone, is not sufficient for understanding learning as a social construction in which an individual shapes, and is shaped by, the actions of the collective.

Understanding Learning and Development as Constructed: An Interactional Ethnographic Approach

Conceptualizing the reflexive relationship between individual and collective development from an interactional ethnographic perspective involves identifying opportunities for learning that members of a social group (e.g., a pair, a reading group, a class) construct in and through their moment-by-moment interactions and examining over time the take-up and transformation of these opportunities by individuals (Tuyay, Jennings, & Dixon, 1995). These analyses provide a basis for exploring both collective and individual development and for understanding what constitutes a zone of proximal development. This approach differs somewhat from what is often undertaken in the study of learning within a zone of proximal development. We use the concept of *opportunities for learning* rather than *zone of proximal development*, given our focus on understanding the constructed nature of everyday life. This emphasis allows us to first examine how the "opportunity" for learning is constructed. We can then explore whether or not this opportunity is within the zone of proximal development for any individual or for the group as a whole. By examining how individual and group interactions contribute to the completion of a particular task or the construction of a particular event, we are able to explore learning as an outcome of collective activity and to identify what counts as a zone of proximal development, or rather, what counts as a learning context to those guiding the learner's development.

Central to this perspective is a theory of culture as constructed by members, an issue recognized by Vygotsky but not realized in his own research (Watson-Gegeo, 1992). To illustrate how a theory of culture as constructed informed our understanding of individual–collective development and the consequential nature of this relationship, we describe further what constitutes interactional ethnography. This approach combines a cultural anthropological perspective on the study of social life (Spradley, 1980) with an interactional sociolinguistic perspective on the study of language in use. The ethnographic approach provides a logic of inquiry (Birdwhistell, 1977; Gee & Green, 1998) that we use to guide our study of the developing collective, and how this development shapes the opportunities for constructing cultural knowledge that members are afforded in and across time and events. The sociolinguistic perspective provides ways of examining how members, in and through their face-to-face interactions, shape and are shaped by mutually constructed social activity.

The dynamic and ongoing relationships among discourse, social action, learning, and development within an ethnographic perspective are captured by Spindler and Spindler (1987). They argue that within any social setting, people carry on a culturally constructed dialogue that is "expressed in behavior, words, symbols, and in the application of cultural knowledge to make instrumental activities and social situations work for one. We learn the dialogue as children, and continue learning it all of our lives, as our circumstances change" (p. 2). By arguing that this dialogue is one of action and interaction, the authors place the study of dialogue in the center of ethnographic work, seeking to identify what members of a social group need to know, produce, predict, interpret, and evaluate in a given setting to participate appropriately and, through that participation, to learn (i.e., to acquire, construct, and transform the cultural knowledge of the group) (Heath, 1982). These assumptions provide a conceptual approach for analyzing discourse data from an emic perspective and for examining how discourse shapes both what is available to be learned and what is displayed as learning within and across events and time. Thus, members of a classroom (a collective) can be viewed as acting as a culture (Collins & Green, 1990, 1992; Santa Barbara Classroom Discourse Group, 1992a, 1992b).

Three key analytic constructs from an anthropological approach to ethnography are central to understanding how interactional ethnography informs the study of the consequential relationships between individual and collective development: exploring part–whole, whole–part relationships; using contrastive relevance; and exploring the history of intertextual and intercontextual relationships within a social group. Erickson (1977) argues that one goal of the ethnographer is to arrive at a holistic understanding of the overall historical, cultural, or social context rather than coding discrete behaviors, events, or strips of talk (cf. Moll, 1990, p. 11, for a similar argument from a sociocultural perspective). To frame how the part–whole, whole–part relationship can be understood, Erickson and Shultz (1981) proposed a situated, socially constructed view of context that captures this process, arguing that contexts are made up of people and their situated social action, embedded in time and changing from moment to moment. Members thus provide contextual cues to whole–part, part–whole relationships. Therefore, to understand the importance or consequence of particular actions and interactions, researchers ground their descriptions in the actions and discourse of members, who signal to each other what they are orienting to and what they are holding each other accountable for.

Durán and Szymanski (1996) argue that the constructed nature of context is consequential for participants. In a study of dyadic interactions within classroom events, they found that as students negotiate tasks at hand within their peer group, they construct a procedural representation of activity, orienting to each other based on their past negotiations and in relation to the eventual progress of their current interaction. "This representation," they say, "is constructed through the participants' initiation and responses to talk based upon the demands of the task and beliefs about the interactional constraints of the social context" (p. 5). Therefore, the interaction is a negotiated production with an implicated future and an intertextual past (Bakhtin, 1986), which they call *consequential progression*. In this chapter, we build on and expand this concept to explore the within-event and across-event nature of such progressions, the intertextual relationships between and among such progressions, and how knowledge constructed in one context becomes socially and academically consequential in others.

The second analytic construct used by interactional ethnographers, *contrastive relevance*, is critical to identifying the consequential nature of the unfolding events of everyday life in classrooms and other social settings. This approach provides a way of grounding analysis in an emic perspective and of exploring what is consequential in the interactions among members. Hymes (1974) argues that by using contrastive relevance, the ethnographer is able to demonstrate the functional relevance of a particular action. The ethnographer examines the choices members of a social group make in particular interactional situations to ascertain the relevance of particular choices of form, code, or meaning within a local context and to explore what difference those choices make to the patterns of life within and across time. Contrast can occur at any level of analysis; the size of the unit does not matter (Erickson, 1977). The key is to show the relevance of this contrast in understanding what members are doing together and the social significance or consequences of these actions. Thus, through the use of contrastive analysis, a researcher is able to identify what meanings, processes, and forms count to members; how they construct form, process, and meaning; and how meanings are related to, and constituted by, the forms of interaction constructed.

That these dimensions of life in classrooms are consequential may appear on the surface to be self-evident. However, what is consequential and how it is or becomes consequential, not only in the moment but over time, is not well understood. To examine this aspect of social life, the interactional ethnographer engages in the third analytic construct, *an exploration of the historical and over-time relationship between and among texts and contexts*. As Watson-Gegeo (1992) argues, "for an ethnographic description to be adequate, it must cover whole events and behavior in light of both the long-term history of relationships in the immediate setting and the relevant larger historical and institutional processes" (p. 53). In arguing that a history of relationships frames the immediate actions of members, she provides a means of understanding, both in time and over time, dimensions of context and the reflexive relationship among individuals, as well as between the individual and the collective. This distinction is far from insignificant, as our analysis will show.

To frame the link between in-time and over-time relationships, we draw on Bloome and his colleagues' (Bloome & Bailey, 1992; Bloome & Egan-Robertson, 1993) view of intertextuality, Floriani's (1993) notion of intercontextuality, and Bakhtin's (1986) view of speaker–hearer relationships. These three theoretical constructs are central to an expanded view of consequential progressions and historically relevant relationships. Bloome and Bailey (1992) frame how members signal to each other ties across time, texts, and events through the notion of intertextuality as socially constructed. They argue that people engaged in a language event "are engaged in intertextual juxtapositions of various conversational and written texts. . . . Intertextuality is a social construction in that these juxtapositions must be interactionally recognized by the participants in an event, acknowledged by those participants, and have social significance within the event" (p. 198). By observing what actions members take up, what they referentially propose and acknowledge, and how they take up and build on what is proposed within an unfolding event, we can identify what counts as socially significant in the local context. Further, by exploring the intertextual ties across contexts, both verbal and nonverbal, we can identify what members bring from prior events and how participating in those prior events is socially relevant and significant. Through the analysis of the social significance to members of particular types of intertextual relationships, we can identify how cultural knowledge from one social setting is consequential in the current interactions and/or future ones (see Dyson, Lee, Moll, this volume).

Building from this work on intertextuality and on context as constructed (Erickson & Shultz, 1981), Floriani (1993) introduced *intercontextuality* as part of a larger argument that students and teachers negotiate the nature of everyday life in classrooms. She proposed a relationship between an actor and a text that shapes ways of engaging with, using, and interacting with that text. Members establish this relationship, like the text itself, as they interact to construct text and context (see Smagorinsky & O'Donnell-Allen, this volume). These ways of engaging with text become cultural practices, which in turn become resources members draw on to interact with and construct text in subsequent contexts, thus forming an intercontextual tie that members recognize, acknowledge, interactionally accomplish, and signal as socially significant.

Underlying this view of intertextuality and intercontextuality is a reflexive relationship between speakers and hearers. As Bakhtin (1986) argues, speech is inherently responsive:

Any understanding of live speech, a live utterance, is inherently responsive, although the degree of this activity varies extremely. Any understanding is imbued with response and necessarily elicits it in one form or another: the listener becomes the speaker.... An actively responsive understanding of what is heard...can be directly realized in action ... or it can remain for the time being, a silent responsive understanding (certain speech genres are intended for this kind of responsive understanding...), but this is, so to speak, responsive understanding with a delayed reaction. (pp. 68–69)

The possibility of a delayed reaction or response is a key aspect in understanding the over-time nature of consequential progressions and provides a way of understanding the importance of examining intertextual and intercontextual relationships across time and events. Additionally, the concept of delayed response has consequences for our approach to studying learning as a social process. If researchers take this concept seriously, they will be unable to assume that actions that they observe in an event or at a moment in time represent what members meant, understood, or learned. Although claims about particular aspects of meaning and understanding can be constructed using the chains of action and interaction among members in a local context to make claims about learning, ethnographers need to analyze what individuals display to each other through oral, non-verbal, graphic, and written modes of communication within and across time and events.

Underlying this position is Bakhtin's view that "Sooner or later what is heard and actively understood will find its response in the subsequent speech or behavior of the listener. In most cases, genres of complex cultural communication are intended precisely for this kind of actively responsive understanding with delayed action. Everything we have said here also pertains to written and read speech" (pp. 59–60). The reflexive nature of speaker–hearer relationships and the view of delayed responses as culturally appropriate and ordinary suggest a way of expanding the discussion of learning from a sociocultural perspective. One way of viewing these two conceptualizations is to see them as suggesting that the link between individual and collective is reflexive both in the moment and over time. We argue that as members of a group construct a public or group text, individuals within the group are simultaneously constructing personal texts and contexts, ones that may match or differ from that public or collective text and context (Kelly & Crawford, 1997; Kelly, Crawford, & Green, in press). The developing group–public text and the context constitute the opportunities for learning afforded to members. These opportunities may or may not lead to learning in the moment, but rather may represent a form of procedural display (Bloome, Theordoreau, & Puro 1989). That is, members may act appropriately, but these actions may meet local demands for participation and may not represent changes in knowledge or the acquisition of new cultural knowledge (Kelly & Green, 1998; Tuyay, Jennings, & Dixon, 1995).

In conceptualizing interactions as entailing and representing a multiplicity of reflexive relationships (e.g., between speaker and hearer, text and context, personal and public texts, and individual and collective), we implicate a particular view of learning, one consonant with sociocultural/sociohistorical theory as discussed in the previous section of this chapter. Individuals do not merely internalize or transform texts or contexts; rather, they actively produce/reproduce them as they contribute to the developing opportunities for learning (Tuyay, Jennings, & Dixon, 1995) through the texts they construct, the discursive practices used to construct these texts, and the social practices guiding their interactions (cf. Fairclough, 1993).

The discussion in this section has shown potential links between Vygotsky's perspective on the relationship between learning and development and an interactional ethnographic approach to the study of classroom life. As we have argued, by viewing classrooms as cultures and learning as related to collective and individual development, links between these two theoretical perspectives become mutually informing. Through the analyses that follow, we illustrate how the dialogue between perspectives leads to new understandings of the consequential nature of the relationship between collective and individual and to the construction of an enhanced expressive potential for research on this issue.

Data Collection and Analysis Design

The data analyzed in the sections that follow were drawn from the an ongoing ethnographic study of social construction of knowledge in a bilingual fifth-grade classroom in a small city in California (e.g., Brilliant-Mills, 1993; Floriani, 1993, 1997; Fránquiz, 1995; Green & Yeager, 1995; Heras, 1993; Putney, 1997; Santa Barbara Classroom Discourse Group, 1995; Yeager, Floriani, & Green, 1998). The data collection for this ethnography began prior to the first day of school in September. Once school began, an ethnographer systematically collected data for the first 3 weeks of school. This involved videotaping the actions among members in the classroom, collecting all artifacts constructed on that day (for particular students), and collecting materials sent home. An intensive period of participant observation was undertaken all day, every day, followed by focused periods of data collection across particular cycles of activity (Green & Meyer, 1991) over the school year. These focused periods provided a way of tracing part–whole relationships, contrastive relevance, the history of relationships, and delayed responses within particular cycles of activity, and of exploring intertextual and intercontextual links. Through this approach we were able to explore what was constructed over time as opportunities for learning; what individual members did to learn; and what members displayed as learning, knowing, and understanding within this constructed world. Also, in identifying how members tied these cycles together intertextually and intercontextually, we were able to examine the consequentiality for particular students of participating in those events and to make visible the socially significant nature of the progression from one cycle to the next.

The analyses that follow provide particular angles of vision on collective and individual-within-the-collective development. The first analysis establishes Jared's interactions with the teacher as a telling case for exploring individual-within-collective development of one concept, *point of*

view. To show how Jared learned and then used point of view as a resource in future discursive events, we engage in a series of analyses called
backward and forward mapping (Tuyay, Floriani, Yeager, Dixon, & Green,
1995). This process allows us to trace intertextual and intercontextual ties
backward and forward in time. The first analysis presented focuses on a
discursive event in October initiated by Jared with the teacher partway
through a cycle of activity on point of view (*The Three Pigs*). This event
serves as a *key event* (Gumperz, 1986) or as what Vygotsky calls a *germ
cell* (Shepel, 1995); that is, it is a pivotal event that anchors all subsequent analyses. We begin the next phase of analysis by moving backward
in time across events involving point of view to identify the roots of the
knowledge that Jared displayed during his interactions with the teacher,
and then we move forward in time to see how what Jared was afforded
shaped his performance in subsequent events. In this way, we illustrate
the opportunities for learning and for constructing common knowledge
(Edwards & Mercer, 1987) or local knowledge (Geertz, 1983) that formed
the history of this discursive event.

The choice of Jared to explore these relationships was purposeful. The
teacher, who is a coresearcher with us and has a background in social
science and ethnography (e.g., Yeager et al., 1998; Yeager, Pattenaude,
Fránquiz, & Jennings, 1999), initiated this analysis as a means of examining what students had learned and then how they used this learning
in new ways. This sampling process provided a basis for her exploration
of student learning across time and events. Her research interest led her
to identify this event with Jared and to locate written and graphic texts
related to being a social scientist in this classroom. Because this key interaction occurred on a day when university researchers were not present,
the teacher's *head notes* (memories of dialogue and social activity) and subsequent reconstruction of this discursive event became important sources
of data for this study. To these written and reconstructed texts we added
analyses of the ethnographic records of the first day of school and of the
practices constructed across the first 3 weeks of school.

Establishing the Telling Case: Tracing Jared's
Take-up of Point of View

In this section we explore what members needed to know, understand, produce, and predict in order to accomplish an assigned task
by identifying the textual, intertextual, and intercontextual referents of
the discursive event constructed by Jared and his teacher. This discursive

event, while a whole in itself, was part of a larger collective event on that day. The teacher asked students to construct a graphic history of the story of the Third Pig in the *Three Little Pigs* from a particular point of view: the mother pig, the stick salesperson, or an ethnographer/detective. During this event, Jared approached the teacher to discuss his confusion about what to do to complete the assignment, thus initiating this discursive event with the teacher.

Analysis of the discourse between Jared and the teacher presented in Table 5.1 shows that as they interacted, the teacher helped Jared make textual, intertextual, and intercontextual links to past and present events and activities within the classroom. In this brief dialogue, they constructed intertextual references to previous texts (the actions of class members on the first-day video), to the current text they were constructing (their present dialogue), and to the memory of events as texts. These references also included intercontextual ties to practices (i.e., ways of being with and/or constructing texts) that the class had previously constructed, such as looking at things from a different angle, acting as ethnographers, needing to use insider knowledge, acting as observers, and exploring positioning to illustrate point of view.

Through these references the teacher helped Jared revisit and expand his understanding of what counts as taking a point of view. This dialogue also shows *how* the teacher served as a social and cultural mediator by bringing to the fore key shared opportunities for learning about point of view constructed previously and then making their academic and social significance for this assignment visible to Jared. Analysis of this chain of activity also made visible the range of discourse practices that the teacher used to support Jared in revisiting past practices and events as shared historical texts: invoking a particular past event, positioning Jared in relationship to this text, asking Jared to compare his point of view with that of someone not present, asking Jared to clarify his response, confirming his understanding, expanding Jared's response using technical language (angle of vision) and thus acknowledging its significance (what can and cannot be seen), and then refocusing on the assignment.

Analysis also shows how Jared contributed to the construction of his own understanding. After initiating the event, he signaled to the teacher/speaker that they were examining a common context. After each query by the teacher, he provided appropriate information and through this information helped to reconstruct the past context in the present. His responses became a text that the teacher then responded to, drawing on her knowledge of Jared's position on the first day's tape as well as his

Table 5.1. *The Reconstructed Dialogue: Jared and Teacher Talk About the Three Pigs Project, October 1994*

Actor	Dialogue	Textual/Intertextual and Intercontextual Reference
J:	I don't understand. Can you explain what you mean about looking at things from a different angle?	• teacher's talk about "looking at things from a different angle" as text
T:	Well, remember the video of our first day that we observed? We were the ethnographers then.	• past actions from first day as text • first day video as text • point of view as ethnographers
J:	Okay.	
T:	What were you able to see?	• memory of events as text
J:	S and V and N moving around, changing tables...	• actions of everyday actors as text • class discussion as text
T:	Now, if someone watching that video who wasn't here the first day wanted to know if you were in the class, would they be able to tell?	• point of view of outsider • needing to use insider knowledge • teacher leading inquiry
J:	Not really.	• memory as insider
T:	Why?	• leading inquiry
J:	Because of where the camera was pointed.	• seeing through camera angle as text
T:	Exactly. From the angle of the camera, there were things you could observe and see and things you could not see, and what you couldn't see was maybe as important as what you could see.	• point of view as the relationship between the camera angle, what can be seen or not seen • actions of observer as text • strategy that text does not represent the whole
J:	Okay. I get it.	• further internalizing
T:	So, you know, you have to position our scientist or ethnographer...	• future referent of positioning to illustrate point of view
J:	So he's looking at it from a certain angle, probably.	• using current dialogue as text
T:	You've got it.	• confirming Jared's understanding of the social and academic practices as well as the concept

participation in previous events. Each of Jared's responses showed how he was able to use this prior experience as a source for further examination in the current event. Further, Jared showed that he was aware of the form of the discourse, that is, the means of production. By contrasting his participation across each interaction, we see that Jared took up and then transformed for his own use the teacher's practice of stating what members were doing in each instance: "So he's looking at it from a certain angle probably." In making this statement, he provided explicit information that showed the teacher that he understood what he was to do and had clarified the task.

Throughout this brief dialogue, the teacher and Jared displayed to each other a reflexive relationship. Each responded as if they had a common text between them, allowing forward progression observed within the event. Through these interactions they signaled how participation in prior events was consequential for both of them. In being able to reinvoke and reconstruct a past event, they were able to revisit collectively, as well as individually, the historical context as a text and to reinterpret it in the present event. This brief analysis demonstrates how a shared or common prior history becomes a cultural resource that is consequential in shaping opportunities for learning in the present.

To determine whether Jared understood point of view, we examined written artifacts from this day. This analysis, a form of intertextual analysis and forward mapping, led to identification of two texts, one written and one graphic (drawing) with written inserts, that showed how Jared used the understandings he claimed that he now had. Analysis of the drawing showed that Jared had added a "detective" at the side of the house in each picture, affording the detective a particular point of view or angle of vision on the event. We then examined a reflexive text in which he wrote about what the detective would see:

Jared 10/11/94

I asked a scientist about what he saw the day he was observing the wolf and the pigs. He was in pig town California. The scientist was always at the side of all the houses at the time he was observing the wolf. I think he took the wolf's side because he was always at an angle that he could only see the wolf.

In writing his text, Jared changed the actor to a scientist from a detective (the name in his pictorial history), which raised questions for us. A re-examination of the text of the discursive event provided evidence of the teacher using the term in one of her final comments to Jared. Additionally, she used two terms interchangeably, "*scientist* or *ethnographer*." Jared's use of a detective in the pictorial history can also be traced to a previous event. The teacher had equated an ethnographer with a detective looking for clues in a note-taking event on a previous day. Thus, in both instances, Jared's choices represented discourse that was available to be appropriated and used. They also represented evidence of a discursive practice, choosing among options, that was part of the language of the classroom

(Lin, 1993). Further, he used the concept of angle of vision and point of view appropriately in this reflexive text; that is, he located the position of the scientist in relationship to the house and the wolf and then provided a rationale for why the scientist would record only one point of view: what the wolf was doing. He also used a sequence of activity that was similar to the one used by the teacher, that is, he located the place, positioned the actors, and then provided a rationale for what could be seen.

This brief analysis shows that Jared took up the content and form of the discourse as a cultural resource for accomplishing this task and then appropriated the discourse strategies used by the teacher in the oral text of previous events to communicate with others in his written text. In this way he demonstrated that he had taken up and internalized the language of the classroom. Additionally, in using it appropriately, he demonstrated his cultural knowledge, as well as his understanding of its social and academic significance within this community of practice.

Exploring Consequential Progression: Jared's Opportunities for Learning Point of View Across the Year

To examine how this history shaped Jared's subsequent understandings and actions, we analyzed ethnographic records (videotape, field notes, teacher plan book, and written artifacts provided by the teacher) across the school year. One set of events identified focused on note taking and note making. Table 5.2 provides a representation of the events identified before and after the dialogue. As indicated in Table 5.2, the collective constructed a range of events that afforded students opportunities for learning and then applying a related set of practices: note taking and note making across time and events. As represented by events in Table 5.2, the teacher began this process by introducing note taking across content areas (i.e., taking notes as a mathematician, as a writer, and as an ethnographer). Analysis shows a contrastive approach used by the teacher to introduce this practice. For example, on September 27, students had three opportunities to explore note taking, two as a writer and one as an ethnographer. On this day, students engaged in a saturation observation in a K-1 classroom. In the saturation observation they recorded observations of sights and sounds in their Writer's Notebooks in order to have them available for use in writing texts at a future time. In contrast, in the Tangram event, students observed a set of four peers, each constructing a square, and recorded their observations in the Social Science

Table 5.2. *Events Focusing on Observing, Note Taking, and Note Making*

Practices of Observing as Literate Action	Activities Involving Observing as Literate Action	Activity Timeline
Observing as note taking	• Day 1 Watermelon Project (estimating weight/cost of watermelon as individual/small group/whole class activity)	9/8/94
	• Saturation Observation of K-1 class (recording sights, sounds, actions in writers' notebooks for future use)	9/22/94
	• Tangrams – observing actions of classmates constructing a square with Tangrams to introduce note taking (university ethnographer as teacher)	9/22/94
	• Observing at home as writers (saturation observation at home)	9/22/94
	• First Day of Class Video – observing actions of class from camera angles and discussing what/who could be seen on tape	9/23/94
Observing as note taking	• Maps – observing same data presented in different ways (multiple types of maps)	9/27/94
Interpreting as note making	• M&M Investigation – observing from personal knowledge and direct experience (counting, graphing, interpreting findings about distribution of colors in M&M packages)	9/27/94
	• Three Pigs – observing same data from three different points of view: that of the third pig, the stick salesman, and the ethnographer/ detective	10/5/94
	JARED'S INTERACTION WITH THE TEACHER THE WRITTEN HISTORY OF THE THIRD PIG THE REFLEXIVE STATEMENT ABOUT THE DRAWING AND THE POSITION OF SCIENTIST	10/11/94
Observing as note taking	• Ice Man Video – observing processes and practices, comparing work of different scientists working as an interdisciplinary team	11/4/94
Interpreting as note making	• Quotations from text juxtaposed with interpretation from personal experience	ongoing
	• Art as text – interpreting "The Starry Night" by Vincent Van Gogh	11/5/94

(continued)

Table 5.2. *(Continued)*

Practices of Observing as Literate Action	Activities Involving Observing as Literate Action	Activity Timeline
Application of point of view – point of view as cultural resource	• North Carolina essay – taking notes and writing a report about an American colony for the Americana Museum – cultural practice as material resource	3/24/95
	• Community Essays (revisiting classroom life as text, writing to next year's students about life in this fifth-grade class)	5/22/95
	• Myself as a Learner (revisiting self across year, writing about what student had learned across time)	5/22/95
	• Dear Reader Letter (observing self across year, selecting items for Showcase Portfolio, telling readers how to understand this portfolio at end of year)	6/5/95

section of their Learning Log. This event also involved students in sharing their note taking and in comparing similarities and differences in what they recorded. Students also located their point of view as an observer. The saturation observation for homework involved students in a second saturation observation at home. This contrastive approach provided opportunities for students to examine and explore differences in discourse processes and practices relevant to each context, as well as to compare and contrast observations across different members. These two types of observation activities enabled students to see their world, actions of members of the local group, and their written recordings as different kinds of texts.

After providing opportunities for students to develop understandings and ability to engage in note taking and observing, the teacher moved to events involving a relationship between note taking and note making, creating a progression across time, events, and content areas. Through this progression she provided students with a range of opportunities for developing an expanding understanding of relationships among observing, recording (note taking), and interpreting (note making) different texts across time, events, modes of communication, and academic disciplines. Analysis of this progression shows that the teacher added a new dimension to the progressive understanding of note taking: the concept of note making. Again, using a contrastive approach, she helped students

Table 5.3. *North Carolina by Jared*

I am a Native American from the Cherokee living in the Southeast. When the English came we knew they had more power then us so we thought that maybe if we did things like them they would let us stay. We developed our own republic. We had writing and had our own newspaper. It really was our land before they came. After a long time they wanted us to pay taxes to them but we didn't. Then in the 1830's the Americans came and walked my descendents from North Carolina to the plains. A lot of us died during the walk. We started out as one Colony at first and in 1665 we divided into two Colonys.
I am an English man who went to North Carolina. When we got there there were Indians on our land. We ignored them for a while. Then we decided to have them as slaves or pay taxes. They didn't want to do either. Years later the Americans made them walk from North Carolina and Georgia to the plains. People died but they didn't mean for anyone to be hurt. We settled in North Carolina in 1652. Our King, King Charles II, sent an army to North Carolina to take it over. North Carolina was founded so England could have three expensive things, wine, silk, and olive oil. We grow rice and indigo to trade and sell. When the Indians wouldn't do the work we brought in slaves from Africa.

understand the differences between recording what they saw and heard and interpreting and/or responding to what they observed. Through a series of events across discipline areas, she helped students expand their understanding of observing and note taking while developing a new practice. The contrastive approach also provided them with opportunities to examine differences in language and discourse practices associated with each, as well as point of view and angle of vision.

With this analysis of what was afforded at the collective level as background, we further examined Jared's understanding of point of view and his understanding of discourse practices related to this concept. The most telling example of Jared's claim of understanding point of view was visible in his North Carolina report (Table 5.3) in social science, written in March. In this essay, Jared writes about North Carolina history from two different points of view. A conversation with the teacher indicated that Jared elected to take two points of view because he could not present what he learned from only one. In writing from two points of view, he demonstrated that he had taken up, internalized, and transformed the concept of point of view, and that he could use it as a cultural resource for academic purposes in social science. He also demonstrated knowledge of what it meant to write history, and to represent others' positions and experiences in history.

By juxtaposing these historically constructed texts (written, oral, and graphic), and by examining these texts for "traces" of other texts, we were able to identify what Jared viewed as consequential and how his understandings were progressively constructed in and through particular opportunities for learning. These analyses showed the intertextual, intercontextual, and expanding nature of learning in this classroom, and made visible the importance of examining social and academic practices in the classroom. They provided a view of what one student took up from the opportunities afforded him. By focusing on Jared, we made visible the progressive nature of conceptual development in this classroom. Further, by focusing on both in-the-moment construction of conceptual understanding and analysis of written artifacts produced across time, we were able to show how the discourse of the collective shaped actions and understandings of individuals.

Exploring Consequential Progression and the Shaping of the Collective

In this section we shift from an individual-within-the-collective focus to an examination of how the collective itself developed across time and events on the first morning. We explore further the concept of consequential progression and show the developing nature of communities of practice. These analyses are informed by Vygotsky's argument that development of the individual is tied integrally to development of the collective itself (cf. Souza Lima, 1995). To understand both individual and collective development, it is necessary to understand the historical dimensions of the group and the relationship among its members, as well as historically developed opportunities for learning constructed by and afforded members. Viewed in this way, individuals are not socialized to the culture of the collective. Rather, members of a group construct cultural tools and practices through joint activity, and individuals learn the means of constructing knowledge as they engage in joint activity. Thus, they are transforming the developing culture as they take up and transform the resources of that culture for themselves (Corsaro & Miller, 1992; John-Steiner et al., 1994; Shepel, 1995; Watson-Gegeo, 1992; Wertsch, 1990).

John-Steiner et al. (1994) describe the methodological implications of this perspective when they argue that a sociocultural analysis seeks understandings of "how this activity has come to be routinely reenacted, how this routine expresses values of the group and relates to other cultural practices, and what part this activity plays in general patterns of the culture" (p. 11). This view of routines as constructed and reenacted within a group, as expressing a particular set of values and beliefs about what counts as a cultural practice, and as contributing to the shape of the general pattern of life suggests the importance of examining ways in which the collective constructs such routines or patterns of practice. Central to this analysis is the view that such patterns of practice (repetitive routine activity) become cultural resources for the collective itself, as well as for the individual within the collective. In the section of *Jared as a telling case*, we were able to illustrate Vygotsky's argument that children internalize the means of social interaction as well as Bakhtin's (1986) notion of delayed reaction.

In the remainder of this section, we present three sets of analyses that draw on constructs to examine the developing collective and how patterns of practice were constructed across time and events. We begin with a series of analyses of events on the first morning of school (September 8, 1994). Each analysis in this series takes a more selective look at how members constructed events of this morning; how, through this process, they constructed processes and practices that shaped the activity of the morning; and how particular practices became cultural resources in subsequent activities for the collective. The second analysis builds on patterns of practice identified on this morning. We use these practices to examine patterns of activity across the first 3 weeks (13 days of school) in order to identify principles of practice (Frake, 1977; Spradley, 1980; Tuyay, Floriani, ct al., 1995). We conclude this section with an analysis of Jared's community essay, examining it for traces of cultural practices and texts (Fairclough, 1992). In particular, we examine this text for intertextual and intercontextual references that make visible how Jared viewed life in the Tower Community as consequential.

Initiating the Collective: Events, Practices, Identity, and Activity on the First Morning of School

Initial analysis of the developing collective involved construction of an event map that represented events and subevents members constructed as they spent time together on the first morning. Map construction began by examining a transcript of talk among members while simultaneously viewing videotaped records. The transcripts represented the ebb and flow of talk and activity as message units (what Green & Wallat, 1979, and Green & Wallat, 1981, call *minimal units of conversational meaning*, i.e., communicatively significant actions on the part of a speaker). By tying event construction to the transcript representation, we were able to identify the contextualization cues (Gumperz, 1992) that members used to signal to each other what they were doing together; what they were holding each other accountable for; how they were constructing the event; what they viewed as socially significant; and how routines and patterns of practice were relevant in the current event.

As indicated in Table 5.4, events of the first morning began at 8:30 with the official school bell and concluded at 12:15 with the transition to lunch. Three events were identified on the first morning: initiating community, the Name Game, and the Watermelon Project. Analysis of the sequence of activity across the morning showed that the teacher initiated community with an event (a period of concerted activity) in which students were afforded an opportunity to begin establishing their positions at a table group and to begin shaping local identities within this developing collective (e.g., Fernie, Davies, Kantor, & McMurray, 1993; Lin, 1993). This event consisted of two subevents: an arrival period and a period of establishing instrumental rules for daily life.

Analysis of the next subevent showed that the teacher continued an instrumental phase of the morning. She initiated this subevent by shifting from an earlier organizational pattern of table group and individual-within-the-table group to one characterized by a whole group interactional space. In this interactional space she introduced and described a set of practices needed to support collective activity at the whole class level and introduced a range of people she defined as members of this community (i.e., the student teacher, teacher aide, and university ethnographers). As part of this activity, she foreshadowed particular dimensions of classroom life (i.e., becoming ethnographers) and drew intertextual connections between life in this class and in previous communities, signaling that this class would do similar activities but would do them differently. In discussing practices in other classrooms, the teacher signaled that she was aware of practices they had used previously. In signaling that these practices would be used differently, she made students aware that they would construct local definitions of such practices in this class. In contrasting past and current practices, she made visible the consequential nature of the language and activity of the local classroom (Lin, 1993).

The contrast in organizational structure of these two subevents provided students with opportunities to explore roles and relationships, norms and expectations, and rights and obligations associated with different types of participant structures used in the classroom. For example, during these activities, students were able to work on an individual project (name tile) within a small group context, interacting with others as they worked. They then moved to a whole-group interactional space with a common focus in which they took up roles as listeners (a type of audience) and responders to the teacher's questions.

Table 5.4. *Map of the Events Constructed through Actions of Class Members on the First Morning*

Events and Phases in Classroom Activity	Literate and Social Actions and Practices	Type of Interactional Spaces and Relationships	Texts Produced and Used
8:30 School begins			
Initiating Community	* selecting name cards	individual	* name cards
* arriving, forming unofficial table groups and making names tiles	* choosing where to sit in table groups	individual	* positioning self at a table
* establishing roles and relationships, norms and expectations	* drawing on name tile	individual in whole class	* decorated name card (for quilt)
	* talking with table group members	individual in table group	* student–student interpersonal
	* introducing chime as signal	whole group	* chime as signal – word on white board
	* explaining active listening	whole group	* the look of listening
	* introducing adults in community student teacher, teacher aide, university ethnographers	individual–whole class	* roles of other adults
			* person as text
	* introducing ethnography as community practice	whole class	* study of own class
	* discussing life in prior communities	individual in past groups	* definition of historical self
	* defining ways of living in Tower community	individual in whole class	* definition of Tower member
	* explaining insider knowledge as member of McKinley community	individual–class–school	* definition of school member

(continued)

Table 5.4. (Continued)

Events and Phases in Classroom Activity	Literate and Social Actions and Practices	Type of Interactional Spaces and Relationships	Texts Produced and Used
Name Game activity	* introducing the Name Game procedures	whole class	* descriptors for teacher on white board in English and Spanish
	* selecting adjective to represent self: joyful Judith	individual in table group	* descriptor of self (choice of language)
	* introducing self to table group	individual in table group	* introducing self – adjective + name (choice of language)
	* introducing self to whole group	individual in whole class	* stating names of students who have already introduced self – adjective + name (use of both languages)
	* naming members of the class who have been introduced	individuals of class – help from class members provided when needed	
Watermelon Project * utilizing Learning Logs	* defining mathematicians	whole class	* definition of student mathematicians
	* introducing how to use and name first part of Learning Log – mathematics	whole class	* Learning Logs (spiral notebooks) as class textbook
	10:50 *Recess (20 minutes)*		
Watermelon Project * transitioning to problem	* explaining tradition of watermelons	individual–present class–past classes	* teacher narrative on personal tradition: linking local class to previous classes
	* formulating questions as part of investigating	individual in whole class	* questions written in Learning Logs
	* asking particular question to be answered	individual in whole class	* question as problem to be solved
	* making a guess	individual in whole class	* entry in Learning Logs
	* making an estimate, collecting data	table group	* entry in Learning Logs
	* revising the estimate from data collection	table group	* entry in Learning Logs
	* explicating the process used so far	whole class	* chart on white board to be copied
	12:15: *Lunch and play period (50 minutes)*		

Expanding Opportunities for Collective Development:
Constructing Identity, Language Choice, and
Participant Structures as Cultural Resources

Analysis of the next event, the Name Game, showed how organizing practices were taken up and used as resources for this new event. In
this event the teacher afforded students another opportunity to present
themselves to others, that is, to construct an identity and to examine further the range of activity associated with different types of participation
structures (Erickson & Shultz, 1981). The teacher began this event with
a whole group interactional space in which she presented procedures that
students needed to follow to be able to introduce themselves during the
Name Game. They needed to choose an adjective that began with the
same letter as their first name to represent themselves. For example, she
told them that she was "Beautiful Beth/bella Beth." By giving her example in both English and Spanish, she signaled both the appropriateness
of language choice and that the languages students brought to the class
were resources for members.

Following the introductory phase of activity, the teacher explicitly indicated that students could receive help from tablemates to complete the
assigned task of choosing their representational adjective. In this way she
afforded students opportunities to work interactively and to provide support for others using the language of their tablemates. After this phase,
students reassembled in a whole class formation, using a new organizing
pattern – forming a circle in an open space in the center of the classroom.
This organizational pattern further defined the range of interactional
spaces that they would use within this developing collective.

Within the circle structure, each student was given an opportunity to
be introduced to the group in the language of his or her choice. Each
student was also acknowledged by others through a practice in which
subsequent speakers repeated the names of those who had preceded them
and provided support to those who did not remember all of the names.
In this activity the teacher also provided students with opportunities for
speaking and/or hearing the languages of members, primarily English
and Spanish, although there was also one Hebrew-English bilingual student and one Vietnamese-dominant student in this particular year. She
thus helped students understand that language choice was a community
resource and that members of the class, as well as the class itself, were
texts that could be heard, seen, and interpreted. In her choice of practices
and organizational patterns, the teacher afforded students opportunities

for learning ways of being in a community that would serve in later events for academic activity. Each variation in pattern helped students expand their repertoires for action (Kantor, Green, Bradley, & Lin, 1992). These patterns set the stage for the first academic event in which participation structures constructed previously (individual–small group–whole group relationships), as well as identity and language choice, would be used to support academic learning.

Mathematics as a Social Construction: Analyzing Discursive Construction of an Academic Discipline

As indicated in Table 5.4, the first academic event, the Watermelon Project, completed the morning. In this event, the organizational patterns previously established were used for academic and instrumental purposes (Christie, 1995). The first of two subevents in the Watermelon Project used a whole class organizational pattern so that the teacher, using both English and Spanish, could establish a common focus and introduce a common understanding of what counted as mathematics. In the first subevent, the teacher introduced knowledge from the intellectual ecology of mathematicians (an intercontextual relationship) and helped students see what they needed to know and do to take up positions as mathematicians (Strike & Posner, 1992; Toulmin, 1972). The teacher also introduced Learning Logs that would serve as student-generated textbooks or historical records of their thinking and learning.

In the second subevent the teacher introduced a problem to solve involving the watermelons. This problem afforded students a range of opportunities for constructing personal estimates of the cost and weight of a watermelon, for negotiating group estimates, for revising personal and group estimates, and for reporting group estimates to the class. She also introduced the practice of asking "why" questions, signaling to students that they would need to do the task and be able to explain why they needed to know this information. The second subevent ended with a phase of activity in which the teacher reestablished a whole class interactional space. In this space she introduced further terms needed to become a mathematician, *data* and *evidence*, and tied these terms to what students were to do now and to the fact that they had been gathering data all morning. In this way, she established intertextual ties between the text of the classroom as data and information gained from actions that students were taking as mathematicians in table groups (i.e., intercontextual ties). Through this approach she helped students construct a particular language for learning in mathematics (and science), particular interactional spaces for exploring similarities and differences in interpretations, and particular practices that served as repertoires for actions.

Examining Student Take-up: Small Group-Collective Interactions

To explore how students took up common opportunities for learning afforded them, we shift the angle of vision from teacher actions in shaping collective activity to student actions in table groups. By examining how individual table groups and members within this collective interpreted and took up particular dimensions of the Watermelon Project, we examine the negotiated and constructed nature of collective-individual knowledge. The specific sequence that we examine is one in which each table group reported its estimates. The message, action, and sequence units of this phase of the event are presented in Table 5.5.

Table 5.5. *Examining Student Take-up of the Collective Response*

905.		everybody's in agreement
906.		you have the same answer
907.		every single person
908.		and written out
909.		in your logs
910.		that means
911.		did you get the calculator
912.		and did you multiply the forty-seven cents by
913.	Sharifah	oh
914.		eleven
915.	Ms. Y	by eleven
916.		and you should all have that answer written down
917.		you should all agree about it
918.		make sure everybody has it
919.		check it out
942.	Ms. Y	alright
943.		watermelon number one
944.		your estimated weight
945.		after you weighed it
946.		how much
947.		out on those scales
948.	FS	eleven pounds

(continued)

Table 5.5. *(Continued)*

949.	Ms.Y	how much do you think your
950.		estimated cost of your watermelon
951.	MS	of our table
952.	Ms. Y	yea
953.		for your group
954.		it's the only answer I want
955.		is for a whole group
956.		cause your group has to be agreed
957.		I don't want it unless you are in agreement
958.	MS	a dollar and five
959.	Ms. Y	that's not
960.		I don't know
961.		that's not the answer
962.		that your group told me
963.		when I was over there
964.	Student	I know
965.	Ms. Y	when your group was over there
966.		they told me a dollar ten
967.		so I think you better
968.		you better discuss it together
969.		Hablen juntos
970.		then I'll come back to you okay
986.	Ms. Y	okay
987.		watermelon number two
988.		que es su
989.		que es su peso estimado
990.	Student	eleven pounds
991.	Ms. Y	what
992.	MS	eleven pounds
993.	Students	two o nine
994.	Ms. Y	what
995.	Students	two o nine
996.	Ms. Y	okay
997.		numero tres
998.	Students	eleven
999.	Student	eleven pounds
1000.	Ms. Y	interesting
1001.		y
1002.	Students	five seventeen
1003.	Ms. Y	five seventeen
1004.	Ms. Y	number four
1005.	Students	fifteen pounds
1017.	Ms. Y	table five

(continued)

Table 5.5. *(Continued)*

1018.		que
1019.		que es su
1020.		que es su estimado
1021.	Students	once libras
1022.	Ms. Y	once libras
1023.		okay
1024.	Ms. Y	y su
1025.		costo
1026.	Students	(inaudible)
1027.	Ms. Y	que
1028.	Students	dos setenta y cinco
1029.	Ms. Y	okay
1030.		the people
1031.	Ms. Y	okay
1032.		number six
1033.	students	we got twelve pounds
1034.	Ms. Y	how many pounds
1035.	Students	twelve pounds
1036.	Students	just twelve
1037.	Ms. Y	and how much
1038.	Students	five dollars
1039.	Students	three dollars
1040.	Ms. Y	you guys need to talk more
1041.	Ms. Y	okay what do we got over here
1042.	Students	eleven pounds
1043.	Students	five thirty-six
1044.	Ms. Y	eleven pounds and five dollars and thirty six cents
1045.	Students	yea
1046.	Ms. Y	that's change from a dollar fifty
1047.		okay
1101.	Ms. Y	Personally
1102.		I think those scales are way off

The data presented in Table 5.5 begin with a sequence in which the teacher established what students were to do. This statement served as a summary of the preceding phases of activity that shaped the meaning of "everybody's in agreement" and was instrumental in nature. In this sequence, lines 905–919, the teacher defined what they were to do, where data were to be recorded, and what mathematical actions were involved; she then restated conditions that shaped a collective, not a personal, estimate. With this as background, we now examine what different table groups did as they reported their estimates to the whole class.

The teacher began by calling on Table Group 1 (lines 942–943), asking for particular information. Analysis of the dialogue between the teacher and group members showed that a female student (FS, line 948) provided the group's estimate of weight. However, when the teacher asked for the cost, a male student asked her if the cost to be reported was "of our table" (MS, line 951). His question showed that he had not understood that the task was to shape a collective response, even though this had been previously stated, checked, restated, and rechecked across different types of interactional spaces (whole group, table group). The teacher repeated what she wanted (lines 952–957). A second male student (MS) gave an answer. What the teacher did next provided insights into the knowledge that she had constructed as she interacted with and observed the group. She stated, "that's not the answer/that your group told me/when I was over there" (lines 961–964). The student responded by saying that he knew this. The teacher then told him, and by extension the group, that they had originally told her that it was a dollar ten (lines 965–966). She then redirected them by telling them to talk it over, speaking in both English and Spanish. The students turned toward each other and began renegotiating a collective estimate using English and Spanish.

The teacher continued to query each table group, looking for them to provide their group solution to the problem thus far. The table groups gave appropriate responses until she called on Table 6. As with Table Group 1, a member of Table Group 6 provided an individual estimate, not the appropriate information (lines 1031–1040), and she told them that "you guys need to talk more" (line 1040), thus redirecting them to the task and sending them back to talk, just as she had done with Table 1. She then returned to Table Group 1, whose members now gave her an appropriate (group) answer (lines 1041–1047). She ended this discussion by introducing her personal reactions to the scales, "personally/I think those scales are way off" (lines 1101–1102).

In this brief phase of activity, the teacher's actions showed how she mediated students' actions by providing support for appropriate participation, how she valued the languages that students spoke as both personal and collective resources, and that appropriate actions and answers were expected. Thus, she continued to shape what counted as collective knowledge, actions, and practices. Students' actions showed that different table groups took up the task differentially (cf. Alton-Lee & Nuthall, 1992, 1993), with some following the explicitly stated practices and processes and others (Table Groups 1 and 6) following the practices but not the full process. When the reporter for a group (Table Groups 1 and 6) did not provide appropriate information, the teacher asked those groups to renegotiate appropriate responses so that they could participate in and provide appropriate data needed for the next part of the collective's task. Ethnographic data across days show that information from these groups recorded at the collective level was used in subsequent days to graph similarities and differences among groups and between estimated and actual weights and costs.

Analysis of student take-up across groups shows that the activity jointly constructed at the class level was not always taken up in ways that the teacher anticipated. This discrepancy suggests that individuals and small groups of students working collaboratively do not simply internalize what is available to them in the intersubjective space (see Dyson, Gutiérrez & Stone, Smagorinsky & O'Donnell-Allen, this volume). Rather, individual members of a class or a small group of members may take up and interpret the requirements of a common task in uncommon ways, and may require additional mediation from the teacher to complete a task in an appropriate manner. Further, the analysis of the differential take-up of students illustrated how opportunities for learning were jointly constructed at the whole class level, as well as the types of support students needed to "grow into the intellectual life of those around him [or her]" (John-Steiner et al., 1994, p. 141).

Student Inscriptions of Consequentiality and Community Development

In previous sections we constructed an argument about the nature of relationships between individual and collective development by analytically juxtaposing a range of texts of classroom life (oral and written) that members signaled were intertextually and intercontextually related. Through that analysis we constructed an argument about the interrelated and transformative nature of life within the developing collective. Additionally, we showed how patterns and practices of life within and across time became material resources for members, and how their use across time and events was consequential for members.

In this section we examine the issue of consequentiality further through an analysis of patterns of life that Jared inscribed in his Community Essay, a text written in May of the school year (see Table 5.2). These essays are one of three types of reflexive texts that the teacher asks students to write in the last month of the school year: Community Essays, Dear Reader Letters for their Showcase Portfolios, and Myself as a Learner Essays.

Through this analysis, we illustrate what Jared viewed as socially significant, as cultural resources, and as situated knowledge, and explore how he used this knowledge to describe principles of practice that members needed to guide their participation and learning within this particular community of practice. To undertake this analysis, we needed to draw one additional theoretical perspective to expand the expressive potential of our approach: critical discourse analysis as framed by Fairclough (1992, 1993; Ivanic, 1994). Ivanic argues that writers make "discourse choices" that are often unconscious, based on the social context of writing and drawn from a range of available discourses.

By building on this argument, we were able to analyze the discourses that Jared used, and to explore how he perceived his world and what he valued as a member. To accomplish this goal, we examined his essay for traces of cultural practices and prior texts in his choice of content, sequencing, and wording. Specifically, we examined each text for intertextual and intercontextual references that make visible what Jared inscribed as knowledge needed to participate as a member. Analysis of the topics selected by Jared is presented in Table 5.6, where each topic is represented in a cell of the table. Once we identified topics, we examined the content, wording, and sequences for constructs that reflect Jared's claims about life in this classroom. For this analysis, we present those claims using constructs from sociocultural theory.

Jared began his essay by locating the classroom in space, by describing patterns of organization, by defining how members worked together, by contrasting ways of working, and by naming one type of cultural practice (projects). He then shifted from a description of collective activity to a discussion of what occurs when a new member enters, indicating awareness of insider knowledge. He then described cultural practices that must be understood, using the contrastive approach we saw in his writing and interactions with the teacher earlier in this chapter. In providing an example of what occurred when two students entered from another teacher's class, he made visible both what they needed to know and how the class members helped new students become members of the Tower Community. Once again, Jared used contrast as a means of making his point of view clear.

He then shifted from a discussion of what outsiders needed to know to a discussion of how he and others felt on the first day of school, showing how identity was constructed in this classroom. In this sequence of text, he illustrated how members formulated membership in the community,

Table 5.6. *Jared's Community Essay: Topic and Sociohistorical Constructs*

Jared's Community Essay	Vygotskian Constructs Related to Student Statements
Our community of the Tower works in separate groups, one big group and sometimes alone. We do projects sometimes in our table groups or just with a partner	• intersubjective spaces • patterns of organization • problem solving – inter/intrapersonal
When new kids came to the school, we showed them around, told them how we switch teachers on some days, and what certain things in the class were for. We not only help new kids coming to the Tower community, but students in this community as well. For example, when Shawn and Josefina came here after they were in Mr. Thedorffi's class for only about one month, everyone took pictures of them and we showed them what a Learning Log and Literature Log were for.	• classroom as culture • cultural transmission • inter-intrapersonal relationships • formulating membership in community • formulating difference between classroom communities • centrality of community
When we did the Watermelon Investigation of the first day, nobody really knew each other, but we still did it as a group. I think in the first week of school, we were still a little nervous and doing what we did the year before, so nobody knew what the Tower community was going to be like (yet).	• formulating class as community, community as constructed • intersubjectivity as constructed • identity as community member constructed through activity

(continued)

Table 5.6. (Continued)

Jared's Community Essay	Vygotskian Constructs Related to Student Statements
	• working in groups as cultural practice brought to the classroom • cultural specificity
On the Spaghetti Dinner, we worked in groups, figuring out what other people couldn't. When we did the Spaghetti Dinner, we argued a lot and learned things from it.	• inter–intrapersonal sharing within groups and across group, zone of proximal development through *leading* activities • interpersonal is both individual and group-level phenomenon • common knowledge constructed within and across group
When we did the Island History Project, I worked with only a partner.	• different pattern of intersubjectivity and interpersonal opportunities afforded students through grouping
I think working in a group means letting each other talk, listening to each other, and having good times and bad times. I think working in a group with people you really don't know that well is good and bad in a way. The good part is that you don't get to fool around, because when you know the people, it is easier to talk to them.	• organizational pattern influences nature of intersubjectivity • different types of intersubjectivity influence task accomplishment
What I'm trying to say is that in the Tower community, you have to respect each other and everyone has responsibilities. Respecting other people means listening when it's	• community has an identity – Tower community • membership entails respect and responsibility

(continued)

their turn to talk, being friendly to each other, and if there is something you don't agree with, saying it in a nice way. Responsibility means other people have the responsibility to listen to me when I talk, be friendly to me, and if there is something they don't agree with me, they tell me in a nice way.

That is what it means to be a part of the Tower community.

- different points of view exist within community
- bringing unconscious processes to conscious awareness through reflection on practices

- classroom is more than a group; it is a community that is constructed by members through their actions and cultural practices
- classroom roles and relationships shape intersubjectivity

again using contrast to make cultural differences in activity and knowledge visible. Additionally, in describing the purpose of particular cultural objects, he established the material presence of the language of the classroom and how this language was tied to the type of activity within this classroom.

The theme of identity formation tied to community development is articulated further in the next sequence of text. In this sequence Jared shifted from a discussion of the collective to how he felt on the first day of school, arguing that "nobody knew what the Tower community was going to be like (yet)." Further, in writing about the Watermelon Investigation on the first day and tying it to the lack of familiarity among members, he showed the significance of this project for collective development. The shift in pronoun from "We" to "I" is also significant in that it showed that he was positioning himself as having a particular point of view at this time in the class, again making visible a contrast with previous contexts (classes).

The next two sequences focused on two different class projects (the Spaghetti Dinner and the Island Project). He located what they did, how members interacted, and how the project was organized. By locating his actors ("we") in times and spaces within this classroom, he demonstrated awareness of the intersubjective nature of classroom life and how the dialogue of action, as well as talk, is important to know and understand.

In the next two sequences of text, Jared made explicit his personal view on "what it means to be a part of the Tower community." These two sequences focused on the rights and responsibilities of membership, both on a personal level and on a collective level. Jared's descriptions also showed awareness of the interdependent nature of interactions in this classroom, and of how these interactions shaped a community identity in which different points of view were resources, and not divisive, given a set of discourse practices related to what he called "respecting other people." In tying together respect and responsibility, Jared further showed that membership in the collective was not a position that was given, but rather one inscribed in actions and activity among members. He made explicit norms and expectations, roles and relationships, and rights and obligations that shaped and were shaped by membership in the Tower Community. Jared demonstrated understanding of the situated nature of life in classrooms; of opportunities for learning; of cultural practices that members needed to read, interpret, and use; and the constructed and local nature of identity for both the collective and the individual.

Conclusion

John-Steiner et al. (1994) capture the interdependent nature of individual and collective development when they state that "the development of the individual is . . . cultural development" (p. 141). In this chapter we have illustrated the complex, negotiated, and constructed nature of life in classrooms. We have also shown that students, in the role(s) afforded them in classrooms, do not grow into a preexisting world; rather, they construct the world in which they live and the opportunities for learning within this world. Further, in bringing Interactional ethnography together with sociocultural theory and critical discourse analysis, we have demonstrated the expressive potential formed by integrating these mutually informing theories and have illustrated how we can explore the distributed (Cole & Engeström, 1993), interactive (Wells & Chang-Wells, 1992), and contextual (John-Steiner et al., 1994) nature of learning. In tracing life within the collective across time and events, and by taking a focused look at how individuals within the collective developed particular knowledge and understandings across time and events, we showed the potential of this approach for identifying the result of the learners' participation in a particular community of practice (Rogoff, 1994). Finally, we constructed an argument about the consequential nature of life within and across time and events. By moving across levels of analysis, from moment-to-moment discourse to examination of intertextual and intercontextual ties across time and events, we demonstrated the importance of understanding the consequential nature of actions and activity at different levels and the progressive nature of particular aspects of everday life.

The questions that this chapter raises for our future research are the following: When is learning? What counts as evidence of learning to various members as well as outsiders? What is the relationship between the opportunities constructed by and afforded to class members, and what members do to learn and construct knowledge? And finally, how can a language of learning be developed using Interactional ethnography, critical discourse analysis, and sociocultural theories that inform the practices and actions of teachers, administrators, students, and parents, as well as the interactions among these and others concerned with what students learn in and across particular communities of practice? We argue that without close examination of the lived experiences of students, we will repeat the history of the past and continue reforming again and again and again. The task facing researchers, as well as teachers and students, has been captured in the saying from the Talmud that two of the bilingual teachers in our community share with their students (Yeager et al., 1999).

> To look is one thing.
> To see what you look at is another.
> To understand what you see is a third.
> To learn from what you understand is still something else.
> But to act on what you learn is
> All that really matters.

References

Alton-Lee, A., & Nuthall, G. (1992). Children's learning in classrooms: Challenges in developing a methodology to explain "opportunity to learn." *Journal of Classroom Interaction, 27*, 1–6.

Alton-Lee, A., & Nuthall, G. (1993). Reframing classroom research: A lesson from the private world of children. *Harvard Educational Review, 63*(1), 50–84.

Bakhtin, M. M. (1986). *Speech genres and other late essays* (C. Emerson & M. Holquist, Eds.; V. M. McGee, Trans.). Austin: University of Texas Press.

Birdwhistell, R. (1977). Some discussion of ethnography, theory, and method. In J. Brockman (Ed.), *About Bateson: Essays on Gregory Bateson* (pp. 103–144). New York: E. P. Dutton.

Bloome, D., & Bailey, F. M. (1992). Studying language and literacy through events, particularity, and intertextuality. In R. Beach, J. L. Green, M. L. Kamil, & T. Shanahan (Eds.), *Multidisciplinary perspectives on literacy research* (pp. 181–210). Urbana, IL: National Conference on Research in English and National Council of Teachers of English.

Bloome, D., & Egan-Robertson, A. (1993). The social construction of intertextuality in classroom reading and writing lessons. *Reading Research Quarterly, 28*, 305–333.

Bloome, D., Theodorov, E., & Puro, P. (1989). Procedural display in classroom lessons. *Curriculum Inquiry, 19*, 265–291.

Brilliant-Mills, H. (1993). Becoming a mathematician: Building a situated definition of mathematics. *Linguistics and Education, 5*, 301–334.

Christie, F. (1995). Pedagogic discourse in the primary school. *Linguistics and Education, 7*, 221–242.

Cochran, J. (1997). What's "common" in a common core: How course structure shapes disciplinary knowledge. *Journal of Classroom Interaction, 32*(2), 45–55.

Cole, M., & Engeström, Y. (1993). A cultural-historical approach to distributed cognition. In G. Salomon (Ed.), *Distributed cognitions: Psychological and educational considerations* (pp. 1–46). New York: Cambridge University Press.

Collins, E. C., & Green, J. L. (1990). Metaphors: The construction of a perspective. *Theory Into Practice, 29*(2), 71–77.

Collins, E. C., & Green, J. L. (1992). Learning in classroom settings: Making or breaking a culture. In H. Marshall (Ed.), *Redefining student learning* (pp. 59–85). Norwood, NJ: Ablex.

Corsaro, W. A., & Miller, P. J. (Eds.). (1992). *Interpretive approaches to children's socialization* (Vol. 58). San Francisco: Jossey-Bass.

Durán, R. P., & Szymanski, M. H. (1996). *Assessing framing of literacy activity among bilingual students*. Santa Barbara: University of California at Santa Barbara.

Edwards, D., & Mercer, N. (1987). *Common knowledge: The development of understanding in the classroom*. New York: Falmer.

Erickson, F. (1977). Some approaches to inquiry in school/community ethnography. *Anthropology & Education Quarterly, 8*(3), 58–69.

Erickson, F., & Shultz, J. (1981). When is the context?: Some issues in methods in the analysis of social competence. In J. L. Green & C. Wallat (Eds.), *Ethnography and language in educational settings* (pp. 147–160). Norwood, NJ: Ablex.

Fairclough, N. (1992). Intertextuality in critical discourse analysis. *Linguistics and Education, 4*, 269–293.

Fairclough, N. (1993). Discourse and text: Linguistic and intertextual analysis within discourse analysis. *Discourse & Society, 3*, 193–218.

Fernie, D., Davies, B., Kantor, R., & McMurray, P. (1993). Becoming a person: Creating integrated gender, peer and positionings in a preschool classroom. *International Journal of Qualitative Research in Education, 6*(2), 95–110.

Floriani, A. (1993). Negotiating what counts: Roles and relationships, texts and contexts, content and meaning. *Linguistics and Education, 5*, 241–273.

Floriani, A. (1997). *Creating a community of learners: Opportunities for learning and negotiating meaning in a bilingual classroom*. Unpublished doctoral dissertation, University of California at Santa Barbara.

Frake, C. (1977). Plying frames can be dangerous: Some reflections on methodology in cognitive anthropology. *Quarterly Newletter of the Institute for Comparative Human Development, 3*, 1–7.

Fránquiz, M. (1995). *Transformations in bilingual classrooms: Understanding opportunity to learn within the change process*. Unpublished doctoral dissertation, University of California at Santa Barbara.

Gaskins, S., Miller, P. J., & Corsaro, W. A. (Eds.). (1992). *Theoretical and methodological perspectives in the interpetive study of children* (Vol. 58). San Francisco: Jossey-Bass.

Gee, J. P., & Green, J. L. (1998). Discourse analysis, learning, and social practice: A methodological study. *Review of Research in Education, 23*, 119–169.

Geertz, C. (1983). *Local knowledge: Further essays in interpretive anthropology*. New York: Basic Books.

Green, J. L., & Meyer, L. A. (1991). The embeddedness of reading in classroom life: Reading as a situated process. In C. Baker & A. Luke (Eds.), *Towards a critical sociology of reading pedagogy* (pp. 141–160). Philadelphia: John Benjamins.

Green, J. L., & Wallat, C. (1979). What is an instructional context? An exploratory analysis of conversational shifts over time. In O. Garnica & M. King (Eds.), *Language, children and society* (pp. 159–187). New York: Pergamon.

Green, J. L., & Wallat, C. (1981). Mapping instructional conversations: A sociolinguistic ethnography. In J. Green & C. Wallat (Eds.), *Ethnography and languages in educational settings* (pp. 161–195). Norwood, NJ: Ablex.

Green, J. L., & Yeager, B. (1995, July). *Constructing literate communities: Language and inquiry in bilingual classrooms*. Paper presented at the meeting of the Australian Literacy Educators' Association, Sydney.

124   *L. G. Putney et al.*

Gumperz, J. J. (1986). Interactional sociolinguistics in the study of schooling. In J. Cook-Gumperz (Ed.), *The social construction of literacy* (pp. 45–68). New York: Cambridge University Press.

Gumperz, J. J. (1992). Contextualization and understanding. In A. Duranti & C. Goodwin (Eds.), *Rethinking context: Language as an interactive phenomenon* (pp. 229–252). New York: Cambridge University Press.

Heath, S. B. (1982). Ethnography in education: Defining the essentials. In P. Gillmore & A. A. Glatthorn (Eds.), *Children in and out of school: Ethnography and education* (pp. 33–55). Washington, D.C.: Center for Applied Linguistics.

Heras, A. I. (1993). The construction of understanding in a sixth grade bilingual classroom. *Linguistics and Education, 5*, 275–299.

Hymes, D. (1974). *Foundations in sociolinguistics: An ethnographic approach*. Philadelphia: University of Pennsylvania Press.

Ivanic, R. (1994). I is for interpersonal: Discoursal construction of writer identities and the teaching of writing. *Linguistics and Education, 6*, 3–15.

John-Steiner, V., Panofsky, C. P., & Smith, L. W. (Eds.) (1994). *Sociocultural approaches to language and literacy: An interactionist perspective*. New York: Cambridge University Press.

Kantor, R., Green, J. L., Bradley, M., & Lin, L. (1992). The construction of schooled discourse repertoires: An interactional sociolinguistic perspective on learning to talk in preschool. *Linguistics and Education, 4*, 131–172.

Kelly, G. J., & Crawford, T. (1997). An ethnographic investigation of the discourse processes of school science. *Science Education, 81*, 533–559.

Kelly, G. J., Crawford, T., & Green, J. L. (in press). Common task and uncommon knowledge: Dissenting voices in the discursive construction of physics across small laboratory groups. *Linguistics and Education, Special issue on language and cognition*.

Kelly, G. J., & Green, J. L. (1998). The social nature of knowing: Toward a sociological perspective on conceptual change and knowledge construction. In B. Guzzetti & C. Hynd (Eds.), *Theoretical perspectives on conceptual change* (pp. 145–182). Mahwah, NJ: Erlbaum.

Lave, J., & Wenger, E. (1991). *Situated learning: Legitimate peripheral participation*. New York: Cambridge University Press.

Lin, L. (1993). Language of and in the classroom: Constructing the patterns of social life. *Linguistics and Education, 5*, 367–409.

Mitchell, J. C. (1984). Case studies. In R. F. Ellen (Ed.), *Ethnographic research: A guide to general conduct* (pp. 237–241). San Diego, CA: Academic Press.

Moll, L. (1990). *Vygotsky and education: Instructional implications and applications of sociohistorical psychology*. New York: Cambridge University Press.

Putney, L. G. (1996). You are it: Meaning making as a collective and historical process. *The Australian Journal of Language and Literacy, 19*(2), 129–143.

Putney, L. G. (1997). *Collective-individual development in a fifth grade bilingual classroom: An interactional ethnographic analysis of historicity and consequentiality*. Unpublished doctoral dissertation, University of California at Santa Barbara.

Rogoff, B. (1994). Developing understanding of the idea of communities of learners. *Mind, Culture, and Activity, 1*, 209–229.

Rogoff, B. (1995). Observing sociocultural activity on three planes: Participatory appropriation, guided participation, and apprenticeship. In J. V. Wertsch, P. del

Río, & A. Alvarez (Eds.), *Sociocultural studies of mind* (pp. 139–164). New York: Cambridge University Press.

Santa Barbara Classroom Discourse Group. (1992a). Constructing literacy in classrooms: Literate actions as social accomplishments. In H. Marshall (Ed.), *Redefining student learning: Roots of educational change* (pp. 119–150). Norwood, NJ: Ablex.

Santa Barbara Classroom Discourse Group. (1992b). Do you see what we see? The referential and intertextual nature of classroom life. *Journal of Classroom Interaction, 27*(2), 29–36.

Santa Barbara Classroom Discourse Group (1995). Two languages, one community: An examination of educational opportunities. In R. Macias & R. Garcia (Eds.), *Changing schools for changing students: An anthology of research of language minorities, schools and society* (pp. 63–106), Santa Barbara, CA: Linguistic Minority Research Institute.

Shepel, E. N. L. (1995). Teacher self-identification in culture from Vygotsky's developmental perspective. *Anthropology and Education Quarterly, 26*, 425–442.

Souza Lima, E. (1995). Culture revisited: Vygotsky's ideas in Brazil. *Anthropology and Education Quarterly, 26*, 443–457.

Spindler, G., & Spindler, L. (Eds.). (1987). *Interpretive ethnography of education: At home and abroad.* Hillsdale, NJ: Erlbaum.

Spradley, J. (1980). *Participant observation.* New York: Holt, Rinehart & Winston.

Strike, K. A. (1974). On the expressive potential of behaviorist language. *American Educational Research Journal, 11*, 103–120.

Strike, K. A., & Posner, G. J. (1992). A revisionist theory of conceptual change. In R. Duschl & R. Hamilton (Eds.), *Philosophy of science, cognitive psychology, and educational theory and practice* (pp. 147–176). Albany: SUNY Press.

Toulmin, S. (1972). *Human understanding, Volume 1: The collective use and evolution of concepts.* Princeton, NJ: Princeton University Press.

Tuyay, S., Floriani, A., Yeager, B., Dixon, C., & Green, J. L. (1995). Constructing an integrated, inquiry-oriented approach in classrooms: A cross-case analysis of social, literate, and academic practice. *Journal of Classroom Interaction, 30*(2), 1–15.

Tuyay, S., Jennings, L., & Dixon, C. (1995). Classroom discourse and opportunities to learn: An ethnographic study of knowledge construction in a bilingual third-grade classroom. *Discourse Processes, 10*, 75–110.

Vygotsky, L. S. (1978). *Mind in society: The development of higher psychological processes* (M. Cole, V. John-Steiner, S. Scribner, & E. Souberman, Eds.). Cambridge, MA: Harvard University Press.

Vygotsky, L. S. (1981). The genesis of higher mental functions. In J. V. Wertsch (Ed.), *The concept of activity in Soviet psychology* (pp. 144–188). White Plains, NY: M. E. Sharpe.

Vygotsky, L. S. (1986). *Thought and language* (A. Kozulin, Ed. & Trans.). Cambridge, MA: MIT Press.

Watson-Gegeo, K. A. (1992). Thick explanation in the ethnographic study of child socialization: A longitudinal study of the problem of schooling for Kwara'ae (Solomon Islands) children. In W. A. Corsaro & P. J. Miller (Eds.), *Interpretive approaches to children's socialization* (pp. 51–66). San Francisco: Jossey-Bass.

Wells, G., & Chang-Wells, G. L. (1992). *Constructing knowledge together: Classrooms as centers of inquiry and literacy.* Portsmouth, NH: Heinemann.

Wertsch, J. V. (Ed.). (1981). *The concept of activity in Soviet psychology*. Armonk, NY: M. E. Sharpe.

Wertsch, J. V. (1990). The voice of rationality in a sociocultural approach to mind. In L. C. Moll (Ed.), *Vygotsky and education* (pp. 111–126). New York: Cambridge University Press.

Wertsch, J. V. (1995). The need for action in sociocultural research. In J. V. Wertsch, P. del Río, & A. Alvarez (Eds.), *Sociocultural studies of mind* (pp. 56–74). New York: Cambridge University Press.

Yeager, B., Floriani, A., & Green, J. L. (1998). Learning to see learning in the classroom: Developing an ethnographic perspective. In D. Bloome & A. Egan-Robertson (Eds.), *Students as inquirers of language and culture in their classrooms* (pp. 115–140). Cresskill, NJ: Hampton.

Yeager, B., Pattenaude, I., Fránquiz, M., & Jennings, L. (in press). Rights, respect, and responsibility: Toward a theory of action in two bilingual classrooms. In J. Robertson (Ed.), *Elementary voices: Teaching and learning about genocide and intolerance*. Urbana, IL: National Council of Teachers of English.

6   Linking Writing and Community Development through the Children's Forum

Anne Haas Dyson

Paddy Clarke, the 10-year-old hero of Roddy Doyle's (1993) novel of the same name, wanted to minister to lepers. He'd read a story about Father Damien, the 19th-century Belgian missionary, who had made lepers his particular cause. Paddy rounded up the neighborhood boys to be his lepers, and he, of course, was Father Damien. "Our Father who art in heaven," he prayed, as each boy "wobbled a bit" (p. 52). And the lepers were properly grateful.

But when Paddy told his parents he had a vocation, they did not react as he expected.

"Good boy," said his mother to him, dry-eyed.
"[You've been] encouraging this rubbish," said his father to his mother, with anger in *his* eyes. (pp. 52–53; emphasis in original)

And Paddy Clarke's own vision of a good life, appropriated from a loved text, was disrupted.

In the project reported herein, I studied child writers who, like Paddy, were envisioning possible lives by appropriating heroes from other people's stories. Their heroes came primarily from the popular media rather

This work was partially supported by the Spencer Foundation and by the Educational Research and Development Center Program (grant number R117G10036 for the National Center for the Study of Writing), as administered by the Office of Educational Research and Improvement (OERI), U.S. Department of Education. The findings and opinions expressed in this chapter do not reflect the position or policies of the Spencer Foundation, the OERI, or the U.S. Department of Education.

I would like to thank the fine graduate students who contributed to the work reported herein, especially Elizabeth Scarboro, Wanda Brooks, Gwen Larsen, and Sheila Shea.

than from books, and their peers were not always so cooperative. But, like Paddy Clarke, they sometimes found that their imagined lives met with unexpected responses from others.

Consider a sample of this classroom scene, which I will present more completely later:

Sammy and Patrick had worked for almost an hour on their Power Rangers [a superhero team] story (Saban, 1994); they had eagerly looked forward to Author's Theater, that time in the third grade day when written texts could be acted out by author-chosen peers. Now, the performance has just concluded, and Kristin, their teacher, has asked for "questions and comments." The first to speak is Sarah, one of their actors:

Sarah:	See, I don't watch the [*Power Rangers*] show [on television], so I don't know what to do. It doesn't make sense to me. I couldn't hear you [reading above the actors], and it's like all of a sudden people are [play] fighting.
	. . . [omitted data]
Edward:	But I know why kids want that fighting. . . . 'Cause, you know how boys are. They get bored. They like fighting.
Lena:	Oh God.

Like Paddy, Sammy and Patrick had used cultural material to form a pleasing imagined world; that world reflected and reinforced their sense of social connection and their common desire to be good guys saving the world from evil. But, also like Paddy, when the relationships being mediated by that story shifted – when the story moved to a different social context – the text did not seem to have the same meaning. It generated social tensions in the classroom community as a whole.

By studying Sammy and his peers, I aim to understand more clearly the link between learning to write and learning to participate in a complex community marked by sociocultural differences. Influenced by Vygotsky, those working from sociocultural perspectives *have* stressed the link between children's literacy learning and their participation in community life (e.g., Dyson, 1989; McLane & McNamee, 1990; Moll & Whitmore, 1993; Putney et al., this volume). Through involvement in literacy activities with others, children learn to interact by writing in particular social circumstances. To help them in that learning, adults and more expert others "loan" children their own consciousness about language and language use (Bruner, 1986, p. 175, building on Vygotsky, 1978); they negotiate the developmental gap between themselves and the children, helping them to choose, encode, and reflect on their written choices. It is that deliberateness of language use that supposedly marks writing development (Vygotsky, 1987).

But classroom communities may be much more conflicted sites for language use than these discussions tend to suggest. To incorporate Bakhtin's (1981) dialogic perspective, in addition, to *developmental gaps* between children and more skillful others – and, of course, *interactional gaps* between composers and their addressees – there are also *ideological gaps* among community members, gaps that reveal larger societal fault lines related to gender, class, race – and, in Paddy Clarke's case, religion. Children struggle to use written signs to bring order to their inner thoughts and simultaneously to reach out to address others, but their signs are themselves symbols of societal order – they are public signs, drenched in community experience, not just in the child's social experience (see Wertsch, this volume, for an account of the *designative* functions of speech). And thus the ideological content of children's chosen words positions them in a contested world. If the resulting tensions become the occasion for public deliberation, learning to write may become linked to learning to participate in a complex community of differences – that is, to members' increasing deliberateness or consciousness about words, textual worlds, and their consequences.

In my work, then, I interweave Vygotskian and Bakhtinian concepts: When children's meaning-making, their imagining of pleasurable worlds, is "completed" in words (Vygotsky, 1987, p. 205; cf. Newman & Holzman, 1993), the ideological "force" of those words may reverberate in their classroom communities and, simultaneously, in their own inner sense or consciousness of themselves as social agents in those communities (Volosinov, 1973, p. 90). As authors, children may thus learn that they do not own their text's meaning, but they are responsible for that text nonetheless and, moreover, they are responsible through it (Bakhtin, 1981). Through what they choose to say and choose not to say, they respond to the world around them.

Social and ideological tensions among children, then, are potential developmental mechanisms for learning to write in what we hope is a pluralistic and democratic society. But, of course, this potential may not necessarily become linked with such idealistic ends. On the one hand, children, like adults, may use their growing consciousness to exploit written performance as a means of participating in and transforming community dialogues (Freire, 1970; Volosinov, 1973); on the other hand, they may choose to exploit the power of such performance for silence or circumvention (Graff, 1987).

The Project: Site, Participants, and Method

These ideas about the social and ideological dynamics of learning to write have come from studying child writers in an urban classroom crisscrossed by differences. The children's school served primarily two neighborhoods – one a primarily African American, low-income, and working-class community and the other a primarily European American, more middle-class community. The children's teacher, Kristin, had begun teaching in March of their second-grade year, and she stayed with the class through their third-grade year.

During the classroom free writing time, the differences among the children were visible whenever they chose their own work partners and their own seating arrangements: They sat within clusters of friends separated by the interplay of gender, race, and class. These same differences were visible (and audible) when the children brought their stories, usually written in the company of friends, to the community as a whole – the public – through Author's Theater. And the differences were especially evident when the children appropriated their story heroes from the popular media.

These media stories are central to many children's social lives as friends and peers. Like Sammy and Patrick, many children play with these stories; they rework them to declare and explore visions of pleasure, power, and goodness. These visions may reveal (and sometimes challenge) societal stereotypes, especially those related to gender (Douglas, 1994). As children grow older, there may be class-related differences in their display of popular culture in school where it is not typically valued. Middle-class children may be more likely to criticize commercial culture in the company of parents and teachers than working-class children are, which does not mean that they are any less involved with it (Buckingham, 1993).

In Kristin's room, media-based stories were written mainly by boys; girls were much more apt to write about their experiences and relations at home and at school. However, in the third grade, non-middle-class girls, all of whom were children of color – unlike their middle-class female peers, all of whom were white – also drew relatively often on the popular media for their free writing, and working-class boys of color did so almost exclusively. The children's use of media-based stories thus seemed linked to their identities as girls and boys and as members of different sociocultural referent groups. And thus, the stories were interesting to me as a researcher with a long-standing interest in young children's use of story composing as a means of negotiating their identities as friends, peers, and students.

In my project, then, I studied children's use of the popular media as source material for their own stories. Although I observed children both in the classroom and on the playground, I focused on the official free writing time. I studied the children's talk during writing to identify the sorts of social processes energizing and shaping their composing – processes like affiliating with others, resisting others, distancing oneself from them, or, more equitably, negotiating with them. And I also identified the ways in which written texts figured into those processes. For example, at first many children used written texts mainly as *props* for (or, more accurately, as tickets to) the Author's Theater – they stood up and pretended to read texts that were not actually written. Over time, though, their texts became more important. They began to serve *as representations of valued characters and actions*, as *reinforcers of their authority*, their right to say how the world is, and as *dialogic mediators* between themselves and others, as ways of anticipating and responding to others' reactions to their stories (see Wells, this volume). (Appendix A lists these analysis categories and provides their behavioral indexes; for extended discussion of methodological procedures, see Dyson, 1995, 1996, 1997).

Finally, I appropriated two terms from Bakhtin's colleague Volosinov (1973) – *reflection* and *refraction* – to describe the ideological processes through which texts reflected and refracted the children's professed values, interests, and beliefs about human relations. These text-generated processes were most visible and audible in Author's Theater, which functioned as a kind of public forum. In that forum, social identities were voiced ("you know how [we] boys are") and different interpretive frames were revealed ("oh God").

As a result, social processes, like using valued texts to affiliate with one's friends, intersected with the ideological processes reverberating in the classroom community as a whole, and thus emerged authorial processes, conscious decision making about the portrayal of human relations and human experience, that is, about composing stories. Over the course of the project, the children made more – and more complex – authorial decisions as texts became more central to community life. Thus, in the Vygotskian fashion, children's texts were both the means for and the result of participation in the composing life of the classroom.

This is a very complex study; it lends itself better to a novel-like form, which can trace changes in the social imaginations and written texts of key characters (like Sammy) and the dynamics between those characters and the community as a whole (Dyson, 1997). By explaining more fully Sammy's event with Patrick, and another centered on Lena and Melissa, I aim to illustrate the social and ideological dynamics that linked children's more differentiated understanding of their social worlds to their more differentiated understanding of their textual ones. (Both of these events come from the third-grade data set; therefore, Appendix B provides pseudonyms for and demographic information on all third graders.)

Illustrating the Link between Literacy and Community Learning

Chapter 1: Sammy, Patrick, and the Questionable Details

Local Negotiations: The Gathering of Tough but Good Guys

One day in late May, two old friends in the third grade, Sammy and Patrick, decided to write a superhero story together. Sammy, who was African American, and Patrick, who was European American, had overlapping but not identical social affiliations in the class. Both boys, though, enjoyed a good superhero tale.

The boys' story was about the Power Rangers, a multiethnic team of middle-class teenagers, including two girls – the lead characters in a live-action television show. In the following excerpt from their composing talk, Sammy and Patrick had already introduced the Power Rangers in their story, and they had also decided on Hercules as the bad guy. (The third grade had been studying Greek myths.) The boys had also already chosen the actors who would be the "good guys" and the one who will be the "bad guy," Hercules. As they wrote, Bryant, Thomas, and Michael came by, one by one, seeking roles. The first to come was Bryant.

Sammy:	Bryant, you could be [Hercules'] friend. . . .
Bryant:	I'm a bad guy? . . . Take me off.
Sammy:	Man! Why you always have to be a bad – see, you always wanta be a good guy. . . .
Bryant:	Pretend like he's [Hercules] a bad guy, and I'm a good guy. And when he wanta do something bad, I don't. I don't wanta join him.
Sammy:	Okay. Yeah.
Patrick:	But you always do.
Sammy:	Yeah.

Bryant:	No, I don't join him. . . .

. . .

Thomas:	Oh! Oh! . . . Can I be in [your story]?
Sammy:	Okay. You could be a bad guy, 'cause there's no more good guys.
Patrick:	Sammy! Sammy! I don't like so many people in my story. . . . It's too hard to control. Everybody gets out of hand.
Sammy:	If they do, let's just make 'em go home.

This was a common director's strategy for Sammy: when actors got "out of hand" in his performances, he improvised his storyline so that characters, for example, went home or even died.

Patrick:	NO! If they do, [Kristin] makes us stop. And we won't be able to do the rest.
Sammy:	But there's only two bad guys! That don't make sense [given the number of Power Rangers].

The boys agreed that Hercules would have one friend, and they returned to their writing.

Sammy:	(rereading) "And they turned into Power Rangers. And they fought Hercules and his friend. And Hercules still won."
Patrick:	No, Hercules didn't win. It was a tie.
Sammy:	No –
Patrick:	'Cause that would be fair to both.
Sammy:	Yeah but that ain't gonna be the end. [That is, Hercules can win now; the Power Rangers will win later.] We gotta have more parts. Let's do it longer, until lunch.

Sammy and Patrick, then, worked to meet their social goals with the cultural and ideological material provided by the superhero genre. They tried to be inclusive and fair to their actors; for example, they deliberated on how many characters to include and what sort of plot developments would allow all the characters an opportunity to win. And they also worked to make a "good" story, one with sufficient action and sensible human relations.

In fact, the pressure of the immediate social milieu helped transform their text so that it served not only as a ticket to social play and affiliation with friends, but also as a valued representation and as a dialogic medium – as a means to negotiate with others' desires. And yet, despite

their deliberations, Sammy and Patrick were not considering gender relations or questioning their depiction of power. These issues were not
salient in the local social world their text reflected, a world constructed
with other male admirers of superhero stories. But these issues *would*
become salient when the social milieu shifted.

Public Negotiations: Questioning the "Tough," the "Good," and the "Guys"

After composing time was over, Sammy and Patrick went to
the front of their classroom to organize for Author's Theater as the
rest of the children gathered on the rug. The boys called their actors.
The seven male actors were superhero regulars, but the two females,
Melissa and Sarah, were not. The girls, who were middle class, white,
and outgoing, had been chosen for female roles during the second-grade
year. During the third grade, the superhero authors were much more
responsive to girls who *requested* roles in these stories – and Sarah and
Melissa did not. Rather, they identified themselves as people who neither knew about nor valued superhero texts. In this they differed from
a group of primarily non-middle-class girls, who identified themselves
as people who found acting out a superhero story quite fun (see Dyson,
1997).

In fact, immediately after the play was over, Sarah made a comment
that emphasized her distance from – her lack of affiliation with – the
superhero audience.

Sarah:	See, I don't watch the show, so I don't know what to do. It doesn't make sense to me. I couldn't hear you, and it's like all of a sudden people are fighting.

. . .

Kristin:	Sarah's comment is that she doesn't know how to do [act out] the character because she's never seen it [the media show] before. So, Sarah, what would help you out there?
Sarah:	If there were more details.
Kristin:	What kind of details?
Sarah:	Like, what led to what. They [the authors] didn't say what they [the bad guys] did bad. It's more like, this character did this. But *why*?

. . .

Melissa:	And one thing that I really don't like is, I don't like when the story is just fighting, 'cause that's what that story was mostly about.

A number of boys immediately made faces, among them Edward and Aloyse (who was Sammy's best friend).

Kristin:	When she said that, I saw you guys kinda go "Uh!" Why did you react that way?
Aloyse:	Because that was his story and that's how he did it. You [Melissa] don't have to tell them what to do.

Offering an apparent compromise, Demario suggested that perhaps non-physical fighting – "arguing" – would be acceptable (although it is hard to imagine a superhero calling others to battle with some variant of "Come on, boys, let's argue!"). Kristin probed further:

Kristin:	How many of you don't like fighting in stories?

Sarah's and Melissa's friend Susan raised her hand, but she had a comment.

Susan:	In this book I'm writing, Pluto will go to battle.
Kristin:	You're saying that this is a story where there is some fighting in it that you like? (Susan nods.) Those of you who like fighting ... do you like the story when all it *is* is fighting ... ?
Aloyse:	Just fighting.
Victor:	No way. Like, sometimes if you write a story like that, it's boring when it's just fighting.
. . .	
Michael:	I don't like stories just fighting. In *my* X-men story, I'm gonna make 'em fight for the Professor [their leader], and then they gonna stop fighting and they're gonna become friends.

When Sarah made her original objection, fracture lines appeared that accentuated not only gender but also the interrelated borders of race and class: Those objecting to the story were white and middle class; those reacting to the objections were non-middle-class children of color. But even as the class fractured and social distance was revealed, a complex discussion of authorial decisions began.

A consensus seemed to be forming (a polymorphous one, but a consensus) that, to be good, any fighting must have a place in an evolving story. The "good" in question had, in part, to do with being a coherent story – a story with a narrative structure, a thematic point, and enough variation to keep audience interest. But it also had to do with being a worthy world – one in which any fighting has some motivation and is eventually ended.

After all, being good *was* important to the superhero fans, as Bryant illustrated with his fervent efforts to become a "good" friend of the designated "bad" guy. The consensus continued to evolve even as Edward fractured the community once again:

Edward: But I know why kids want that fighting. . . . 'Cause, you know how boys are. They get bored. They like fighting.

Lena: Oh God.

Kristin: Why're you getting mad, Lena?

Lena: It's sick. There's some girls that like fighting.

. . .

Edward: I think boys like all that fighting.

Demario: I don't like a story that has all just fighting in it, 'cause it wouldn't be a story. It would just be fighting, and you wouldn't know when to stop.

Kristin: Good point.

Sarah: It seems to me that if it's just fighting from beginning to end, without any story, it wouldn't be like "So one day they go into battle."

"Going into battle" is the language of the Greek myths studied by the class; and, indeed, Sarah herself (somebody who does "not like fighting" in stories) had gone to battle in a playground game of "gods and goddesses," as had her friends Melissa and Susan. In fact, there was a fair amount of violence in these girls' playground games, as they enjoyed running from the unmitigated evil of sharks on the loose and dinosaurs run amok. (Since the girls usually played victims, perhaps a role as a superhero would not be such a bad addition to their play repertoire.)

So Sammy and Patrick had gotten together to compose a good story – a fun story – for Author's Theater. But when that text was displayed in the public forum, social tensions emerged and, with teacher guidance, so did talk about authors' decisions about the representation of human relations, about stories. And those decisions, in turn, reconnected class members as decision-making children informed by certain shared values. Thus, the children did not make "flat judgments for or against" certain works but rather had "a fluid conversation about the qualities of the company [they] keep [in their stories] and the company [they themselves] provide" (Booth, 1988, p. 18).

In other events, Kristin helped the children discuss the decisions implicit in genre choice – for example, the kinds of conflicts and resolutions evident in superhero stories, video games, Greek myths, and biographies of varied historical heroes, especially leaders of nonviolent movements. After all, as Aloyse said at the end of the excerpted discussion, if we want to win in life, we have to "fight with the inside of [our] head[s]." That is, if we want stories in which those who are not physically strong (like the very slight Aloyse) are powerful, then we need different kinds of stories.

As for Sammy, during his next and last composing event of the school year, he included action other than fighting, wrote dialogue as part of the fight scene, and (for the first time) detailed the characters' feelings both before and after the fight between the good guys and the bad ones. These are all written actions consistent with articulated community values.

However, a growing consciousness of the social and ideological conflicts that can be generated by words in a particular community does not necessarily lead to authorial decisions to negotiate, explore, or even provoke those conflicts. Authors may simply decide to circumvent possible problems, as illustrated by the next chapter, featuring Lena and Melissa.

Chapter 2: Lena, Melissa, and the Unmediated Matter

Local Negotiations of Differing Interests

Near the end of the school year in June, Lena, who was Black and an immigrant student from Eritrea, decided to write a romantic text about Jason and Amber. Jason was a college student who volunteered regularly in Kristin's classroom, and Amber was his girlfriend who sometimes came with him. Jason was a light-skinned African American, and Amber was a very blond European American. Jason in particular was greeted with great enthusiasm by everybody in the class, and he was "liked" by many girls across racial lines.

In his interactions with the class (including his formal presentations), Jason stressed his African American identity. When he was a child, he had lived in an urban neighborhood much like that of the African American children in Kristin's class – a neighborhood regarded with affection by the children but also a neighborhood with evident problems of poverty and crime. During adolescence, his life changed dramatically; he and his mother lived in Africa with his new stepfather, who was a diplomat there. Jason formally shared maps and cultural artifacts from his African experiences with the class. Despite this emphasis on his African American identity and his strong sense of connection with Africa, Jason's racial identity was made problematic in the course of Lena's composing experiences –

and this was especially so because of Melissa's intense interest in Lena's composing.

Melissa, who was European American, was one of Jason's most enthusiastic female admirers. (She had even written him a poem in her journal.) Melissa was enormously pleased when Lena decided to write about Jason. Melissa sat next to Lena as the latter wrote, announcing her topic with pleasure to whomever happened by: "Lena's writing about Jason!"

Lena and Melissa had different but overlapping peer affiliations, and those different affiliations became salient in their talk about the planned story and its eventual performance. Sammy and Patrick too had overlapping but distinctive places in the classroom's social landscape. But their Power Rangers story emphasized their common interests as boys, not their differences in race. This was not true for Lena's story about (and not about) interracial romance.

Both Lena and Melissa had previously written stories based on films featuring such romance; Lena had written about *Jungle Fever* (Lee, 1991) and Melissa about *Dragon, The Bruce Lee Story* (DeLaurentis & Cohen, 1993). Moreover, Melissa had transformed her source material so that the couple was racially matched. The ideological uneasiness suggested by that literary action was made explicit in the social pressures she brought to bear on the diplomatic Lena.

Melissa very much wanted to play the role of Amber, Jason's beloved girlfriend. For her, Lena's story was a ticket to appealing social play – despite the fact that, in the story, Amber is not faithful to Jason. Following is Lena's text:

Once there was a girl named Amber. She had a baby named Kristin. She had a boy friend. His name was Jason. But she had another boyfriend. His name was Matt. Matt was at her house. The telephone rang. Matt answered it. Then Lily said, "Hello, is Amber there?" "No but I'm her boy friend." "You don't sound like Jason." "Who is Jason?" "Um um um good bye." And then Lily said to Linda, "Amber is cheating on Jason. And his name is Matt." Then they ran to her house. But they were too late. They [Matt and Amber] were yelling at each other. . . . Then Matt said, "I don't want to be your boy friend." He went out of the house and slammed the door. And Amber started to cry. Amber went out the back door and went to Jason's house. . . . (Spelling and punctuation corrected for ease of reading)

Amber and Jason do get married. However, "they got divorced in '92 and they did not see each other until '94 but the mother had the baby."

In the following excerpt from Lena's and Melissa's talk during composing, the divisive issue of race had just surfaced in what had been excited, good-humored talk. Melissa had just asked Lena if Rahda (who was light-skinned and an Indian American) could be Jason. Lena replied that she had promised the role to Victor (who was dark-skinned and of Mexican heritage), but Rahda could have the part if Victor was absent. Melissa then suggested Kevin (who was white) for Matt.

Lena:	I do not want Kevin. I do not want Kevin. I'll take Demario [who was Black]. Demario will not fool around [on the stage].
Melissa:	'Cause Amber's *White*.
Lena:	Yeah. But Jason's not White. He's Black.
Melissa:	Yeah. But he's pretty White.
Lena:	He's mixed.

Lena later explained to me that Jason was "mixed" because he was partly from Africa and partly from America. Lena's own status as an African immigrant may have influenced her definition of "mixed." The children continued to disagree on who should play Matt. Melissa was adamant; Matt planned "to marry Amber," she said. Lena finally agreed to Melissa's request, but referred to the official class policy that anyone could play any role, whatever the character's sex or race.

Lena:	[Matt and Jason can be White], but I'm not going to say they're White. They'll [the actors] act like theirselves. They're not even going to know they're White.
Melissa:	Okay.

Lena thus used her decision-making power as author to mediate her tense encounter with Melissa; that mediation resulted not in textual explicitness, but in textual silence.

The Fracturing of Community and the Circumvention of Text

On the last day of the project, Lena had an Author's Theater turn, and she chose to present the story of Jason and Amber. As her turn began, Lena called her actors. Melissa was named as Amber, as promised, and Melissa's friends Sarah and Susan were given their promised roles as Amber's two friends, Lily and Linda. Rahda was given Jason's role because Victor did not want it.

"Who wants to be Matt?" asked Lena.

Ordinarily, most boys avoided romantic roles. But the role of Matt was different; it allowed one to be in Jason's world. Indeed, many boys raised their hands, among them Demario, Thomas, Aloyse, and Sammy, all African American. Two girls, Tina (who was Black) and Lynn (who was

White), raised their hands as well. But before Lena could respond, Melissa leaned over and whispered in her ear. Lena then chose *not* Demario, the child promised the role, but Lynn, a White girl.

The Author's Theater performance went smoothly, although Demario and Thomas mumbled throughout the performance. Indeed, in the discussion that followed, the two boys seemed to continue to speak in muffled voices. Lena had finished her performance and asked for questions and comments. Thomas could not contain himself, so anxious was he to comment.

Thomas: The boys – they had their hand up. She [Lena] didn't pick nobody.

Demario: I know. Melissa told her to pick somebody else. She didn't say my name!

. . .

Kristin: You need to tell Melissa that.

Thomas: (to Melissa) [I'm] *mad*. 'Cause me, Aloyse, Demario – we all had our hands up but nobody pick us.

. . .

Lena: Because I wanted a girl to play a boy. I didn't pick Demario because sometimes he plays around.

This was exactly the reason Lena originally gave Melissa for rejecting *Kevin* and choosing Demario. Moreover, in singling out Demario from Thomas's list of boys, Lena indicated her particular responsibility to that child.

Thomas: No no. *Look* –

Lena: *Sometimes* [he plays around], I said. I didn't say all the time.

Thomas: But Melissa told her [Lena] to pick Lynn.

. . .

Melissa: Thomas, the reason why I picked Lynn – I *told* Lena when I was whispering to her that – I said, if you want, you should pick Lynn because she hardly ever gets to play a boy's part and she likes acting, and she doesn't care if it's a boy or a girl. . . .

Note Melissa's opening self-corrections, which distance her from the actual decision ("if you want").

Demario: When she be playing outside, she be playing boys' parts. Yes, ma'am!

Demario was disputing the claim that Lynn did not regularly play boys' roles; she did in fact regularly play male roles in superhero dramas.

. . .

Kristin: I'm just really confused, Demario and Thomas, why it's causing such trouble. Thomas, I understand that you're upset that Melissa said she should pick Lynn. Is that your only problem?

Thomas: Yes. 'Cause it was Lena's choice.

Kristin: Demario, I don't understand why you're so upset. Can you help us figure it out?

Demario: No.

I think it would have been very difficult indeed for Demario to sort out the complicated social scene that had just evolved. Kristin did not know that Demario had been promised the role. Nor did she know about the *representational* issue involved, an issue mediated by a silent text. The children went on to discuss the issue of acting, reaffirming the long-standing class rule about the individual's right to play any role without regard to sex or race. That rule had, in fact, been central to Lena's rationale for allowing Demario unwittingly to play the role of a White man.

But in the class discussion, the issue of participation was not linked to the issue of textual representation. The children had just enacted a story inspired by Jason, an African American man – and there were no African American children in the production. Moreover, in this school, there were a substantial number of children from families that identified themselves as mixed race on school forms. If Jason and Matt had been written explicitly as White, the ideological tensions that may have resulted could have given new meaning to the common school theme of the "different kinds of families" in "our" community and of the different choices people make inside and outside of texts. But as it happened, the text's unwritten words were hard to read, to speak, and to contest in public places.

The Public School as Public Forum

Lena, Melissa, Sammy, and Patrick were all intensely engaged in learning how to write in the company of their teacher and peers. But from a dialogic perspective, they were learning to manipulate more than words. They were manipulating ideological symbols of power and weakness, love and hostility, good and evil, and, at the same time, they were manipulating their social relations with classroom companions.

In the intersection of the social processes of affiliation and negotiation, and in the ideological processes of reflection and refraction, issues of human relations emerged, including those related to gender, race, and class. These issues were in no way caused by the children's composing, dramatizing, and talking. But they were thus made visible in the official world and, at least potentially, made subject to more deliberate manipulation, more conscious control.

The specific nature of the children's common interests and values cannot be generalized beyond this class, nor can the local effects of the Author's Theater events. But the social and ideological processes evident in this classroom seem applicable to other settings that offer young students open-ended composing periods. And Kristin's text-based public forum seems an example of the sort of arena envisioned by the educational reformer Deborah Meier (1995). In her words:

We cannot assume everyone will react the same way to the theory of evolution, the "discovery" of America, the Gulf War, or the value of "lifestyle" choices [nor, I would add, to the popular media]. Differences make things complicated. But dealing with the complicated is what training for good citizenship is all about.... [Public schools] could provide an exciting opportunity to use our often forgotten power to create imaginary worlds, share theories, and act out possibilities. This time not just on the playground but in all the varied public arenas in which we meet with our fellow citizens. (p. 7)

The arena Kristin negotiated with her children was both socially fun and instructionally focused, as well as a place where respectful listening was required. Moreover, the issues that were raised in that forum were couched in the familiar language of playground encounters (e.g., "that's not fair") and, at the same time, those issues were linked, through teacher guidance, to child agency and textual possibilities (e.g., "Could you imagine a story where...? What kind of details...?").

The preceding description of Kristin's socially organized, goal-directed public forum, with its linking of spontaneous (i.e., playground) and more scientific (i.e., school) language, seems quite Vygotskian to me (see especially Vygotsky, 1987, Chapter 6). What does not seem so Vygotskian to me is the analytic emphasis on the ideological tensions that emerged in and energized this forum.

As ideological gaps opened up – these differences in interpretations and in perspective on cultural capital (i.e., on "taste" [Bourdieu, 1984]) – those gaps could become moments for collective consideration of text fairness and goodness and also for individual play with newly salient aspects of text (e.g., the qualities of certain characters and actions). In time, community considerations became a guiding influence on individual authors' deliberations. And, in turn, those authorial deliberations were increasingly addressed to the community of the whole; even Lena's and Melissa's decisions, however problematic, were rooted in a sensitivity to the micropolitics of their classroom community.

One reason this guided focus on text could potentially support the elaboration of child writing *and* the deepening of community was, in fact, the very focus on a specific world. Decisions about what's powerful and good, what's fair and worthy, cannot be determined by universal law but rather by principled consideration of each case (Williams, 1991). And this consideration, I think, is what Kristin and the children were attempting when, for example, they wrestled with the nature of power, the possibilities of female and male action, and the relevance of race.

In the forum, dramatic play allowed the children to enter each other's text worlds, and discussions of writing allowed them to hold those worlds still so that texts could be jointly reconsidered, reimagined (Freire, 1970). Indeed, without a written word to contest, it was hard to speak, to untangle the complexities of identity and community. Thus textual reconsideration and social reconsideration were linked in the details of specific plots and actions, created and enacted by specific children, whose fictional (and nonfictional) fates were themselves linked.

As the children continue to grow, as the social configurations of their daily lives change, as their own bodies change, there will be new issues to consider. I am sure that my analytic narrative about Melissa and Lena left no sense of closure, and none was intended. There *is* no end – the suggestions of the children's growing awareness of romance and sexuality suggest changes in their intertextual worlds to come; their grappling with the themes and plots of life inside and outside texts will continue to need adult guidance and symbolic materials with which to work. And this leads me to a few closing reflections on both teaching and research.

First, how often, I wonder, will the children find teachers like Kristin in their futures, teachers willing to engage with the issues of children's lives that we as adults may choose not to see (Derman-Sparks, 1995)? Such teachers will require comfort with their own identities (Sleeter, 1993), an understanding of our pluralistic society (Takaki, 1993), and a depth of disciplinary knowledge and pedagogic skill that supports their efforts to pursue academic ends in ways that serve human ends consistent with democratic values, values like active inclusiveness, respect for the dignity of the individual, and joint responsibility for the common good (Lagemann, 1994).

Moreover, such teachers will require the support of their schools and communities, their own forums within which to explore the complexities and contradictions they themselves may feel about their children's words and worlds. In the tense, pressured atmosphere of many big-city schools, there is little time for teachers to discuss and develop their ideas with each other, to themselves become a community respectful of differences and aware of their common principles. Those trying new ways can feel isolated, as did Kristin (see Moll, Wells, this volume, for arguments in favor of the need for such professional communities).

Second, I wonder what kinds of source materials the children will have available to them in the official school world. There is no direct line from source material to child writer's rendition, but the source material does matter: It provides a universe of possible characters, relations, and actions. If children do not have available or cannot use in the official world text materials that explicitly foreground significant dimensions of their experience (e.g., race, class, gender), then they may be left to their own unexamined assumptions (Gutiérrez & Stone, this volume; Harris, 1992; Lee, Moll, this volume; Sims, 1982).

In this chapter I have foregrounded the children themselves – and the complex social and ideological dynamics of their social lives – as a potential source of individual and collective growth. I wonder, finally, what if any influence contemporary children, living in such complex circumstances, might be allowed to have on researchers like us, who are so inspired by the past. In my view, there is far too little in classroom research labeled Vygotskian that suggests the ideological fluidity of cultural symbols or human identities. Moreover, children themselves are seen primarily as apprentices to adult experts within adult-dominated worlds – despite the fact that many children are participating and forming a social and historical childhood that we ourselves have not experienced, and they are in need of a language to talk about and amid differences that we, the supposed masters, do not have (Smith, 1993; Williams, 1995).

And yet, at least for me, the young children presented herein made abundantly sensible Vygotsky's belief, inspired by Marx, in the link between human nature and human history and in the necessity for researchers to focus on process and on change. That belief suggests that no one ever masters a mediational tool like written language. Written words, like oral ones, are a means for participating in an always changing social community, a never-ending process of societal history-making; and thus, their meaning, their appropriate use, is always changing too. And maybe that is what contemporary children most need to learn.

This chapter began with a story of Paddy Clarke, a child playing out his imagined world with his friends – and being startled by the reactions of adults. Those reactions suggested that there were complexities the child was not seeing, ramifications of a spiritual calling that he was not grasping. I have hoped, however, to suggest that children have their own startling message, a message about complexities to be grappled with and ramifications of a sociocultural point of view to be explored. In their own classroom community, Sammy, Patrick, Lena, and Melissa were entering, however imperfectly, a more complex social and cultural dialogue, and this, I hope, can be said for us all.

Appendix A: Data Analysis Categories

Social Processes

Affiliating: Children refer to common knowledge, common pleasures, or common miseries or injustices, thereby emphasizing their similarity to others in a particular group. (For example, boys often built conversations about the media by displaying their knowledge about a group-valued media program; "oh yeah," each boy would say after each contribution, implying his own prior knowledge of the shared scene before adding his own recollections.)

Soliciting: Children seek others' desire to be included in their own plans. (For example, children often announced their desire to write about a commonly valued character or story [an implicit assumption of affiliation] in order to solicit others' requests for a part in their story; sometimes children directly requested others' involvement or inquired about their desires: "You wanta be in it [my story]?")

Allowing or Denying: Children allow or deny desiring others to be included in their own plans. (For example, children could agree to give others their desired roles ["You could be a good guy"] or another requested role. Usually the allowed requests had been indirectly solicited [e.g., by an announcement that one was writing about a popular character]. But sometimes unanticipated others solicited roles. Denying others who desired a role could have clear ideological echoes: "You're not no bad guy. You a lady.")

Controlling: Children direct others to comply with their own plans and/or anticipate how others will have to comply with their own words. (For example, children directed others to act out their words during Author's Theater events; sometimes children anticipated what their words would make others do: "Jonathan's gonna' hafta kiss Melissa [when they act out my story]!")

Complying or Resisting: Children comply with or resist others' plans. (For example, children could voice dissatisfaction with others' planned roles and actions. Like denying, resisting could have clear ideological echoes: "Amber's *White*," so her boyfriend in a child's romance story should not be Black.)

Distancing: Children dissociate themselves from others' chosen characters or actions. (For example, children could distance themselves from superhero stories by proclaiming them "not original" or full of "too much fighting.")

Negotiation: Children attempt to interact in ways that involve mutual accommodation between two or more participants, each seeking some control. (For example, child authors could agree to include character roles desired by another child in their own texts if the latter would return the favor.)

Textual Functions

Text as Ticket: The written text allows children to have a turn at directing or controlling their peers; the paper is thus both a ticket allowing access to the author and a prop for the child enacting the role of the author – the authority – in an Author's Theater event. (For example, sometimes children's texts were invisible, as it were; they pretended to read texts that were not actually written.)

Text as Memory Support: The written text functions to help children remember information relevant to their stories or the stories themselves. (For example, children often jotted down names of story characters, matched with names of child actors, even when they used an "invisible" text.)

Text as Representation: The written text functions to represent valued characters, relations among characters, and actions. (For example, boys often chose superhero thematic material, which marked their maleness in this class.)

Text as Authority (the "Reified" Text): The written text functions to reinforce the control of the author. (For example, when girls complained that boys did not include female characters in their stories, the boys often replied by repeating their complaint but without any sense of personal responsibility [i.e., with a variant of "Yes, there *are* no girls in this story"]; that is, they implied that the matter was out of their hands as authors – the texts were set.)

Text as Dialogic: The written text functions fully as a mediator of relationships among author, actors, and audience members. Its mediational role is not only interpersonal but also ideological. (For example, in response to the objections of others, the author might change the written relationship between males and females; most often, such changes occurred in a forthcoming text, not in the one being criticized.)

Appendix B: Sex and Ethnicity of Third-Grade Children

Sex	Ethnicity
FEMALE	
Lena	Eritrean American
Lettrice	African American
Liliana*	European American
Lynn*	European American
Makeda	African American
Melissa†	European American
Rhonda	African American
Susan*	European American
Sarah*	European American
Tina	African American
MALE	
Adam	European American
Aloyse	Ethiopian American (immigrant)
Bryant	African American
Demario	African American
Edward	Mexican American
James	Korean American
Jonathan*	Chinese American/European American†
Kevin	European American
Michael	African American
Patrick	European American
Rahda	Indian (Asian) American
Sammy	African American
Thomas	African American
Victor	Mexican American

* Children from homes in which at least one parent had a middle-class, white-collar job.

† Jonathan was biracial. However, he looked Caucasian, and his racial identity as Chinese did not seem salient to the children, unlike that of James and Rahda, the other Asian American children. (For example, Melissa included James and Rahda as potential leads for her Bruce Lee story because of "their hair." She did not consider blond Jonathan.)

References

Bakhtin, M. (1981). Discourse in the novel. In C. Emerson & M. Holquist (Eds.), *The dialogic imagination: Four essays by M. Bakhtin* (pp. 259–422). Austin: University of Texas Press.

Booth, W. C. (1988). *The company we keep: An ethics of fiction*. Berkeley: University of California Press.

Bourdieu, P. (1984). *Distinction: A social critique of the judgment of taste* (R. Nice, Trans.). Cambridge, MA: Harvard University Press.

Bruner, J. (1986). *Actual minds, possible worlds*. Cambridge, MA: Harvard University Press.

Buckingham, D. (1993). *Children talking television: The making of television literacy*. New York: Falmer.

DeLaurentis, R. (Producer), & Cohen, R. (Director). (1993). *Dragon, The Bruce Lee Story* [film]. Universal City, CA: Universal Pictures.

Derman-Sparks, L. (1995). How well are we nurturing racial and ethnic diversity? In D. Levine, R. Lowe, B. Peterson, & R. Tenorio (Eds.), *Rethinking schools: An agenda for change* (pp. 17–22). New York: Free Press.

Douglas, S. J. (1994). *Where the girls are: Growing up female with the mass media*. New York: Random House.

Doyle, R. (1993). *Paddy Clarke Ha ha ha*. London: Minerva.

Dyson, A. H. (1989). *Multiple worlds of child writers: Friends learning to write*. New York: Teachers College Press.

Dyson, A. H. (1994). The ninjas, the X-men, and the ladies: Playing with power and identity in an urban primary school. *Teachers College Record, 96*, 219–239.

Dyson, A. H. (1995). Writing children: Reinventing the development of childhood literacy. *Written Communication, 12*, 4–46.

Dyson, A. H. (1996). Cultural constellations and childhood identities: On Greek gods, cartoon heroes, and the social lives of school children. *Harvard Educational Review, 66*, 471–495.

Dyson, A. H. (1997). *Writing superheroes: Contemporary childhood, popular culture, and classroom literacy*. New York: Teachers College Press.

Freire, P. (1970). *Pedagogy of the oppressed*. New York: Continuum.

Graff, H. (1989). *The labyrinths of literacy: Reflections on literacy past and present*. New York: Falmer.

Harris, V. (Ed.) (1992). *Teaching multicultural literature in grades K–8*. Norwood, MA: Christopher-Gordon.

Lagemann, E. C. (1994). For the record: Character and community. *Teachers College Record, 96*, 141–147.

Lee, S., with 40 Acres and a Mule Productions (Producer), & Lee, S. (Director). (1991). *Jungle fever* [film]. Universal City, CA: Universal Pictures.

McLane, J., & McNamee, G. (1990). *Early literacy*. Cambridge, MA: Harvard University Press.

Meier, D. (1995). *The power of their ideas: Lessons for America from a small school in Harlem*. Boston: Beacon Press.

Moll, L., & Whitmore, K. (1993). Vygotsky in classroom practice: Moving from individual transmission to social transaction. In E. Forman, N. Minick, C. A. Stone

(Eds.), *Contexts for learning: Sociocultural dynamics in children's development* (pp. 19–42). New York: Oxford University Press.

Newman, F., & Holzman, L. (1993). *Lev Vygotsky: Revolutionary scientist*. New York: Routledge.

Saban, H. (1994). *Mighty Morphin' Power Rangers*. New York: Saban Entertainment.

Sims, R. (1982). *Shadow and substance: Afro-American experience in contemporary children's fiction*. Urbana, IL: National Council of Teachers of English.

Sleeter, C. (1993). How white teachers construct race. In E. McCarthy & W. Crichlow (Eds.), *Race, identity, and representation in education* (pp. 157–171). New York: Routledge.

Smith, A. D. (1993). *Fires in the mirror*. New York: Bantam Doubleday.

Takaki, R. (1993). *A different mirror*. Boston: Little, Brown.

Volosinov, V. N. (1973). *Marxism and the philosophy of language* (L. Matejka & I. R. Titunik, Trans.). Cambridge, MA: Harvard University Press.

Vygotsky, L. S. (1978). *Mind in society: The development of higher psychological processes* (M. Cole, V. John-Steiner, S. Scribner, & E. Souberman, Eds.). Cambridge, MA: Harvard University Press.

Vygotsky, L. S. (1987). Thinking and speech. In L. S. Vygotsky, *Collected works* (Vol. 1, pp. 39–285) (R. Rieber & A. Carton, Eds.; N. Minick, Trans.). New York: Plenum.

Williams, P. J. (1991). *The alchemy of race and rights*. Cambridge, MA: Harvard University Press.

Williams, P. J. (1995). *The rooster's egg: On the persistence of prejudice*. Cambridge, MA: Harvard University Press.

7   Synchronic and Diachronic Dimensions of Social Practice

An Emerging Methodology for Cultural-Historical Perspectives on Literacy Learning

Kris D. Gutiérrez and Lynda D. Stone

The significance of developing a deep understanding of schools and their social organization is that it can inform policies and practices of urban education. Although there is much to be learned from research that has helped to locate educational problems in the larger social context, educators also need research methodologies and theoretical frames that provide the possibility of more local explanations for the dilemmas and problems facing urban education. Situated understandings of education provide insight into the cognitive and social consequences of educational policies and practices (Moll, this volume). We endeavor to provide these situated understandings by examining more critically the theoretical constructs that currently underlie the educational treatment of students in general, but particularly of linguistically and culturally diverse students and of the routine practices of urban classrooms and schools (see Ball, Dyson, Lee, this volume). The goal of our research, then, is not only to provide a language for describing urban schooling and its literacy practices, but also to provide a critical analysis of their outcome. We draw on our body of research in urban education, literacy learning and its social organization, and the relationship of literacy learning to the practices of the local community to propose the following *syncretic framework* for the study of literacy in formal and nonformal educational settings. *Syncretic* here refers to the principled and strategic use of a combination of theoretical and methodological tools to examine individual actions, as well as the goals and history of those actions (see Putney et al., Smagorinsky & O'Donnell-Allen, this volume).

In our studies of literacy learning and development, we have attempted to account for the reciprocal relationship between literacy learning and the social practices of the classroom. In doing so, we have begun to recognize how much we have underestimated the complexity of classroom life and its relationship to literacy development (Gutiérrez, 1992, 1993b).

150

Classrooms, as institutional settings, have a social and cultural history that allows them to have both stable and emergent characteristics (Gutiérrez, 1993a, 1993b). Further, classrooms are constitutive of multiple activity systems that interact to promote learning. Learning, however, is not always a benign activity; thus conflict, tension, and contradiction contribute to the idiosyncratic nature of learning activity (Gutiérrez, Rymes, & Larson, 1995). To capture the complex, persistent, and emergent character of classroom social practices, we use a cultural-historical theoretical view of learning and development to understand socially and culturally organized phenomena such as literacy practices in classrooms (Cole, 1985, 1995, 1996; Engeström, 1993; Moll, 1990; Rogoff, 1990; Vygotsky, 1978; Wertsch, 1991). From this theoretical perspective, learning is not an individual process but rather a *transactional* (Dewey & Bentley, 1949) process mediated by the use of cultural tools such as writing or spoken language as people participate in routine activities in communities of practice such as classrooms (Cazden, 1988; Dyson, this volume; Gutiérrez & Stone, 1997; Lave & Wenger, 1991; Stone, 1994, 1996a; Mehan, 1979; Wells, this volume). Participation in social interactional processes promotes individual knowledge production.

In this chapter we will discuss how cultural-historical activity theory (Cole, 1996; Leont'ev, 1981; Wertsch, 1981) as an overarching frame affords us the possibility of bringing to bear a range of theoretical lenses that yield a repertoire of methodological tools to examine the mutual and interdependent relationship between the individual and the social world. We will also illustrate how we use a syncretic approach as a principled means to make visible and document the intricate and dynamic social processes of literacy practices. Following Duranti and Ochs (1998), through a syncretic approach we use a combination of theoretical and methodological tools to examine social phenomena. This approach necessitates transdisciplinary perspectives for the theoretical and methodological treatment of the social practices of literacy learning. Specifically, our shift in focus or unit of analysis from either the individual or the larger social context to an activity system allows an examination of the interrelationship between the individual and the cultural setting. In this view, social settings are not discretely circumscribed phenomena but instead occur as a part of laminated, overlapped, and interwoven social phenomena that occur in the moment and across time and space (Gutiérrez et al., 1995; Putney et al., this volume). Following Engeström (1987) and Giddens (1979), we define *activity system* as a social practice that includes the norms, values, division of labor, and goals of the community; this framework for activity allows

152   *K. D. Gutiérrez and L. D. Stone*

us to move across and within various levels of analysis. The syncretic approach we use, then, systematically and strategically blends theoretical constructs from social, psychological, and anthropological theories and yet allows us to remain anchored in cultural-historical and activity theories of development (Cole, 1995, 1996; Rogoff, 1990, 1995; Wertsch, 1991). Specifically, we use this explanatory theory to rethink and reevaluate how we look at the literacy learning of linguistically and culturally diverse students of urban learning contexts.

Our framework, then, is dependent upon a rich theoretical network that arises from the goodness of fit between our theoretical constructs and the complexity of social phenomena. This goodness of fit allows us to draw, in a principled or syncretic way, from critical social theories, developmental theories, and literary and language theories to link the particular to the larger social context. Thus, methodologically we attempt to look at both the social practice of literacy learning and the moment-to-moment construction of that practice. As a consequence, we also use theoretical perspectives of such scholars as Bakhtin (1981), Bourdieu (1977, 1991a, 1991b), Foucault (1977), Goffman (1959, 1961, 1974, 1981), and Luke and Gore (1992) to more richly understand social phenomena such as social identities, hybridity, and hierarchies and power relations in learning contexts. Thus, by integrating micro and macro analyses of learning environments, we are able to investigate the social, spatial, and temporal organizational dimensions of literacy learning practices, that is, diachronic and synchronic dimensions of activity (Gutiérrez, 1993a, 1993b, Stone, 1996b). These multiple layers of analysis reveal that the complex and situated nature of learning can be analyzed not only for its cognitive and social implications but also for its political consequences. Like others, then, we stress the importance of dealing with units of analysis that include but extend beyond the individual.

Our syncretic perspective helps account for the complexity of social phenomena and is consonant with the broader definition of literacy as a set of practices (Ball, this volume; Gutiérrez, Baquedano-Lopez, & Alvarez, 1998; Putney et al., this volume). Literacy learning, from this perspective, is situated in a social milieu and thus arises from participation in a community's communicative practices, both proximal and distal. From this view, literacy practices are constituted through the junction of cultural artifacts, values, beliefs, and normative practices known as an *activity system* (Leont'ev, 1981). Conceptualizing literacy learning as an activity system links thinking and doing in social practices. This theoretical approach necessarily eschews more narrow views of literacy learning that do not account for the social and cognitive consequences of literacy practices in urban schools. Accounting for these consequences is an essential goal for those concerned with urban schools and their diverse student populations (Ball, this volume).

Thus, we study the culturally informed and culture-producing nature of literacy practices. By using ethnography and discourse analytic methods of inquiry, we examine the meaning-making processes in which members of a community construct knowledge and a worldview individually and collectively as they participate in schooling practices (see Moll, this volume). The slice of life that we observe and analyze is informed by an evolving set of ethnographic questions that grow out of our body of work (see Gutiérrez, 1987, 1992, 1993a, 1993b, 1994; Stone & Gutiérrez, 1997). These questions include:

- What is the relationship between local practices and learning and developmental processes?
- What is the nature of the social and discursive practices in the teaching and learning of literacy?
- How can we account for developmental change through participation?
- In what ways are routine literacy practices socially and culturally constituted?
- What does the social organization of learning reveal about social relationships, hierarchies, rituals, knowledge exchanges, and belief systems in particular learning arenas?
- What are the potential contributions of conflict, tension, and contradiction to literacy learning and development?
- What are the social and cognitive consequences of literacy practices for urban student populations?
- What constitutes successful instructional practices, and how can they be sustained?

Guided by these questions and by our syncretic framework, we look both at language and through language to examine the interrelationship among literacy, culture, and learning (Ochs, 1988; Schieffelin & Ochs, 1986; Wells, this volume). Thus, the study of literacy becomes an important domain in that the practices and problems of urban education, as well as literacy learning, can be investigated in concert.

We have observed that literacy learning, its context and social organization, continue to be narrowly conceptualized and examined. For the most part, formal learning arenas such as classrooms, because of their seeming predictability, have been examined in ways that have not accounted for their stable yet improvisational character. In contrast, we understand

Literacy Practice as Social Practice

Social organization of literacy practices as they temporally unfold.

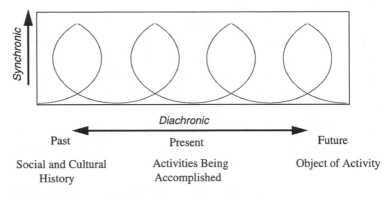

Figure 7.1 History of actions.

literacy practices as complex, overlapping, and intertwined social spaces and events. Thus, *social practice* becomes the unit of analysis that can be analyzed from various analytical perspectives. In this way we can develop and use multiple perspectives to explain more richly the relationship between social and cognitive phenomena.

Moreover, to understand better the relationship between literacy learning and its contexts, we examine the *gestalt*, or the whole practice and the history of those practices, *in situ*. Practices are socially and culturally organized and thus encode a social and cultural history. Practice becomes a rich unit of analysis because practices are constituted over time by multiple activities that stretch and change (Putney et al., this volume). Accordingly, a focus on practice makes visible the social and cultural history of the practice, an understanding of what is being accomplished in the moment, and an understanding of the future goal or object of activity. In Figure 7.1 we illustrate the relationship between the history of actions and the face-to-face interactional sequences that constitute the historical nature of those actions.

Figure 7.1 portrays the interrelationship between the regularized acts of situated practices occurring in the moment and the history of actions that constitutes the background meaning or source of mutual knowledge used for the social production of knowledge (Giddens, 1979). One means of talking about the routine discursive practices of the various social spaces of learning contexts is to use the notion of *script* to account for the temporal or diachronic constitution of social activity. Script here refers to a range of recurring patterns of activity within and across events in which members' actions display stable ways of engaging with others (see Gutiérrez, 1992, 1993a, 1993b for a detailed discussion of script). These scripts, characterized by particular social, spatial, and language patterns, become resources that participants use to interpret the activity of others and to guide their own participation.

The notion of script has become a useful construct for understanding how these normative practices qua literacy learning provide a range of opportunities for students to participate in constructions of literacy knowledge (Gutiérrez, 1992). An expanded definition of script explicates it as an orientation that members come to expect after repeated interactions in contexts with particular social and language patterns constructed in both local moments and over time (see Putney et al.'s discussion of *intercontext* elsewhere in this volume). These frames of reference with their range of participation structures lead to patterned ways of being and doing in particular contexts within classrooms. Script, then, helps account for the stability and variance of the classroom, the spontaneous and repetitive aspects of the social practices of the literacy learning we have observed (Gutiérrez, 1992, 1993a, 1995).

Script, in our earlier work (Gutiérrez, 1992, 1993b), focused analysis on the diachronic dimensions of social practices. Because it focused exclusively, although not intentionally, on the temporal dimension, it privileged the official space of the classroom and, thus, a particular discourse and curriculum. It is not surprising that much of classroom literacy research concerns itself with classroom teaching and thus also focuses on official spaces of the classroom.

Notwithstanding the significance of the interlaced relationship between ongoing activities and their cumulative history, our more recent work has addressed the multiple fields of activity in the classroom. In doing so, we recognize the importance of closely examining the social organization of activities that occur simultaneously in social practices – the synchronic dimension of activity. It is an analysis of this social and spatiotemporal level that reveals how social actions during activities both produce and reproduce cultural phenomena and how cognition is distributed among participants in the social space itself (Gutiérrez et al., 1995; Gutiérrez & Stone, 1997; Stone, 1996b; Stone & Gutiérrez, 1997). Thus Figure 7.1 reflects the relationship between the history of actions and their moment-to-moment construction and accounts for the various spaces in which these actions simultaneously occur.

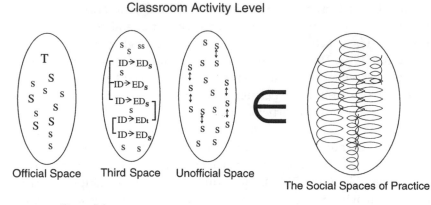

Figure 7.2

We propose the theoretical construct of *social space* or *habitus* (Bourdieu, 1991b) to describe the various patterns of participation that occur in overlapping and mutually informing but seemingly exclusive places where teacher and students reside and interact. Thompson (1991) describes Bourdieu's notion of habitus as "a set of *dispositions* which incline agents to act and react in certain ways. The dispositions generate practices, perceptions and attitudes which are 'regular' without being consciously co-ordinated or governed by any 'rule'. The dispositions which constitute the habitus are inculcated, structured, durable, generative and transposable" (p. 12; emphasis in original). Within the habitus of the classroom we have found *official*, *unofficial*, and *third spaces* within which various scripts or normative practices are employed (Gutiérrez et al., 1995). Representation of the official space found in Figure 7.2 illustrates the teacher's habitus; note that some students contribute to and participate in the teacher script or the official activity of the learning event. Those students who resist the normative institutional practices of the classroom, or whose local and cultural knowledge are often displaced, often form their own counterscript. This displacement of student knowledge motivates a different social space in which counterscript develops, that is, the underlife of the unofficial space (Goffman, 1961; Gutiérrez, 1993a; Gutiérrez et al., 1995). These counterscripts, however, are neither harmonious nor necessarily overlapping (Dyson, this volume; see also Smagorinsky & O'Donnell-Allen, this volume, for an analysis of *offstage* student discussion). Yet, as illustrated later, counterscript in the unofficial spaces of the classroom may often be linked. These linked actions form a more sustained and inclusive counterscript (see the bidirectional arrows linking student discourse).

We have previously argued against the seeming monologism of learning spaces in classrooms – that is, the seeming univocal discourse emanating from the teacher as the classroom's official and only script. Regardless of the dominance of the official script, we argue that classrooms are, in fact, intrinsically dialogical. The potential for multiple spaces exists. The emergence of a less apparent counterscript again reveals the inherently multivoiced and dialogic nature of any learning context (Gutiérrez et al., 1995). From this view, the social spaces of the classroom are constitutive of the history of the social practices of schools, the particular habitus of the teacher, and individual responses to the normative practices. Through this analytic lens, the conflicts, tensions, and contradictions that emerge within and across the various social spaces are made visible.

In particular, we use the theoretical category of the third space to identify and describe the competing discourses and epistemologies of the different social actors in the social practice of literacy learning (Gutiérrez, Baquedano-Lopez, & Turner, 1997; Gutiérrez et al., 1995, 1998). The third space is a discursive space in which alternative and competing discourses and positionings transform conflict and difference into rich zones of collaboration and learning. In this way, the third space provides the mediational context and tools necessary for future development. Thus, as Figure 7.2 depicts, the third space differs from the other spaces in that the dialogue among participants occurs as nonrandom associations between their scripts and is a genuine exchange of perspectives and worldviews. Accordingly, in these contexts, we can observe and document the collective negotiation of meaning. In Figure 7.2 we illustrate these spaces and show that although they are not exclusive, and although they are necessarily overlapping and mutually constituted, for purposes of analysis these spaces are identified as theoretically distinct categories.

The *Social Spaces of Practice* in Figure 7.2 illustrate the laminated and conflicting nature of the communicative actions observed in classrooms and other learning contexts. Our methodology, then, provides the theoretical and methodological tools to explain how these spaces are not monologic and unidimensional, but rather are complex social spaces that are inextricably related to what gets learned and how. By examining the face-to-face interaction and the resulting products, we understand both the history and thus the construction of the social practices of the classroom. As a result, we have access to the products and the means for assessing both the products and their processes. The significance here is that we challenge the limitations of the exclusive use of more traditional measures of learning and propose a more expanded understanding of measures of learning and achievement. Later, we will demostrate how this view of assessment is understood within the framework of apprenticeship (Gutiérrez & Stone, 1997; Rogoff, 1990).

Although we will not elaborate here, we held to ethnographic principles of research and developed theoretical categories from our corpora of data. Because our intention is to understand situated practice, our instrumentation grows out of theoretical categories that emerge from the data. For this reason, we can shift perspectives on the data while remaining anchored in the overarching theoretical orientation of cultural-historical activity theory. The rationale for developing and revising instruments in relation to the classroom and school contexts is eloquently stated by Miles and Huberman (1994): "Prior instrumentation is usually context-stripped; it lusts for universality, uniformity, and comparability. But qualitative research lives and breathes through seeing the context; it is the particularities that produce the generalities, not the reverse" (p. 35). Using multiple and layered data collection strategies and analytical methods such as discourse and conversational analysis, we mine the data to make visible the layers of context (cf. Goodwin & Goodwin, 1992; Goodwin & Heritage, 1990; Green & Wallat, 1981; Schegloff, 1991). These data were specifically derived from participant-observation field notes, interviews, archival data, audio and video recordings, a retrospective dialogic analysis of classroom videos and their transcription, and classroom artifacts including student-generated oral and written texts.

By studying everyday literacy activities across time and space, then, we study how literacy practices are constituted and how these practices influence teaching and learning. By analyzing the constructed script of the classroom, we attempt to account for what occurs at the individual and interpersonal levels over time. By examining the stable and improvisational attributes of scripts or the social practices of the learning context, we document how multiple social spaces come into existence in a single moment. We employ discourse analytical tools to account for what occurs in these moment-to-moment interactions among individuals, insofar as discourse analysis allows the indexing of the relationship between the larger community values and individual actions (Atkinson & Heritage, 1984; Levinson, 1983; Ochs, 1979).

Activity theory in particular allows us to examine the relationship between the interpersonal and the larger community (Engeström, 1987, 1993; Leont'ev, 1981). It is important to note that *activity* refers to the structural organization of a social practice (i.e., a cultural system) or the social plane that promotes cognitive growth and ideological views in both

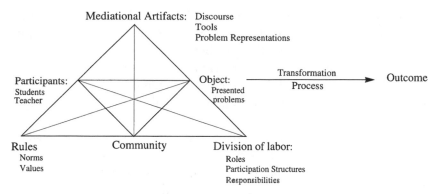

Figure 7.3 Adapted from Engeström (1993).

adults and children. Activity theory affords the possibility of focusing simultaneously on the critical elements of learning practices: the community and interpersonal levels, the macro and micro levels. An understanding of the community level accounts for how the social and discursive practices of the learning community shape what gets learned, who gets to learn, and how that learning is organized. A community's rules of production create values and beliefs that influence the habitus or social spaces of the learning context.

Following Engeström (1993), we seek to investigate the relationship of community organization to individual and interpersonal actions. Figure 7.3 diagrams how practice at the community and individual levels represents an interrelated system in which the object of activity, or that which animates social action during situated practices, motivates participants to make meaning out of a cultural object. The object of the activity or larger cultural goal here does not in any predetermined way direct the unfolding nature of social action, which is inherently opportunistic and creative. Rather, the durable qualities of practices and the improvisational nature of social actions interact to both maintain and change situated practices. This relationship among action, goal, and practice explains why cultural practices such as literacy events change over time while retaining some continuity. For this reason, as students participate in literacy events, they are both creating and re-creating situated practices during the construction of literacy knowledge. Framed in this way, cultural practices, learning, and development exist in a reciprocal relationship.

The activity theoretic characterization of a social practice considers the pragmatic actions of students and teachers in classrooms as inextricably related to cognitive products such as the strategies and skills of writing. In other words, the normative practices exhibit how the social production of domain knowledge is individually and collectively generated within the structure of a practice. Further, because the unit of analysis in its broadest formulation includes the history of patterned, joint, mediated activities of a practice and their current instantiation, an examination of social interactions during literacy practices makes visible the nature of learning.

Our theoretical orientation and methodology discussed earlier lead us to view learning as changing participation over time as a means to document the outcomes or objects of activity in a community (Engeström, 1993; Lave & Wenger, 1991; Putney et al., this volume; Rogoff, 1990, 1997; Rogoff, Matusov, & White, 1996). We draw from Rogoff's (1995) definition of apprenticeship as the mature goals of a community's social practices to examine how competence develops through coparticipation in the joint activities of literacy. Activity theory helps us document changes in roles and thus the changing nature of participation across literacy events. By focusing on the division of labor, access to conceptual tools, and the use of conceptual tools, we can account for the shifts in roles and responsibilities of participants and further tease apart how literacy practices influence teaching and learning. In this way we can also systematically demonstrate how literacy activity itself mediates the learning that gets accomplished.

In addition, we, like Hutchins (1993), challenge more static notions of expertise that assert that the group expertise is simply the sum of the individuals' knowledge. Rather, we can demonstrate and codify how students' knowledge and expertise (in the course of a literacy event or events) are distributed among participants as the nature of their participation shifts. In doing so, we challenge the commonly held notion of expertise as being located in one individual and illustrate instead how expertise exists both in the individual and in the group and their subsequent interactions. In other words, we try to account for the ways in which thinking is distributed in social settings (Gutiérrez & Stone, 1997; Moll, this volume; Salomon, 1993). Moreover, we attempt to demonstrate how knowledge is distributed when multiple forms of expertise become available to all participants. Expertise in this context is redefined as a socially and situated construct. Thus, we can use a framework of changing participation and apprenticeship as theoretical constructs to understand the data, and we have developed categories to describe the range of participation observed in learning contexts. Of significance is our similar treatment of other theoretical categories discussed earlier. In each case, we use the particular construct while remaining grounded in our overarching theoretical orientation of cultural-historical theory.

So far, we have attempted to demonstrate that when classroom literacy practices are reframed as contexts in which cognition, activity, and situation are mutually constituted, the striking complexity of learning and development in social settings becomes a topic for consideration. In order to capture this complexity, we offer a theoretical frame and methodology, through the constructs of social spaces, changing participation, and scripts, to take into account the essential interrelationship of the social and the individual. The dynamics and structure of literacy practices, then, reveal how direct experience occasions the dialogical construction of meaning, self, and knowledge.

In this chapter we have illustrated how our theory and methodology allow for an unpackaging of the social organization of learning communities and provide opportunities to look at various social phenomena. Because literacy learning is a social and cultural process that links language and thinking in a community's practices, we have argued that what is needed is a theoretical perspective that takes into account the interaction between the social milieu and the individual. We have proposed cultural-historical psychology and a syncretic approach as a means of better understanding educational phenomena and of expanding conceptualizations of literacy.

Discussion

The theoretical and methodological approaches that we outline for the study of classroom literacy practices are heuristics intended to provide a measure of clarity to more traditional ways of viewing formal and informal learning settings. On the one hand, the historical and often mistaken identification of classrooms as relatively static settings has underestimated the complexity of classroom life and its inextricable relationship to learning. On the other hand, classroom activity and learning have been seen as disconnected or unrelated activities. As a consequence, a theoretical examination of the mutually constitutive relations between cognition and activity in the classroom arena has not yet been adequately addressed (see other chapters in this volume for efforts to explore this relationship: Dyson, Putney et al., Smagorinsky & O'Donnell-Allen, Wells). It is for this reason that we argue for the syncretic approach as a systematic and strategic consideration of the complexities of literacy practices in educational settings that promote learning and development. We believe that it is this combination of complementary psychological and social theories and a multidimensional analysis that provides us with the possibility of better understanding the conflicting and contradictory practices of urban education, their influence on literacy learning, and their resulting tensions.

References

Atkinson, J. M., & Heritage, J. (1984). *Structures of social action: Studies in conversation analysis.* New York: Cambridge University Press.

Bakhtin, M. M. (1981). *The dialogic imagination: Four essays by M. M. Bakhtin* (M. Holquist, Ed.; C. Emerson & M. Holquist, Trans.). Austin: University of Texas Press.

Bourdieu, P. (1977). *Outline of a theory of practice.* New York: Cambridge University Press.

Bourdieu, P. (1991a). Epilogue: On the possibility of a field of world sociology. (L. Wacquant, Trans.). In P. Bourdieu & J. Coleman (Eds.), *Social theory for a changing society* (pp. 373–387) Boulder, CO: Westview Press.

Bourdieu, P. (1991b). *Language and symbolic power.* (J. B. Thompson, Ed.; G. Raymond & M. Adamson, Trans.). Cambridge, MA: Harvard University Press.

Cazden, C. B. (1988). *Classroom discourse: The language of teaching and learning.* Portsmouth, NH: Heinemann.

Cole, M. (1985). The zone of proximal development: Where culture and cognition create each other. In J. Wertsch (Ed.), *Culture, communication and cognition: Vygotskian perspectives* (pp. 146–161). New York: Cambridge University Press.

Cole, M. (1995). The supra-individual envelope of development: Activity and practices, situation and context. In J. Goodnow, P. Miller, & F. Kessel (Eds.), *Cultural practices as contexts for development* (pp. 105–118). San Francisco: Jossey-Bass.

Cole, M. (1996). *Cultural psychology: A once and future discipline.* Cambridge, MA: Harvard University Press.

Dewey, J., & Bentley, A. (1949). *Knowing and the known.* Boston: Beacon Press.

Duranti, A. (1997). *Linguistic anthropology.* New York: Cambridge University Press.

Duranti, A., & Ochs, E. (1998). Syncretic literacy: Homework in a Samoan American family. In L. B. Resinck, C. Pontecorvo, & R. Saljo (Eds.), *Discourse, tools, and reasoning: Situated cognition and technologically supported environments* (pp. 169–202). Berlin: Springer.

Engeström, Y. (1987). *Learning by expanding. An activity-theoretical approach to developmental research.* Helsinki: Orienta-Konsultit.

Engeström, Y. (1993). Developmental studies of work as a testbench of activity theory: The case of primary care medical practice. In S. Chaiklin & J. Lave (Eds.), *Understanding practice: Perspectives on activity and context* (pp. 64–103). New York: Cambridge University Press.

Foucault, J. (1977). *Discipline and punish: The birth of a prison* (A. M. Sheridan Smith, Trans.). New York: Pantheon.

Giddens, A. (1979). *Central problems in social theory.* Berkeley: University of California Press.

Goffman, E. (1959). *Presentation of self in everday life.* New York: Anchor Books.

Goffman, E. (1961). *Asylums: Essays on the social situation of mental patients and other inmates.* New York: Anchor Books.

Goffman, E. (1974). *An essay on the organization of experience: Frame analysis.* Boston: Northeastern University Press.

Goffman, E. (1981). *Forms of talk.* Philadelphia: University of Pennsylvania Press.

Goodwin, C., & Goodwin, M. H. (1992, August). *Professional vision.* Paper presented at the Plenary Lecture at the International Conference on Discourse and the Professions, Uppsala, Sweden.

Goodwin, C., & Heritage, J. (1990). Conversational analysis. *Annual Review of Anthropology, 19,* 283–307.

Green, J., & Wallat, C. (1981). *Ethnography and language in educational settings.* Norwood, NJ: Ablex.

Gutiérrez, K. D. (1987). *The composing process of four college-aged basic readers and writers.* Unpublished doctoral dissertation. University of Colorado, Boulder.

Gutiérrez, K. D. (1992). A comparison of instructional contexts in writing process classrooms with Latino children. *Education and Urban Society, 24,* 244–262.

Gutiérrez, K. D. (1993a, April). *Scripts, counterscripts and multiple scripts.* Paper presented at the annual meeting of the American Educational Research Association., Atlanta, GA.

Gutiérrez, K. D. (1993b). How talk, context, and script shape contexts for learning: A cross-case comparison of journal sharing. *Linguistics and Education, 5,* 335–365.

Gutiérrez, K. D., Baquedano-Lopez, P., & Alvarez, H. (1998, April). *Building a culture of collaboration through hybrid language practices.* Paper presented at the annual meeting of the American Educational Research Association, San Diego, CA.

Gutiérrez, K. D., Baquedano-Lopez, P., & Turner, M. (1997). Putting language back into language arts: When the radical middle meets the third space. *Language Arts, 74,* 368–378.

Gutiérrez, K. D., Rymes, B., & Larson, J. (1995). Script, counterscript, and underlife in classrooms: James Brown vs. Brown vs. Board of Education. *Harvard Educational Review, 65,* 445–471.

Gutiérrez, K. D., & Stone, L. (1997). A cultural-historical view of learning and the learning disabilities: Participation in a community of learners. *Learning Disabilities Research & Practice, 12,* 123–131.

Hutchins, E. (1993). The social organization of distributed cognition. In L. B. Resnick, J. M. Levine, & S. D. Teasley (Eds.), *Perspectives on socially shared cognition* (pp. 283–307). Washington, DC: American Psychological Association.

Lave, J., & Wenger, E. (1991). *Situated learning: Legitimate peripheral participation.* New York: Cambridge University Press.

Leont'ev, A. N. (1981). *The problem of activity in psychology.* Armonk, NY: M. E. Sharpe.

Levinson, S. C. (1983). *Pragmatics.* New York: Cambridge University Press.

Luke, C., & Gore, J. (Eds.). (1992). *Feminisms and critical pedagogy.* New York: Routledge.

Mehan, H. (1979). *Learning lessons.* Cambridge, MA: Harvard University Press.

Miles, M., & Huberman, A. M. (1994). *An expanded sourcebook: Qualitative data analysis* (2nd ed.). Thousand Oaks, CA: Sage.

Moll, L. (1990). *Vygotsky and education: Instructional implications and applications of socio-historical psychology.* New York: Cambridge University Press.

Ochs, E. (1979). Transcription as theory. In B. Schieffelin (Ed.), *Developmental pragmatics* (pp. 43–72). New York: Academic Press.

Ochs, E. (1988). *Culture and language development: Language acquisition and language socialization in a Samoan village.* New York: Cambridge University Press.

Rogoff, B. (1990). *Apprenticeship in thinking: Cognitive development in social context.* New York: Oxford University Press.

Rogoff, B. (1995). Observing sociocultural activity on three planes: participatory appropriation, guided participation, and apprenticeship. In J. V. Wertsch, P. del Río, & A. Alvarez (Eds.), *Sociocultural studies of mind* (pp. 139–164). New York: Cambridge University Press.

Rogoff, B. (1997). Evaluating development in the process of participation: Theory, methods, and practice building on each other. In E. Amsel & A. Renninger (Eds.), *Change and development: Issues of theory, application, and method* (pp. 265–285). Hillsdale, NJ: Erlbaum.

Rogoff, B., Matusov, E. W., & White, C. (1996). Models of teaching and learning: Participation in a community of learners. In D. R. Olson & N. Torrance (Eds.), *The handbook of education and human development: New models of learning, teaching and schooling* (pp. 388–414). London: Basil Blackwell.

Salomon, G. (Ed.). (1993). *Distributed cognitions: Psychological and educational considerations.* New York: Cambridge University Press.

Schegloff, E. A. (1991). Conversation analysis and socially shared cognition. In L. B. Resnick, J. M. Levine, & S. D. Teasley (Eds.), *Perspectives on socially shared cognition* (pp. 150–171). Washington, DC: American Psychological Association.

Schieffelin, B. B., & Ochs, E. (Eds.). (1986). *Language socialization across cultures.* New York: Cambridge University Press.

Stone, L. D. (1994, April). *Issues in problem-solving discourse: The socialization of planning skills during kindergarten science lessons.* Paper presented at the annual meeting of the American Educational Research Association, San Francisco.

Stone, L. D. (1996a). The social construction of mathematical knowledge: Presented problems in mathematics classrooms. *Issues in Applied Linguistics,* 7(1), 119–133.

Stone, L. D. (1996b). *A cross-cultural study of problem articulation in equivalent fraction lessons.* Unpublished doctoral dissertation, University of California at Los Angeles.

Stone, L. D., & Gutiérrez, K. D. (1997, June). *Problem finding as distributed intelligence: The role of changing participation in problem-solving activities in an after-school learning community.* Paper presented at the meeting of the Jean Piaget Society, Santa Monica, CA.

Thomson, J. B. (1991). Editor's introduction. In P. Bordieu (Ed.), *Language and symbolic power* (pp. 1–31) (G. Raymond & M. Adamson, Trans.). Cambridge, MA: Harvard University Press.

Vygotsky, L. S. (1978). *Mind in society: The development of higher psychological processes* (M. Cole, V. John-Steiner, S. Scribner, & E. Souberman, Eds.). Cambridge, MA: Harvard University Press.

Wertsch, J. V. (1981). The concept of activity in Soviet psychology: An introduction. In J. V. Wertsch (Ed. & Trans.), *The concept of activity in Soviet psychology* (pp. 3–36). Armonk, NY: M. E. Sharpe.

Wertsch, J. V. (1991). *Voices of the mind: A sociocultural approach to mediated action.* Cambridge, MA: Harvard University Press.

8 Idiocultural Diversity in Small Groups

The Role of the Relational Framework in Collaborative Learning

Peter Smagorinsky and Cindy O'Donnell-Allen

Vygotskian theorists share the assumption that the structure of consciousness comes about through situated, goal-directed, tool-mediated engagement in social practices (Cole, 1996; Wertsch, 1991). This axiom implies that in order to understand mental functioning, researchers should analyze the context of development and the ways in which it provides problems, values, structures, tools, and implied trajectories for human action. Operating from this perspective, educational researchers have focused on a variety of *nested contexts* (Cazden, 1988, p. 198) to help account for the ways in which (1) school-age children develop ways of thinking and (2) the primary contexts for development (home and community) prepare children for the primary context for assessment (school). Among the social practices and arenas that researchers have studied in order to account for why people think and act as they do in school are public policy (Brown, 1993), home and community literacy practices (Moll, this volume), disciplinary traditions (Applebee, 1996), instructional approaches (Hillocks, 1995), peer group culture (Dyson, this volume), gender groups (Sadker & Sadker, 1994), cultural discourse communities (Lee, 1993, this volume), school in relation to communities (Peshkin, 1978), whole classrooms (Jackson, 1968), and small groups within classrooms (Smagorinsky & Fly, 1993). By studying development in a variety of settings, researchers have documented the ways in which the contexts of human development provide channels for what Wertsch (1985) has called the *social formation of mind.*

This research was funded by a grant from the NCTE Research Foundation. At the time of the study, Cindy O'Donnell-Allen was a teacher at Norman (OK) High School and a doctoral student at the University of Oklahoma, and Peter Smagorinsky taught at the University of Oklahoma.

Two key aspects of social settings and their influence on concept development are the related notions of *prolepsis* (Cole, 1996) and *telos* (Wertsch, 1996a, 1996b, this volume). Both refer to a social group's view of an optimal outcome for human development and the group's resultant efforts to promote that outcome within members of their community. Vygotsky (1987) used the term *higher mental functions* (p. 127) to describe the culturally sanctioned, ideal ways of thinking that are valued and fostered within formal settings. Wertsch (1985) argues that each activity setting is governed by implicit assumptions that "determine the selection of actions and their operational composition. The guiding and integrating force of these assumptions is what Leont'ev called the motive of an activity.... Among other things, the motive that is involved in a particular activity setting specifies what is to be maximized in that setting" (p. 212). With different motives obtaining in different settings and with different settings providing different problems to solve, people engage in context-specific social practices that lead to the development of community-based, localized higher mental functions (Tulviste, 1991) and that enable them to "live culturally" (Ingold, 1994, p. 330; cited in Moll, this volume).

Every setting, in this view, is governed by particular motives that provide coherence and direction for the human activity that takes place within it. Educators who are consciously aware of this assumption have tried to structure the physical, social, and instructional environments of schools and classrooms in order to direct students' development toward particular ends. With students' social futures in mind, schools privilege certain cultural tools, in particular speech, and reward specific ways of using and ordering them to encourage students to arrive at the optimal developmental destinations. Moll (1990) has argued that

from a Vygotskian perspective, a major role of schooling is to create social contexts (zones of proximal development) for mastery of and conscious awareness in the use of these cultural tools. It is by mastering these technologies of representation and communication (Olson, 1986) that individuals acquire the capacity, the means, for "higher-order" intellectual activity. Thus Vygotskian theory posits a strong, dialectic connection between external (i.e., social and ... extracurricular) practical activity mediated by cultural tools, such as speech and writing, and individuals' intellectual activity. (p. 12)

Stated more simply, a Vygotskian perspective would hold that the social and physical organization of schooling implies and encourages an ideal student and, eventually, an ideal adult and citizen. The notion of what constitutes an ideal adult, however, is under dispute, viewed variously as one who is caring (Noddings, 1993), subversive (Postman & Weingartner,

1987), thoughtful (Brown, 1993), culturally literate (Hirsch, 1987), civic-minded (Stotsky, 1991), imaginative (Bogdan, 1992), democratic (Dewey, 1966), joyous (Newman, 1996), virtuous (Bennett, 1993), politically liberated (Freire, 1970), personally liberated (Montessori, 1964), self-motivated (Csikszentmihalyi & Larson, 1984), scientific (Piaget, 1952), skeptical (Foucault, 1972), reflective (Schön, 1991), free (Greene, 1988), domestic (Martin, 1995), inquiring (Dewey, 1960), and compassionate (Jesus Christ, n.d.) – to name just a few qualities that educators have identified over the years. We should stress that (1) each of these terms may be defined in ways different from the way intended by its advocate, (2) each of these theorists, while foregrounding one trait, endorses others as well, and (3) many of these different qualities of an ideal adult are compatible with one another. Each ideal endpoint can, however, suggest the need to promote specific frameworks for thinking and conceptions of human purpose and thus, for educators, engagement in different social and intellectual practices in school.

In this chapter we look at one effort, by coauthor Cindy O'Donnell-Allen, to deliberately develop a social context in her high school English classes according to principles of progressive education (e.g., Dewey, 1966). We will briefly describe the overall context of instruction and the relationship between Cindy's goals and her instructional approach. We then describe the small group discussions that took place during one classroom episode when students interpreted different characters from Shakespeare's *Hamlet* through the artistic medium of the *body biography*, a life-sized human outline that the groups filled with images and words that represented their interpretation of their character. We see our work as being compatible with the kinds of collaborative communities of inquiry endorsed by Moll, Putney et al., and Wells elsewhere in this volume. (See O'Donnell-Allen & Smagorinsky, 1999, and Smagorinsky & O'Donnell-Allen, 1999a, 1998b, for more detailed accounts of the school and classroom context and some of the transcripts we discuss here and more thorough descriptions of our collaboration.)

Cindy shared Dewey's (1966) view that schooling should promote democratic communities, with the ideal citizen achieving independence of thought and the freedom to express it responsibly within the confines of the greater social good (see Wells, this volume). To encourage these qualities, she set up her classroom so that students had input into the curriculum and classroom organization and had latitude in deciding how to act within the overall structure of the classroom. Students' needs and interests motivated much of their work, thus taking student production in different directions and necessitating flexibility in evaluation, including students' involvement in the development of assessment criteria. Students were therefore given a great deal of responsibility ordinarily assumed by teachers, with Cindy's goal being for them to identify and create paths to guide their social futures. She assumed that given freedom of choice, students would become empowered learners, set worthy goals, regulate their own progress, and share willingly with classmates, who, similarly liberated from adult-imposed school structures, would grow together as a community of learners. Through such action, she believed, students would develop a "continuing impulse to learn" (Oldfather & Dahl, 1994, p. 142), an ongoing intrinsic motivation to learn fostered by their self-directed engagement in the personal construction of meaning. Cindy thus consciously oversaw the creation of a classroom environment that she believed would promote the development of both an immediate democratic community and long-term ways of thinking that would enable the students to become happy and productive members of society.

Ideally, the motive of the activity described by Wertsch (1985), if effectively established by a teacher through the classroom structure and processes, would override any other motives that students might have for their school experiences. The overall values and motives of a classroom environment, as identified and fostered by teachers, could then diminish disaffection, subversion, or other mindsets that might undermine the goals of community and student empowerment.

In this chapter we question the power of any context to overcome all others for all students. Our analysis of the different processes engaged in by the small groups in Cindy's class suggests that, while promoting certain types of behavior, the social context of the classroom, no matter how conscientiously developed, lacks the power to determine action pervasively. Our analysis is based on our observation that, within the overall culture of the class, small groups form their own local cultures, or *idiocultures* (Fine, 1987), that operate within the larger social structure yet may be negotiated in ways that take a different direction from that suggested by the predominant motive of the setting. We consider how one aspect of an idioculture, a *relational framework*, can contribute to social processes that may be at odds with the teacher's sense of prolepsis and that may cause social dynamics to veer in different directions than those suggested by the overall social context orchestrated by the teacher. We come to these conclusions after studying the "offstage" discussions of students (Scott, 1990, p. 4; cited in Finders, 1997, p. 10) as they talk beyond the confines of the formal floor while working in small groups. Following this analysis, we argue for a more complex view of social context that takes into account not just the immediate environment of the classroom but also the overlapping histories that students bring with them to each social encounter. (See Dyson and Gutiérrez & Stone, this volume, for an account of the *counterscripts* that can develop in opposition to a teacher's official script.)

Instructional Context

The research took place in a large (1,662 students) 2-year senior high school in the American Southwest that used a block schedule, with classes meeting on alternating days for 84 minutes. The block schedule fit well with Cindy's progressive emphasis, allowing extended time for discussion and response-centered activities. Instruction throughout the core academic departments in the rest of the school, however, tended to rely on teacher-dominated patterns of discourse designed to impart declarative, authoritative knowledge, thus situating Cindy's approach within a larger school context in which instruction in core subject areas assumed each discipline to be organized around a traditional base of content that a teacher was responsible for transmitting to students. Her instruction more closely resembled that in non-core areas such as home economics and agriculture, in which students chose their own projects and developed them under the teacher's guidance through what Wells (this volume) describes as collaborative, dialogic inquiry (see Smagorinsky, 1995, 1996, for more detailed accounts of these non-core classes).

Cindy typically organized instruction around themes intended to allow students to connect their own experiences to literature. In the unit on Identity that opened the year, for instance, students responded to literature in *response logs*, which served as the basis for small group discussions, which in turn provided the material for whole class discussions. Occasionally students used their response logs as the impetus for collaborative artistic interpretations of literature. Students also kept *writer's notebooks* in which they recorded personal writing related to the unit theme, usually in the exploratory manner that Wertsch (this volume) associates with the *expressivist* intellectual tradition in Western thought. Eventually they could take entries from either their response logs or their writer's notebooks and develop them into polished pieces to be included in the portfolios that constituted their semester exam. Under Cindy's guidance, students generated the criteria for assessing the portfolios. Her approach provided a thematic structure within which students were allowed choice regarding the work that Cindy would assess and the standards by which she would assess it.

The episode we focus on in this chapter took place in February, about a month into the second semester of the year. Following an in-class reading of *Hamlet*, Cindy had students organize into five small groups. Each group chose a central character in *Hamlet* (Hamlet, Gertrude, Claudius, Polonius, Ophelia, or Laertes) to interpret through the construction of a *body biography*, a life-sized human outline that students filled with art and words that represented their understanding of the character (Underwood, 1987; see Appendix A). We tape-recorded four of the five groups as they composed their body biographies, and we then analyzed the transcripts. The whole coding system described both the social processes that structured students' discussions and the context, text, and intertext that provided them with both constraints and substance through which to produce their interpretations (see Putney et al., this volume, for a related discussion). In this chapter we will focus only on one aspect of the social processes, what we call the *relational framework* that they established, and discuss how it contributed to the idiocultures that developed within two groups that contrasted sharply with one another. The idioculture that developed within one of the groups was highly compatible with Cindy's motive of developing a democratic community within the classroom; the other group illustrates how a relational framework can develop that undermines a teacher's efforts to encourage a social future characterized by equity and common cause. In this chapter we will describe the ways in which the same overall instructional context, and thus the same social channels for development, may be negotiated in different ways by different groups of participants. The subversion we see in this group is different from that described by Gutiérrez and Stone (this volume), who discuss students' resistance to a teacher who limits their use of their cultural capital in classroom tasks. Cindy, in contrast, designed her class to enable and motivate students to engage with the literature, the interpretive task, and one another in ways that contributed to their development as responsible members of a community of inquiry.

Social Frameworks within Groups

We next review the codes that helped us identify the relational framework that each group formed and that subsequently guided its interactions. We found that within the classroom, each group operated within both *imposed constraints* and *negotiated constraints*, each following from and in part a consequence of the *intercontext* (Floriani, 1993; Putney et al., this volume) or shared social practices that had taken place in Cindy's class during the school year. Imposed constraints described such structures as the assignment, the time limits within which the students worked, and the availability of materials, and provided the general impetus, direction, and tools for their joint activity. The imposed constraints compelled them to produce a body biography by a certain date (which Cindy extended at the end of the first block class).

More germane to the idea of a relational framework were the negotiated constraints that students developed to structure their interaction as they worked. These relationships varied considerably from group to group and had different consequences for both the equity of contribution within the groups and, in some cases, the appearance of the group product that resulted from their effort. We next describe the codes that enabled us to make inferences about the relational framework of the group work.

We found that, across groups, *social process* codes fell into three areas: those that were *productive* (i.e., that contributed to the body biography production), *constructive* (i.e., that promoted social cohesion), and *destructive* (i.e., that undermined social cohesion). We describe the constructive and destructive codes next because they were the key codes in determining the relational framework. In addition, we describe talk that was *off-task* and seemingly a consequence of the degree of cohesiveness within a group.

Constructive Social Process

Affirmation: These statements affirmed the worth of another group member's contribution. They were more than simple statements of agreement; instead, they praised another group member's contribution and, by implication, the contributor as well.

Inclusion: These statements invited other students to participate in the project. Most often they were offered to more quiet, less assertive students in order to give them roles and opportunities to contribute.

Courtesy: These statements conveyed considerateness toward another student, often in the form of routine civility.

Destructive Social Process

Discourtesy: These statements conveyed lack of consideration for another student and often were insulting or demeaning.

Resistance to Discourtesy: These statements occurred when, following a discourteous statement, a student demonstrated resistance to the affront.

Apathy: These statements explicitly stated a lack of engagement with or motive for school work

Off-Task Statements

Off-task statements were unrelated to the academic task and usually involved discussions of out-of-school events from the students' lives that did not inform their body biography production in any way. Although we looked for ways to interpret off-task statements so that they contributed in some way to the production of the body biography, we found instead that off-task talk was primarily initiated and engaged in by students who made statements we coded as socially *destructive*. Although not itself destructive for the most part, off-task talk tended to detract from, rather than contribute to, students' engagement with the literature and production of their interpretive text.

Relational Framework

We next describe the relational frameworks that each group negotiated. Table 8.1 describes the frequency of each code with each member of each group. Group 1 had relationships characterized by (1) the presence

Table 8.1. *Constructive, destructive, and off-task codes*

	Constructive Affirmation	Inclusion	Courtesy	Destructive Discourtesy	Resistance to Discourtesy	Off-Task
Group 1						
Carly	13	17	10	0	0	3
Sherri	2	0	2	0	0	0
Ann	3	0	2	0	0	4
Maggie	0	0	0	0	0	1
Total	18	17	14	0	0	8
Group 2						
Rita	0	0	2	0	3	83
Jack	6	0	1	28	0	116
Dirk	1	0	1	2	10	68
James	1	0	0	0	0	40
Bob	0	0	0	0	0	8
Total	8	0	4	30	13	315

of constructive statements, (2) the absence of destructive statements, and (3) relatively few off-task statements. Group 2 had relationships characterized by (1) the presence of destructive statements, (2) few constructive statements, and (3) relatively frequent off-task statements.

Group 1

The coding system helped us to identify the constructive processes appearing in the discussion of Group 1. Group 1 interpreted the character of Ophelia (see Figure 8.1) and included four girls: Carly, Sherri, Ann, and Maggie (who was absent for much of the discussion). None of the girls was a member of any stable social group within the class. Sherri, one of two African American students in the class, had moved into town from another state at the semester break and had not developed any friendships that we observed. Ann, a quiet student whose grades fluctuated, had transferred into Cindy's class at the semester break and also did not appear to have settled into a social group. Carly had been in Cindy's class all year and was highly active in school government. In spite of possessing exceptional personal and leadership skills (she was both the school's Homecoming Queen and president of its Student Congress in her senior year), she did not socialize with a particular group within this class or outside it. Maggie was an older student who had dropped out of school the previous year and then reenrolled, only to drop out again due to pregnancy shortly after the *Hamlet* unit ended; her absence during much of the body biography production was typical of her attendance for much of the year. As a whole, the girls had virtually no shared history and were not members of established social groups within the class. They worked together because the assignment required a group effort, not because they shared interests or experiences with one another.

The students in this group established a relational framework that was characterized by their self-assessments (primarily through self-deprecating comments), their affirmation of one another's worth, and their efforts at inclusion. These interactions often appeared in a pattern: One girl would provide a negative self-assessment, and another would immediately respond with a statement of affirmation. In addition to this type of exchange, students would make statements of inclusion designed to involve one another in the project and would make statements of courtesy that promoted social cohesion. Such interactions contributed to a relational framework that allowed them to work in a highly supportive and constructive way.

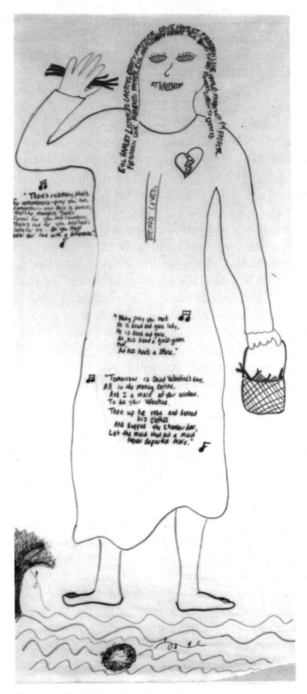

Figure 8.1 Body biography of Ophelia.

The relational framework was negotiated early in the group's collaboration. As noted, the girls were not well acquainted with one another. The beginning of their transcript revealed that their initial conversation served both to initiate their work on the assignment and to develop a relational framework that promoted an emotionally safe environment. The following exchange took place shortly after they began working. Ann had lain down to be traced and worried that her fingers appeared to be fat because the outline had inflated their appearance, a concern expressed by several girls in the groups whose discussions we analyzed:

Ann: Oh, not bad – okay, we could go over it with like the marker and make it look a little thinner.

Sherri: Your fingers are not that fat, so don't worry.

Carly: It is like, oh, finger exercises. Okay, let's – was she wearing a dress? That might be easier, oh, she was wearing the dress, then we'll just put on a dress.

Ann: Yeah, because they went like tight here and then they just, like all the way down.

Carly: Do you want to do that?

Sherri: Yeah, weren't you saying you were just going to do bare feet?

Carly: Yeah, we'll do bare feet, okay.

Ann: You wanna trace your sketch?

Carly: Okay, is it okay if I go ahead and, like, do the dress?

Ann: Yeah.

Carly: You sure?

Ann: Yeah.

Carly: Any of you guys want to do it?

Sherri: No, it doesn't matter.

Ann: I wouldn't know where to begin.

This excerpt illustrates patterns that recurred often during their collaboration. Ann's self-deprecating remark about the size of her fingers was immediately met with an affirmation from Sherri and Carly's humorous effort to dissipate her anxiety. The group then began to discuss how to represent their character on the body biography. The issue of representation was quickly superseded by the girls' efforts to identify the roles each would take in the interpretation. Carly tried to include the others in the production, taking a role for herself only after offering it to the others. Her effort at inclusion was met with Ann's self-deprecating remark about her ability to provide a good drawing, following which they began a discussion of how to depict the character's literal appearance in the play and film.

This initial exchange helped the group set up an egalitarian way of working together. The girls attempted to sort out their roles and relationships but did so by offering roles rather than assuming them. From the very beginning, then, the girls worked not only at negotiating an interpretation of the play but also at negotiating a relational framework that allowed them to work together cohesively and supportively.

A second characteristic we identified that contributed to their relational framework was in the progression of their analysis and interpretation of the play. Initially they discussed literal aspects of the Ophelia character, enabling them to talk about a topic that engendered agreement rather than conflict. During the first 125 of the total 754 coded statements in the transcript, they relied on the Zeffirelli film shown in class for their sense of how the character would look. Of the first 125 statements in the transcript, 25 (20%) were coded as referring to the film; in the remaining 629 statements, only 11 (2%) statements received this code. In addition, the first 125 statements included 21 (17%) statements coded as being a *description* of the character in either the play or their body biography, with description codes appearing in 80 of the remaining 629 (13%) statements in the transcript. In contrast, the first 125 statements included 11 (9%) statements coded as either a *symbol* or *interpretation*, whereas the remaining 629 statements included 132 (21%) such statements.

Taken together, these figures suggest that their initial emphasis contributed to the development of a supportive relational framework because it focused on topics about which there was little disagreement. The following excerpt illustrates the literal focus of their discussion.

Carly: Okay, how does that, how did the dress, it came in and goes –

Ann: It goes down right below the boobs and then they just –

Carly: Is that the waist thing?

Ann: It's not even the waist, right here and then it just –

Carly: Is it like here, you think?

Ann: Up.

Carly: Up here?

Ann: Yeah.

Carly: Okay.

Ann: Your shoulders are a little higher.

Carly: We'll figure it out, we'll redecorate me.

Ann: We'll fix our hair in perfection.

Carly: Yeah, thank God for an eraser. Okay so here's, let me just kind of, it came to right about here or something?

Ann: Yeah, they came all the way down.

Carly: God, I really need some knee pads and I'll be ready for this. Okay, I'll just have to – I'll redo this part make it tighter, but it's a wavy dress. Can you tell?

Ann: It's supposed to be.

Carly: Good, I really don't know how, I'm not like a fashion designer at all. So if you guys have any input on this just let me know.

Ann: Looks good to me.

Carly: Should we give her hair?

Ann: Yeah, her hair was long, wasn't it?

Sherri: Yeah.

Carly: And it was kind of wavy?

Sherri: Yeah, that's her hair, but she always used to have it in a pony tail.

Ann: Or wrapped up.

This segment illustrates both their literal focus and their continued use of self-deprecation, affirmation, and role offering as ways to enable them to cohere. The discussion of the cinematic character's appearance allowed them to begin their discussion with high levels of agreement and accord.

In the remainder of the discussion, the girls turned to the more open-ended problem of how to interpret the character through symbols. One such exchange took place toward the end of the first block period and concerned their symbolic depiction of Ophelia's relationship with her father:

Carly: What are we going to put for her to obey her dad?

Ann: I don't know, we need some kind of symbol.

Carly: Maybe in her hair.

Ann: We could put something and then have like "Listen to Dad" –

Carly: See, we could put on her hair, instead of actually drawing hair, we could write "Dad" in like the curves, do you know what I am saying?

Ann: Yeah, I think so.

Sherri: Okay, but we can't draw it in back of her, she's like –

Ann: We could put like "Listens to Dad, obeys Dad, Dad died," et cetera.

Carly: Yeah, Dad slash Hamlet.

Ann: We could like list all of the things that made her go crazy in her hair.

Carly: Okay, yeah! That's awesome! Good idea, okay.

Ann: Okay, but I don't think I'm going to turn that into a coffin.

Carly: Okay, that's good because that would be – I'm sorry if I put my butt in your face – I'll draw it in her hair.

Ann: And her hair has to be brown, too, that's what color her hair was.

Carly: Okay, can I, with chunks of black, like one letter being black or something. Okay, I'm going to, is it okay if I write a song in here?

Sherri: Uh huh.

Carly: Okay, where is her first song? What does she say first? She says something really interesting first. Where's the, no, okay, maybe not. Should I just put all of her songs because they're not very long and they all say something interesting? Or should I put that – ?

This excerpt illustrates both the kinds of interpretation that the group came up with and the continued maintenance of the social relations that enabled them to produce it. As the discussion and Figure 8.1 reveal, they used Ophelia's hair as the vehicle through which to convey verbal symbols about her situation. In doing so, they continued to use the same courtesies and affirmations that they had established early on in their discussion.

On the whole, then, the relational framework established by this group realized Cindy's ideal notion of how students would perform within the parameters of a progressive pedagogy: Within the overall confines of the required reading of *Hamlet* and the guidelines of the body biography assignment, the students chose a character to interpret, engaged in exploratory discussion as a vehicle for coming to agreement on how to understand the character and depict her artistically, and treated one another with respect and appreciation. We see this group as illustrating the potential for how students negotiate the open-ended structure provided by a progressive pedagogy, in particular the kinds of productive and cohesive social relations that they can establish in this context. (For additional perspectives on the uses of exploratory or expressivist speech, see the chapters in this volume by Ball, Putney et al., Wells, and Wertsch.)

Group 2

Group 2 interpreted the character of Gertrude (see Figure 8.2) and included five students: Rita, Jack, Dirk, James, and Bob. Jack provided the axis for the group's social relations. He was tall, forceful, and talkative, often overpowering other students in the group socially with abusive statements delivered with a chuckle. He directed most of his derogatory comments to Rita, the only girl in the group, and to Dirk, the only African American. Rita, who had been diagnosed with attention deficit disorder, for which she took Ritilin and was assisted academically by a resource teacher, was task oriented and grade conscious and was the impetus for most of the academic work accomplished within the group. Her need for structure and explicit direction often put her at odds with Cindy's open-ended instruction. She frequently made self-deprecating remarks both during this assignment and at other points during the year, being particularly worried about being fat in spite of standing 5 feet 2 inches and weighing 105 pounds. She also revealed insecurity about her appearance in general in spite of being described as attractive by several people interviewed for the study. Rather than being met with affirmations following these self-deprecating remarks, she instead made herself vulnerable to the taunting of Jack. Of the other three students, Dirk served as the foil to Jack's abusive humor, James was largely ignored, and Bob worked quietly on the fringes when present.

Like Group 1, this group included students who were not members of any stable social group within the class; instead, they collaborated because the task required a group project. The group also included a preponderance of students who received poor grades in school: Jack passed Cindy's class with the lowest possible passing grade, Dirk was the only student who failed, and James dropped out of school in the spring after learning that he would not graduate. Rita had received poor grades in prior years before being prescribed Ritilin and working on developing study habits with her resource teacher, but she improved dramatically at that point in all classes. Bob was a member of the school's small neo-1960s counterculture, earning C's in spite of Cindy's belief in his potential for higher achievement.

The group's relations were established early in their discussion. Rita served as the figure for their body biography, and after a girl from a neighboring group had finished tracing her outline, the following exchange took place:

Rita: Don't smell of my breath, whatever you do.

Jack: You already ate one bag [of chips] a minute ago. Rita, you're a pig. That's why we had to size down your thighs. We had to do a little constructive surgery.

Rita: My crotch is not that low.

Figure 8.2 Body biography of Gertrude.

Jack:	No, that is a pretty low crotch. Do you want me to fix that for you?
Dirk:	Well, what are we supposed to do – draw you buck naked or something?
Jack:	No, Dirk, please.
Dirk:	I'm pretty sure –
Jack:	Don't go there, man.
Dirk:	We'll just draw some lines like she had clothes on and that is why her crotch is so low.
Jack:	All right, tell me how high, Rita, like up in there?
Rita:	That's good, I don't care what it looks like.
Jack:	It's a good thing.
Dirk:	We'll draw the chi-chi's now.
James:	Man, that is, that is weird.
Rita:	No boobs. (Laughter) I don't have any, and no, you're not going to draw any.
Dirk:	She lookin' –
Jack:	Yeah, she looks – we can reconstruct, but we can't reconstruct that much.

This early exchange illustrates processes that took place frequently during their discussion. Rita served as the subject of various insults, primarily from Jack. Jack's abusive remarks toward Rita in this excerpt were central to a relational framework that discouraged collaboration and cohesion. On the fringes of these discussions stood James, whose contributions were minimal and rarely acknowledged by the others, and Bob, who was task oriented when present but largely absent from the discussion. The relational framework developed by this group did not support Cindy's intention to have the body biography serve as a vehicle for a cooperative interpretation of the character or a democratic community of learners.

In addition to feeding on Rita's insecurity about her appearance, Jack's comments toward Dirk were at times blatantly racist. In the following segment, Dirk made a reference to a black marker he was using for his contribution to the body biography, and Jack insulted him repeatedly.

Jack:	What's up, Bucky?
Dirk:	I had black.
Jack:	What's so great about black? Black stinks.
Dirk:	You got a point? Huh? I smell good. What're you talking about?

Jack: You smell so good – if you took a bath.

Dirk: I was going to mention that I found some markers in the drawer.

Jack: Hey, what are you doing, son?

Dirk: Same thing you're doing, son.

Jack: Well, now what are you doing? You're just messing everything up.

Dirk: Come on now.

Jack: Just take your black marker and get away from me, man. You hear me, boy?

This segment needs little explanation, other than to say that it illustrates the destructive relationships that Jack initiated within the group. These relationships were unanticipated in Cindy's design of the activity and reveal the ways in which negotiations that take place within a general classroom context are not necessarily as productive as are often assumed in accounts of progressive classrooms (see, e.g., Atwell, 1987).

A second problem that affected the relational framework of this group was the varying degrees of commitment that the different students brought to the class and ultimately to this task. As noted, two of the five students did not pass the class and one passed with the lowest possible grade, though each was given abundant opportunities and incentives to perform. These degrees of commitment resulted in widely varying efforts to contribute to the group effort. One key episode in the small group discussion came early when the students were discussing the time frame Cindy had provided to complete the body biographies. At the time of the excerpt that follows, the students believed that they had one block period, plus time outside class including the ensuing weekend, to finish their interpretation. Cindy also made her room available before and after school and during Overtime, a 30-minute period between class and lunch when students could go to teachers for extra help. In considering how they would need time outside class, the group interacted as follows:

Rita: You guys, we're not coming in for Overtime – I'll do some of this over the weekend.

Jack: Rita's like – sacrifice. We're not coming in. You're right, I ain't coming in.

Rita: She should have given us like two periods to do this in.

James: Shoot, I can't do this, I gotta work.

In discussing this segment during our data analysis, we came up with the image of a balloon that is punctured, releasing all pressure inside: When Rita declared that she would work on the body biography at home, the other group members lost all urgency in contributing equally to the project. From this point on, the transcript became characterized by Rita's efforts to initiate an interpretation and, for the most part, the other group members drifting off into unrelated conversations about the film *Forrest Gump*, an upcoming car wash sponsored by the cheerleaders, the impending state basketball tournament, the merits of different brands of shoes, their preferences in snack foods, and other topics. Roughly one-third of the group's discussion concerned these topics without relating to the body biography production in any way we could identify. We looked for ways to interpret their off-task conversation as contributing to the social relations or intellectual work of the group but could not distinguish it from casual conversation that might take place in any informal setting and could not see any pathways from these topics to their construction of their interpretation.

We present one final excerpt from their discussion, recorded when Rita brought in the body biography she had completed over the weekend. Here Rita explained the decisions she had made to the other group members:

Jack: Where's our little writing that goes around her?

Rita: I know, I haven't done that yet.

Jack: Rita, what are you thinking? What did you do, blow it off again?

Rita: Well, I've got it written down. I just –

Dirk: I see, you closed in the hip a little bit.

Rita: Yeah.

Jack: Oh, the king, the king of hearts.

Rita: Guys, does it look crappy? – I mean is it okay?

Jack: The king of hearts. Pretty sweet. I think it looks pretty sweet, Rita. You did well. Did your little sister help you?

Rita: The reason why I crossed her fingers is because, is because I thought that I was going to explain that. I think she's real, she's crossing her fingers because she's hoping that everything will work out between everybody.

Jack: Did your little sister help you?

Rita: No, I did it last night.

Jack: You done good, Rita.

Rita: It looks kind of stupid but –

Jack: You done plum good.

Rita: I didn't know what to draw down here. I was like – damn, now what do I draw? So, I just –

Jack: So, the Queen. Q for queen, right?

Rita: Yeah –

Jack: And here she is.

Rita: I drew some hair because my body kind of looked like it needed it.

Jack: That's what I thought – I thought she should have hair.

James: Besides, they didn't have chemotherapy back then.

Dirk: So she's crying because of Ophelia? Ophelia was killed.

Rita: I don't know, she's kind of confused.

Jack: She's crying because Rita said she was crying.

This excerpt illustrates the processes that we found consistently throughout this group's discussion. Rita conceived and executed the bulk of the interpretation, her insights about the play providing the substance of their body biography. Jack, though showing some appreciation for Rita's efforts (for which he would receive credit), balanced his praise with discourtesies. James made a single contribution, an attempt at humor that went unacknowledged. Rita worried about her elaborate depiction being "crappy" and looking "stupid." And Jack explained the character's tears as a decision of Rita's that needed no further discussion.

Discussion

In this chapter we have illustrated the contruct we have called the relational framework of a group's interaction. We see this construct as helping to complicate the notion of an instructional context. Educational writers have often described the creation of a healthy social climate as a vehicle for promoting productive social relationships (e.g., Graves, 1983). The case of Group 1 reported in this chapter reveals that, with the right configuration of students, this optimism may be well founded (see also the case study reported in Smagorinsky & O'Donnell-Allen, 1998a). The dynamics taking place within Group 2, however, show that with different sets of students, the social relationships that are negotiated can be counterproductive and establish a motive for the activity that is incongruous with that envisioned by the teacher.

Group 2 illustrates the way in which some aspects of the teacher's overriding motive may be realized in ways that mask the dynamics that produce them. Simply by looking at the completed body biographies of these two groups, a viewer might assume that the groups' interactions were equally fruitful. For this particular task, then, Cindy's goal of having each group produce a compelling and meaningful body biography was achieved. However, her goal of developing a democratic classroom community was unevenly realized across groups; of the four transcripts analyzed for the study as a whole, two were characterized by cohesiveness and two by discourtesy or apathy. We see, then, the ways in which a teacher's effort to envision an ideal citizen and structure a classroom to facilitate students' development toward that end can be reconstructed by students whose past experiences have helped them form goals for schooling that are different from the teacher's. When these incompatible goals do not include the regard of school work as a means of personal development, then the establishment of an open-ended, polydirectional instructional context provides a setting for students to act in ways that are counterproductive to the teacher's goals for the class (cf. Finders, 1997; Lensmire, 1994; Lewis, 1997). One final excerpt from Group 2's discussion illustrates this point well. The students had been discussing the role of a medallion in their body biography, thinking of how it might work symbolically. Cindy circulated past this group and checked on their progress:

Cindy: You guys need to include more things? – Have you gone down this list of all the stuff? Have you talked about that?

Dirk: We're doing it. Now on this medallion here, can we just like – what you want us to do with it? Do you want us to put like –

James: Can we draw a face on there?

Dirk: A face or can we put a name or what?

Jack: Let's put a face. I'll draw a face.

Cindy: It's up to you. You are the artists. You are the bosses.

Dirk: Yeah, but you're the teacher.

Jack: Yeah, but you're the grade giver.

Even in late February, after 6 months of Cindy's systematic efforts to get the students to see themselves as meaning-makers and to view their work as a vehicle for personal development, they interpreted this task as primarily teacher-pleasing.

We see, then, the need to conceive of social contexts in terms of the deeper histories that comprise them. The image of nested contexts runs the danger of being viewed as two-dimensional; that is, we can see how a small group is part of a class, which is part of a school, which is part of a community, with the contexts radiating outward. A third dimension, however, enables us to view the cultural and historical backgrounds that contribute to each context and thus see the ways in which they can be negotiated outside the framework provided by the nesting. The idiocultural diversity illustrated by these two groups in a single class, then, provides a view of classrooms and their subgroups as infinitely complex, dynamic, and difficult to predict from knowledge of the context alone. Rather than being deterministic, as John-Steiner and Meehan (this volume) say is often believed of Vygotskian sociocultural views of development, this perspective leaves room for a social setting to be negotiated and meaning to be constructed by its participants to suit their own ends, for good or ill.

Appendix A: The Body Biography Assignment

For your chosen character, your group will be creating a *body biography* – a visual and written portrait illustrating several aspects of the character's life within the play.

You have many possibilities for filling up your giant sheet of paper. I have listed several, but please feel free to come up with your own creations. As always, the choices you make should be based on the text, for you will be verbally explaining (and thus, in a sense, defending) them at a showing of your work. Above all, your choices should be creative, analytical, and accurate. After completing this portrait, you will participate in a showing in which you will present your masterpiece to the class. This showing should accomplish these objectives. It should

- review significant events, choices, and changes involving your character.
- communicate to us the full essence of your character by emphasizing the traits that make her/him who s/he is.
- promote discussion of your character (especially regarding gender issues in the play).

Body Biography Requirements

Although I expect your biography to contain additional dimensions, your portrait *must* contain

- a review of significant happenings in the play.
- visual symbols.
- an original text.
- your character's three most important lines from the play.

Body Biography Suggestions

1. *Placement* – Carefully choose the placement of your text and artwork. For example, the area where your character's heart would be might be appropriate for illustrating the important relationships within his or her life.
2. *Spine* – Actors often discuss a character's spine. This is her/his objective within the play. What is the most important goal for your character? What drives her/his thoughts and actions? This is her/his spine. How can you illustrate it?
3. *Virtues and Vices* – What are your character's most admirable qualities? Her/his worst? How can you make us visualize them?
4. *Color* – Colors are often symbolic. What color(s) do you most associate with your character? Why? How can you effectively work these colors into your presentation?
5. *Symbols* – What objects can you associate with your character that illustrate her/his essence? Are there objects mentioned within the play itself that you could use? If not, choose objects that especially seem to correspond with the character.
6. *Formula Poems* – These are fast but effective recipes for producing a text because they are designed to reveal a lot about a character. (See the additional handouts I gave you for directions and examples.)
7. *Mirror, Mirror* – Consider both how your character appears to others on the surface and what you know about the character's inner self. Do these images clash or correspond? What does this tell you about the character?
8. *Changes* – How has your character chanced within the play? Trace these chances within your text and/or artwork.

References

Applebee, A. N. (1996). *Curriculum as conversation: Transforming traditions of teaching and learning.* Chicago: University of Chicago Press.

Atwell, N. (1987). *In the middle: Writing, reading, and learning with adolescents.* Portsmouth, NH: Heinemann.

Bennett, W. J. (Ed.). (1993). *The book of virtues: A treasury of great moral stories.* New York: Simon & Schuster.

Bogdan, D. (1992). *Re-educating the imagination: Toward a poetics, politics, and pedagogy of literary engagement.* Portsmouth, NH: Heinemann.

Brown, R. G. (1993). *Schools of thought: How the politics of literacy shape thinking in the classroom*. San Francisco: Jossey-Bass.

Cazden, C. B. (1988). *Classroom discourse*. Portsmouth, NH: Heinemann.

Cole, M. (1996). *Cultural psychology: A once and future discipline*. Cambridge, MA: Harvard University Press.

Csikszentmihalyi, M., & Larson, R. (1984). *Being adolescent*. New York: Basic Books.

Dewey, J. (1960). *The quest for certainty*. New York: Putnam.

Dewey, J. (1966). *Democracy and education: An introduction to the philosophy of education*. New York: The Free Press.

Finders, M. J. (1997). *Just girls: Hidden literacies and life in junior high*. Urbana, IL, and New York: National Council of Teachers of English and Teachers College Press.

Fine, G. A. (1987). *With the boys*. Chicago: University of Chicago Press.

Floriani, A. (1993). Negotiating what counts: Roles and relationships, content and meaning, texts and contexts. *Linguistics and Education*, 5, 241–274.

Freire, P. (1970). The adult literacy process as cultural action for freedom. *Harvard Educational Review*, 40, 205–212.

Foucault, M. (1972). *The archaeology of knowledge and the discourse on language*. New York: Pantheon.

Graves, D. (1983). *Writing: Teachers and children at work*. Portsmouth, NH: Heinemann.

Greene, M. (1988). *The dialectic of freedom*. New York: Teachers College Press.

Hillocks, G. (1995). *Teaching writing as reflective practice*. New York: Teachers College Press.

Hirsch, E. D. (1987). *Cultural literacy: What every American should know*. Boston: Houghton Mifflin.

Ingold, T. (1994). Introduction to culture. In T. Ingold (Ed.), *Companion encyclopedia of anthropology: Humanity, culture and social life* (pp. 329–349). London: Routledge.

Jackson, P. W. (1968). *Life in classrooms*. New York: Holt, Rinehart, & Winston.

Jesus Christ (n.d.). Cited in *The Holy Bible*.

Lee, C. D. (1993). *Signifying as a scaffold for literary interpretation: The pedagogical implications of an African American discourse genre*. Research Report No. 26. Urbana, IL: National Council of Teachers of English.

Lensmire, T. J. (1994). *When children write: Critical re-visions of the writing workshop*. New York: Teachers College Press.

Lewis, C. (1997). The social drama of literature discussions in a fifth/sixth-grade classroom. *Research in the Teaching of English*, 31, 163–204.

Martin, J. (1995). *The schoolhome*. Cambridge, MA: Harvard University Press.

Moll, L. C. (1990). Introduction. In L. C. Moll (Ed.), *Vygotsky and education: Instructional implications and applications of sociohistorical psychology* (pp. 1–27). New York: Cambridge University Press.

Montessori, M. (1964). *The Montessori method* (A. E. George, Trans.). Cambridge, MA: Robert Bentley.

Newman, F. (1996). *Performance of a lifetime: A practical-philosophical guide to the joyous life*. New York: Castillo International.

Noddings, N. (1993). *The challenge to care in schools*. New York: Teachers College Press.

O'Donnell-Allen, C., & Smagorinsky, P. (1999). Revising Ophelia: Rethinking questions of gender and power in school. *English Journal, 88*(3), 35–42.

Oldfather, P., & Dahl, K. (1994). Toward a social constructivist reconceptualization of intrinsic motivation for literacy learning. *Journal of Reading Behavior, 26*, 139–158.

Olson, D. (1986). Intelligence and literacy: The relationship between intelligence and the technologies of representation and communication. In R. Sternberg & R. Wagner (Eds.), *Practical intelligence: Nature and origins of competence in the everyday world* (pp. 338–360). New York: Cambridge University Press.

Peshkin, A. (1978). *Growing up American: Schooling and the survival of community*. Chicago: University of Chicago Press.

Piaget, J. (1952). *The origins of intelligence in children*. New York: Norton.

Postman, N., & Weingartner, C. (1987). *Teaching as a subversive activity*. New York: Dell.

Sadker, M., & Sadker, D. (1994). *Failing at fairness: How America's schools cheat girls*. New York: Scribner's.

Schon, D. A. (Ed.). (1991). *The reflective turn: Case studies in and on educational practice*. New York: Teachers College Press.

Scott, J. (1990). *Domination and the arts of resistance: Hidden transcripts*. New Haven, CT: Yale University Press.

Smagorinsky, P. (1995). Constructing meaning in the disciplines: Reconceptualizing writing across the curriculum as composing across the curriculum. *American Journal of Education, 103*, 160–184.

Smagorinsky, P. (1996). Multiple intelligences, multiple means of composing: An alternative way of thinking about learning. *NASSP Bulletin, 80*(583), 11–17.

Smagorinsky, P., & Fly, P. K. (1993). The social environment of the classroom: A Vygotskian perspective on small group process. *Communication Education, 42*, 159–171.

Smagorinsky, P., & O'Donnell-Allen, C. (1998a). Reading as mediated and mediating action: Composing meaning for literature through multimedia interpretive texts. *Reading Research Quarterly, 33*, 198–226.

Smagorinsky, P., & O'Donnell-Allen, C. (1998b). The depth and dynamics of context: Tracing the sources and channels of engagement and disengagement in students' response to literature. *Journal of Literacy Research, 30*, 515–559.

Stotsky, S. (Ed.). (1991). *Making connections between civic education and language*. New York: Teachers College Press.

Tulviste, P. (1991). *The cultural-historical development of verbal thinking*. Commack, NY: Nova Science Publishers.

Underwood, W. (1987). The body biography: A framework for student working. *English Journal, 76*(8), 44–48.

Vygotsky, L. S. (1987). Thinking and speech. In L. S. Vygotsky, *Collected works* (Vol. 1, pp. 39–285) (R. Rieber & A. Carton, Eds.; N. Minick, Trans.). New York: Plenum.

Wertsch, J. V. (1985). *Vygotsky and the social formation of mind*. Cambridge, MA: Harvard University Press.

Wertsch, J. V. (1991). *Voices of the mind: A sociocultural approach to mediated action.* Cambridge, MA: Harvard University Press.

Wertsch, J. V. (1996a). *Vygotsky: The ambivalent Enlightenment rationalist.* Volume 21, Heinz Werner Lecture Series (pp. 39–62). Worcester, MA: Clark University Press.

Wertsch, J. V. (1996b). The role of abstract rationality in Vygotsky's image of mind. In A. Tryphon & J. Vonèche (Eds.), *Piaget-Vygotsky: The social genesis of thought* (pp. 25–43). East Sussex, UK: Psychology Press.

9 Signifying in the Zone of Proximal Development

Carol D. Lee

In "Oral and Literate Traditions Among Black Americans Living in Poverty," Heath (1989) states:

> The school has seemed unable to recognize and take up the potentially positive interactive and adaptive verbal and interpretive habits learned by Black American children (as well as other nonmainstream groups), rural and urban, within their families and on the streets. These uses of language – spoken and written – are wide ranging, and many represent skills that would benefit all youngsters: keen listening and observational skills, quick recognition of nuanced roles, rapid-fire dialogue, hard-driving argumentation, succinct recapitulation of an event, striking metaphors, and comparative analyses based on unexpected analogies. (p. 370)

The uses of language described by Heath are epitomized in the form of talk known traditionally in the African American community as *signifying*. In this chapter I use a Vygotskian conceptual framework to argue that signifying as a form of social discourse in the African American community has the potential to serve as an effective scaffolding device for teaching complex skills in the interpretation of literature. I will argue that signifying as a construct bridges what Vygotsky called *spontaneous* and *scientific* concepts. I will further demonstrate the cultural dynamics of the process of semiotic mediation through which underachieving African American high school students were apprenticed into a community of literate problem solving by drawing on their knowledge of signifying.

A Vygotskian Perspective on Language and Problem Solving

Lev Vygotsky (1986) saw language as a primary mediator of knowledge for humans. He saw language acquisition as evolving through

191

a series of spiraling stages, each with a particular function in terms of shaping the problem-solving skills of humans. For Vygotsky, language at its core was a communicative tool that evolved within a specific sociohistorical context. He defined language acquisition as a mechanism for communicating to others. However, with the evolution of egocentric speech – the child talking to the self – language in addition becomes a tool for problem solving. (See Wertsch, this volume, for an account of the *designative* and *expressive* traditions that influenced Vygotsky's view of the role of speech for the individual in the social context.) In Vygotsky's studies, children use egocentric speech initially to accompany problem-solving strategies but later to direct problem-solving strategies. With the evolution of inner speech – using attenuated and often silent language – the learner uses language to direct problem-solving strategies. Egocentric speech and inner speech may be distinguished by the qualities of orality and elaborateness. These uses of egocentric and inner speech are examples of language being used to mediate the acquisition of knowledge. Both provide relational, causal, and temporal frameworks through which the learner internally conceptualizes the outside environment. Thus, in the Vygotskian framework, language serves as a conceptual organizer, a primary medium through which thinking occurs.

The use of language as both a socially communicative act and a medium for the internal organization of experience requires give-and-take, a dialectical interaction among interlocutors. Wertsch (1984) calls this dialectical dialogue *semiotic mediation* (Vygotsky, 1986). In many respects, the speech act for Vygotsky represented the quintessential unit for semiotic mediation. Through an ongoing process of semiotic mediation occurring in specific cultural, social, and historical contexts, the young learn the skills, values, and knowledge funds of the community of which they are a part (see Moll, this volume, for an extended discussion of *funds of knowledge*). Through social and language interactions, older and more experienced members of a community teach younger and less experienced members the skills, values, and knowledge needed to be productive members of that community.

According to Vygotsky, learning is a product of the ongoing interaction between ontogenetic development (of which language acquisition is one key variable) and instruction. Vygotsky acknowledged that instruction may occur both within practical experiences and within formal school settings. Within the Vygotskian framework, however, there are fundamental differences in the qualities of concepts developed within the two settings. The concepts that develop within practical community experience he termed *spontaneous concepts*. The concepts that develop within formal school settings he termed *scientific concepts*. Although I question the limitation of scientific concepts to school settings and spontaneous concepts to practical community experience, it is important to point out that Vygotsky did acknowledge the fundamental interconnection between the two categories of concepts. Vygotsky characterized spontaneous concepts as situational, empirical, and practical. He characterized scientific concepts as systematic, as existing within a hierarchical network of related concepts, relative, generalizable, detached from the concrete, and used consciously and intentionally by people. The mental qualities that he believed were necessary to the acquisition of scientific concepts are deliberate attention, logical memory, abstraction, and the ability to compare and differentiate. He said that scientific concepts serve as the "propaedeutic guide" (Vygotsky, 1986) to the development of spontaneous concepts. That is, scientific concepts fine-tune and raise spontaneous concepts to a level of conscious, strategic use, whereas spontaneous concepts are the framework on which scientific concepts are built.

Signifying within a ZPD

Signifying is an oral genre of communication within the African American Vernacular English (AAVE) speech community. In a strict Vygotskian sense, signifying shares many of the characteristics attributed to spontaneous concepts. As a speech event, signifying occurs in specific social contexts (situational) and achieves specific goals for both the initiator and the receiver of the signifying act (practical). As these social contexts and goals may be both diverse and complex, I will save the specific examples until later when a full explication of signifying is offered.

Vygotsky (1986) says, "the absence of a system is the cardinal psychological difference distinguishing spontaneous from scientific concepts" (p. 205). In defining signifying, I will argue, however, that it is systematic, exists within a hierarchical network of related concepts, is used consciously and intentionally, and is both relative and generalizable. It is relative and generalizable because it is a rhetorical stance that must be generalized by its users to a multiplicity of specific situations that are potentially vast in number. In this sense, signifying shares attributes of scientific concepts as defined by Vygotsky. The difference, however, is that adolescents, in particular, who signify are not conscious of the rules of interpretation that operate within that discourse system, rules of interpretation that they know intuitively but not scientifically.

Vygotsky's (1978) analysis suggests that school learning may occur optimally when the novice has sufficiently developed spontaneous concepts learned in practical/community contexts that are related to scientific concepts learned in formal school contexts. The novice who has demonstrated an independent level of problem solving within the realm of a spontaneous concept is then placed in a social context with a more expert teacher who, through prodding, modeling, and questioning, guides the novice closer to a more adult-like, scientific representation of the task at hand. The learning context is considered social in that the learner does not acquire scientific concepts in isolation. Vygotsky called this condition the *zone of proximal development* (ZPD) and defined it as "the distance between the actual developmental level as determined by independent problem solving and the level of potential development as determined through problem solving under adult guidance or in collaboration with more capable peers" (p. 86).

Wertsch (1984) acknowledges that Vygotsky did not adequately and explicitly define "what constitutes problem solving under adult guidance or in collaboration with more capable peers" (p. 8). Inferring from the breadth of Vygotsky's writings, Wertsch states that there are three minimal constraints that define a ZPD. The first constraint is *situation definition*. Initially the student and the teacher may have different representations of the task to be completed. As the learning interaction progresses, the student's representation of the task should evolve to a representation closer to that of the teacher. The second constraint is *intersubjectivity*, which Wertsch defines as the extent to which the student and the teacher agree on what the task is. According to Wertsch, intersubjectivity may exist on a minimal level. For example, student and teacher may initially agree only on the tools to be used to complete the task. Through the process of *semiotic mediation* – the third constraint on any ZPD – the teacher may temporarily give up his or her representation of the task to accommodate the level of understanding of the student, while the student comes progressively closer to the representation of the task that the teacher/expert holds. Wertsch points out that the difference in the initial representation by the novice in the zone is not necessarily quantitatively different later on; rather, it is qualitatively different. Through the process of semiotic mediation, then, the level on which intersubjectivity exists spirals in complexity.

In this chapter, I propose that signifying as a form of social discourse within the speech community of speakers of AAVE demonstrates a useful example of semiotic mediation. Signifying is a linguistic tool that directs behavior and organizes the user's cognitive representation of the external environment.

Thinking in School and Community Contexts

The enterprise of studying similarities in thinking between the contexts of school and community or work is a delicate matter. Scribner (1984) outlines two critical issues in such an enterprise. She resolves that cognition should be studied within the framework of practice:

[1] This view attaches one definite, if not exhaustive, meaning to the ambiguous concept of experience. It particularizes experience as the active engagement of an individual in some pursuit involving socially organized domains of knowledge and technologies, including symbol systems. It conceives of functionality in the instrumental sense of supporting accomplishment of some goal-directed action. . . . (p. 14)

[2] The general construct of practice offers a possibility for integrating social-cultural and psychological levels of analysis and achieving explanatory accounts of how basic mental processes and structures become specialized and diversified through experience. (p. 13)

Scribner raises the question of how "one locate[s] cognitive phenomena that can be classified as similar in kind and that are sufficiently bounded to be amenable to analysis" (p. 14). Scribner concludes that "practice and task" are such units of analysis. These units of analysis parallel the activity unit, as defined by Vygotskian psychologist Leont'ev (1981; Wertsch, Minick, & Arns, 1984). Scribner (1984), Lave (1977), Rogoff (1990), and others have investigated what Vygotsky calls the *higher mental functions* in socially routinized activity or practice. This approach is consistent with Vygotsky's general law of cultural development, in which higher psychological functioning first appears on the social plane, between people as "interpsychological," and then on the psychological plane, within the individual child, as "intrapsychological" (Vygotsky, 1978; see Ball, this volume, for an extended discussion of *internalization*).

In this society (as in many others), the language practices of disenfranchised groups are not only devalued by schools (a condition of diglossia, as defined by Saville-Troike, 1989), but in fact have the effect of negatively impacting learning (Cazden, 1988; Cook-Gumperz, 1986; Delpit, 1990; Michaels, 1986; Philips, 1985). Under these circumstances, the act of analyzing the higher mental functions in socially routinized activity among poor and ethnically diverse student populations is a radical move. Up to this point, the bulk of such research has focused either on higher mental thinking in blue-collar workplaces or on the incorporation of nonmainstream verbal interaction patterns into classroom discourse in order to increase student participation in instructional talk. The major body of research that has investigated similarities in problem-solving strategies in practical/community social contexts among poor and disenfranchised groups and problem solving in schools has been in the area of mathematics (La Rocha, 1985; Nunes, Schliemann, & Carraher, 1993; Reed & Lave, 1981; Saxe, 1988). Despite a popular focus on Vygotsky in literacy research, few studies have investigated the interactions between spontaneous and scientific concepts in language minority communities. Similarly, within the situated cognition framework, clearly influenced by Vygotsky, little attention has been given to the study of formal literacy as social practice outside school. In addition, this line of research has had little observable and lasting influence on schooling. The research that extends the framework offered in this chapter attempts to speak both to the need to locate shared spaces between home and school knowledge in a way that academically empowers underachieving student populations and to offer practical alternatives that schools can use.

I shall attempt here to analyze signifying within a Vygotskian framework and to argue its use in a ZPD as a spontaneous concept – with the restrictions I've already addressed concerning the dubious distinctions defining spontaneous concepts. As a spontaneous concept in the Vygotskian sense, signifying has aspects that parallel literary "scientific" concepts such as irony, metaphor, symbolism, and the various rhetorical tropes through which double entendre and inferred meanings may be expressed in literary texts. Because of these shared characteristics, signifying is ripe for exploitation within a Vygotskian ZPD. Within the framework proposed in this chapter, African American students naive about the formal definitions and applications of these rhetorical tropes in literature are seen as novices within the ZPD, and the literature teacher, skilled in both signifying and literary analysis, is the expert. In such a ZPD the literature teacher scaffolds the spontaneous concept already understood – albeit intuitively – by the novice in order to bring the novice closer to the "expert" or "literary" understanding of these tropes. Signifying may be further defined, through the levels of analysis of activities put forward by Leont'ev (1981), as a series of actions motivated by specific goals and operationalized within a specific cultural context.

Properties of Signifying

Signifying has been formally defined by many scholars, writers, and activists (Abrahams, 1970; Andrews & Owens, 1973; Brown, 1969; Cooke, 1984; Gates, 1984, 1988; Hurston, 1935; Kochman, 1972; Major, 1970; Mitchell-Kernan, 1981; Smitherman, 1977). Some define its characteristics in structural terms as a speech act with delineated functions (Abrahams, 1970; Kochman, 1972). Others define it as a rhetorical stance, an attitude toward language, and a means of cultural self definition (Cooke, 1984; Gates, 1984, 1988; Mitchell-Kernan, 1981; Smitherman, 1977). I do not see these categories as being mutually exclusive. In fact, both are necessary to the argument of this chapter. An understanding of signifying as a rhetorical stance, an attitude toward language, and a means of cultural self-definition is important in assessing the value given to signifying as an art form within the African American community. It is precisely because it is so highly valued and so widely practiced that signifying has the potential to serve as a bridge to literacy skills within a school environment.

Goodlad (1984) has commented on the boredom of American classrooms. If large numbers of African American students are not achieving academically, as measured by rates of high school graduation and standardized measures of literacy, then it is reasonable to assume that these students are often not engaged in the process of literacy instruction. Learning to interpret formal properties of literature is one critical aspect of literacy instruction. Irony, symbolism, and uses of metaphor and point of view are examples of such formal properties. An understanding of the structural properties and functions of signifying is what allows one to conceptualize its potential linkages with these formal literary concepts.

Both Gates (1984, 1988) and Mitchell-Kernan (1981) point to the specialized meanings attributed to the word *signify* within the African American community. Both of these authors contrast the European American dictionary-based definition of signification with the Afro-centric definition. To signify within the African American community means to speak with innuendo and double meanings, to play rhetorically on the meaning and sounds of words, and to be quick and often witty in one's response. There is no parallel usage of the terms *signify* or *signification* within other ethnic, English-speaking communities, although other speech communities have routine forms of language play. Gates punctuates the difference in the use of the term in the two communities by capitalizing the first letter to identify Signifying as a specialized concept of language use within the Black community. In many social settings within the African American community, the adolescent, in particular, who cannot signify has no status and no style, is a kind of outsider who is incapable of participating in social conversation. Although Signifying is a common language phenomenon across Black communities, Mitchell-Kernan (1981) observes:

While the terminological use of signifying to refer to a particular kind of language specialization defines the Black community as a speech community in contrast to non-Black communities, it should be emphasized that further intra-community terminological specialization reflects social structural divisions within the community and related activity specializations. (p. 313)

Thus signifying and its many components may be called by different names in different communities or during different historical periods, and certain skills may be more dominant within one gender. Also, certain individuals may assume more specialized roles than other members of the general community, such as the role of contemporary rappers.

Gates (1984, 1988) and Cooke (1984) argue that signifying is a historical phenomenon within the African American community. Gates (1988) places the origin of signifying in 19th-century spirituals and slave narratives. He quotes from an ex-slave, Wash Wilson, who says, "When de niggers go round singin' 'Steal Away to Jesus,' dat mean dere gwine be a 'ligious meetin' dat night. Dat de sig'fication of a meetin'" (p. 68). Like Cooke, Gates identifies "Signifying as the slave's trope," an indirect way of reversing the relations of slave and master.

Signifying may be called or classified by many names. According to Gates (1984), "The Black rhetorical tropes subsumed under signifying would include 'marking,' 'loud-talking,' 'specifying,' 'testifying,' 'calling out' (of one's name), 'sounding,' 'rapping' and 'playing the dozens'" (p. 286). Other terms include *shucking* (as in "shucking and jiving") and *talking shit*.

Signifying in any given speech event or stretch of talk may fulfill one or many of the following functions:

1. Challenge and maintain a friendly but intense verbal duel.
2. Persuade – to direct through indirection, to use Abrahams's (1970) reference, to drive home a message "without preaching or lecturing" (Smitherman, 1977).
3. Criticize or insult through either carping or innuendo.
4. Praise – Rap Brown (1969) said, "Signifying allowed you a choice – you could either make a cat feel good or bad. If you had just destroyed someone or if they were just down already, signifying could help them over."
5. Reverse a relationship.
6. "Show off," to use Hurston's (1935) term or use it as a "way of expressing your own feelings," to use Rap Brown's (1969) words.

Mitchell-Kernan (1981), Ellison (1964), and Smitherman (1977) describe the formal properties of signifying. Mitchell-Kernan describes signifying as "a way of encoding messages or meanings which involves, in most cases, an element of indirection" (p. 311). She emphasizes that dictionary meanings of words in an act of signifying are not sufficient for constructing meaning. One must recognize the "implicit content or function, which is potentially obscured by the surface content or function" (p. 314). Ellison (1964) talks about "ironic signifying – 'signifying' here meaning, in the unwritten dictionary of American Negro usage, 'rhetorical understatements' " (pp. 249–250). Smitherman summarizes the formal properties of signifying as follows:

indirection, circumlocution; metaphorical-imagistic (but images rooted in the everyday, real world); humorous, ironic; rhythmic fluency and sound; teachy but not preachy; directed at person or persons usually present in the situational context (siggers do not talk behind yo back); punning, play on words; introduction of the semantically or logically unexpected. (p. 121)

A Network of Related Tropes in Literature

The purpose of defining signifying in this chapter is to show its parallels to various formal literary tropes and also to highlight its formal characteristics that have much in common with the attributes that Vygotsky (1986) says characterize scientific concepts. The literary tropes of interest include irony, metaphor, symbolism, and use of unreliable narrators. What these tropes have in common is that where an author employs them, possible intended meanings must be inferred and strictly literal interpretations must be rejected. Use of any of these devices signals to an expert reader that some encoded meaning, some double entendre, is intended. In this sense, all of these literary devices share an attribute with signifying: "encoding messages or meanings which involve in most cases an element of indirection" (Mitchell-Kernan 1981, p. 311).

Once a reader has determined that the surface-level meaning is not sufficient, the reader must decide how to construct the encoded meaning or meanings. According to Winner (1988), if a passage is ironic, readers (or listeners in the case of oral communication) reconstruct an intended meaning in opposition to the literal one; if metaphoric, in addition to the literal one. Symbolism may be thought of as an extension of metaphor in that the image, character, object, event, or action has a potential meaning or set of meanings that are in addition to the literal meaning but also represent a generalizable proposition. Point of view, as represented by the use of unreliable narrators, may be thought of as an extension of irony. In response to the specialized question "Who is

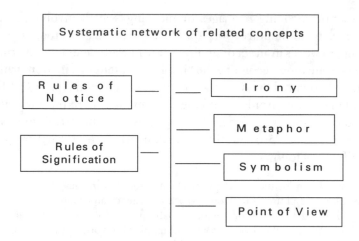

Figure 9.1 Systematic network of related literary concepts.

talking?" when we encounter unreliable narrators, we reject the surface meaning of what they communicate because we do not deem what they say trustworthy. In this sense, these four literary devices are systematically related. Rabinowitz (1987) calls those strategies readers use to recognize that something other than the literal meaning is intended *rules of notice*. The strategies and prior knowledge we draw on to impose meaning Rabinowitz calls *rules of signification*. The system of related literary tropes and devices is accessed by rules of notice and interpreted through rules of signification. Because these tropes and literary devices are systematically related, strategies used to detect irony are also applicable to detecting metaphor, symbolism, and manipulation of point of view through the use of an unreliable narrator. The nexus of related literary devices is represented in Figure 9.1.

In order to demonstrate the links between the spontaneous concept of signifying and formal literary devices, I will construct a case around irony. Because I have argued that irony stands within a nexus of interrelated literary tropes, a cognitive analysis of the act of interpreting irony within the framework of activity theory (Leont'ev, 1981) is theoretically extended to the other related tropes.

In what follows, I will first discuss formal properties of irony in literature and strategies a reader may use in both identifying and reconstructing the meaning of ironic passages. Then, by analyzing several signifying dialogues, I will attempt to demonstrate the systematicity of the cognitive strategies one must use, whether implicitly or explicitly, in order to interpret the motives and goals and the shifts in meaning as the dialogue progresses.

I shall not attempt here to offer any authoritative definition of irony, for as Booth (1974) says, "There is no agreement among critics about what irony is" (p. ix). Yet, irony, like signifying, provides a well-used bridge between Vygotsky's scientific and spontaneous concepts. Booth accurately observes that irony "can be found on almost every page of many great writers, but you will also find it sprinkling the conversation of the railroad workers in Utah and – I am told – the street sweepers in Bombay" (p. 30). A major thesis of this chapter is that the cognitive representations involved in recognizing and reconstructing meaning in acts of signifying are systematic, complex, and akin to similar representations in recognizing and reconstructing the meaning of an ironic, metaphoric, or symbolic passage in literature. Accordingly, Wittgenstein has said, "The tacit conventions on which the understanding of everyday language depends are enormously complicated" (cited in Booth, 1974).

Booth (1974) emphasizes the importance of context in interpreting irony: "The 'context,' then, is not just the words but the words as they relate to our total view of the subject, to our range of inferences about what the author would most probably mean by each stroke, and to our range of possible genres" (p. 99). Booth indicates that his purpose is to describe "the way irony works," and he points out that knowledge of the genre and the author influences how irony functions in particular works. Booth says that in order for the author and reader to engage each other in a shared understanding of the irony of a passage, they must agree on at least three areas of common experience:

1. their common experience of the vocabulary and grammar of English . . . along with understanding of rules which allow for and control verbal inventions
2. their common cultural experience and their agreement about its meaning and value
3. their common experience of literary genres, a potentially large (but almost certainly finite) number of shared grooves or tracks into which reading experience can be directed. (p. 100)

For many African American students (and others whose community culture differs markedly from mainstream school culture), these areas of experience are not shared understandings, particularly when reading literature that does not reflect their common experiences with vocabulary and grammar, cultural values that are not part of their experience, and literary genres with which they are explicitly unfamiliar (see Ball, this volume). On the other hand, in an act of signifying, it is safe to assume that a majority of African American students who speak AAVE will have a common understanding of language conventions and meaning, values around the import of the ritual of the act, and understanding of the the rules of the game that I believe may be analogous to expectations regarding literary genres.

Booth (1974) distinguishes between the act of recognizing irony and the act of reconstructing the meanings of an ironic passage. Smith (1987) outlines five clues that Booth argues an author may use to signal irony in a work or passage:

1. "a straightforward warning in the author's own voice . . . in titles, in epigraphs, and in other direct clues."
2. "when an author has his or her speaker proclaim a known error. . . ."
3. "existence of a conflict within a work."
4. "a clash of style," as when the "language of a speaker is not clearly the same as the language of the author" or when the author uses understatements or exaggerations.
5. "a conflict of belief" between a speaker and the author or "behavior of a speaker that the author could not endorse." (pp. 11–13)

Smith adds, "In each case the reader must bring to bear standards from outside the text onto the world of the text, proceeding from the belief that the author does not hold alien values" (p. 13). The clues identified by Booth and Smith may be classified as rules of notice, as defined by Rabinowitz (1987). Rules of notice are strategies and clues that readers of fiction use to determine that something in a text requires additional and special attention. As framed in this chapter, attention signaling that the surface or literal meaning is insufficient is the issue of focus.

Common Processes in Understanding Irony and Other Tropes in Literature and Signifying in Social Discourse

In this section I provide examples of signifying. I argue that the rules for recognizing each example as signifying parallel the clues for signaling irony, as defined by Booth (1974). Considering that signifying in social discourse does not involve a printed text with such conventions as titles and epigraphs, it is reasonable to distill the following parallel steps in recognizing an act as signifying.

1. *When a speaker proclaims a known error*, as in the following example (Mitchell-Kernan, 1981, p. 317): [Relevant background information: the husband is a member of the class of individuals who do not wear suits to work]

Wife: Where are you going?

Husband: I'm going to work.

Wife: (You're wearing) a suit, tie and white shirt? You didn't tell me you got a promotion.

The surface meaning of the wife's final comment is rejected because of the rule of notice by which the speaker proclaims a known error. An ironic meaning in opposition to the literal one is constructed. In addition, both the husband and the wife recognize the husband as an unreliable narrator.

2. *Existence of a conflict*, as in the following example (Mitchell-Kernan, 1981, pp. 318–319): [Relevant background information: Grace hadn't told anybody that she was pregnant and was starting to show. The following exchange is between Grace and her sister.]

Rochelle: Girl, you sure do need to join the Metrecal for lunch bunch.

Grace: (Non-committally) Yea, I guess I am putting on a little weight.

Rochelle: Now look here, girl, we both standing here soaking wet and you still trying to tell me it ain't raining.

Again, this rule of notice, existence of a conflict, signals that Rochelle's final comment is not intended to be interpreted literally. The intended meaning is in opposition to the literal one, that is, they are not soaking wet. The statement "we both standing here soaking wet and you still trying to tell me it ain't raining" requires that we think analogically, and consider relationships between the tenor of the metaphor and the situation between Rochelle and Grace.

3. *A clash of style*: Smitherman (1977, p. 86) references a cartoon by Ollie Harrington. Two African American men are in what looks like a hotel room, which could be in Paris. One man, dressed in an undershirt and boxer shorts, with a cigar in his mouth, is looking at an open book. The other man, dressed as a dapper dandy in a 1940s-style fancy dress, says:

"That book ain't gonna teach you no French, Bootsie. You got to live it. Now s'posin' you just had a fine feed at some chick's pad. You bows and says, 'Bon soir mademoiselle, et cetera.' Now that means, 'Goodnight, Irene. Thanks for the fine scoff. The chitterlings was simply devine and I'll dig you by and by!"

Harrington, the cartoonist, as the author, is signifying on the men, affecting to be more sophisticated than they really are. There is a clash of styles between the men's attempt to be sophisticated speakers of French and their obvious working-class origins. The scenario is ironic because what we are to infer about the men is the opposite of what they purport to be. Besides being ironic, the cartoon is satirical.

4. *The speech behavior of the signifier could not possibly be one that the speaker would actually do or believe, analogous to Booth's conflict of belief.*

The dozens presents an excellent example. In the dozens, one ritualistically insults another's mother, usually, or another family member. Smitherman (1977) warns that in order for the dozens not to be offensive, the insults must have no basis in fact, as in the following excerpt from Richard Wright's (1963) *Lawd Today*, in which a group of Black men playing cards engage in playing the dozens (thanks to Smitherman, 1977, p. 127, for the example):

"Yeah," he said slowly, "I remembers when my little baby brother was watching with slobber in his mouth, your old grandma was out in the privy crying 'cause she couldn't find a corncob. . . ."

Slim and Bob groaned and stomped their feet.

"Yeah," said Al, retaliating with narrowed eyes. "When my old grandma was crying for that corncob, your old aunt Lucy was round back of the barn with old Colonel James' old man, and she was saying something like this: 'Yyyyou kknow . . . Mmmiister Cccolonel . . . I jjjust ddon't like to sssell . . . my ssstuff . . . I jjjust lloves to gggive . . . iit away. . . .'."

The rule of notice applicable here notifies the reader or listener to reject the surface meaning. This text of signifying is satiric and, in a sense, involves an unreliable narrator.

Booth makes an important point when he distinguishes between the strategies a reader uses to recognize irony from the strategies he or she uses to reconstruct meaning in the ironic passage. The reconstruction process is necessary because once the reader identifies the passage as ironic (or the speaker recognizes the first turn in the speech act as signifying), the reader (or listener) realizes that the surface meaning must be rejected. Smith (1987) recounts four steps that Booth indicates may be used in reconstructing meaning: "rejecting the surface meaning, trying out alternative meanings, applying one's knowledge of the author, and selecting among alternatives" (p. 13). Smith observes that in "the usual case of quick recognition" the alternative meanings of which Booth speaks may come "flooding in." However, Smith is concerned that Booth's explanation does not attend to what variables control a reader's selection of alternative meanings. Smith says that the variable cannot simply be knowledge of the author because readers "understand the irony of unknown authors" (p. 14). To account for this discrepancy, Smith offers his own four steps of reconstruction. Smith believes that readers

1. Reject the surface meaning
2. Decide what is not under dispute in the work
3. Apply their knowledge of the world to generate a reconstructed meaning and, if possible,
4. Check the reconstructed meaning against their knowledge of the author. (p. 15)

Because Smith's reconstructive steps are more specific than Booth's, and because knowledge of the social world as well as knowledge of the signifier is crucial in reconstructing meaning within a signifying speech act, I will apply Smith's reconstructive steps in analyzing signifying. One rarely signifies with a person about whom one has no personal knowledge and especially not with a person outside one's cultural community. There are also restrictions on what kind of signifying may acceptably occur across, for example, age cohorts. It would not be socially acceptable for an adolescent boy or girl to play the dozens with an adult or elder.

The extent to which a reader or listener may use these reconstructive steps as a conscious strategy depends on several key factors. However, Smith's (1989) study on the effects of direct versus tacit instruction of irony with high school students suggests that whether explictly conscious or implictly tacit, readers do seem to employ these strategies in reconstructing meaning in the ironic poems in his study. I agree with Smith that when expert readers read texts with which they are very familiar (familiar with the text, the author, and the author's other texts), it is possible that alternative meanings to the surface meaning may indeed come "flooding in," as suggested by Booth (1974). However, any of the following variables that must be considered in the interpretive process may sufficiently slow down processing to the point where a reader begins consciously to employ the steps identified by Smith: the skill of the reader, the complexity of textual antecedents needed to generalize meaning, knowledge of restrictions or possibilities brought to bear by the genre, and/or real-world knowledge of the reader. On the other hand, a participant in extended dialogue within a signifying speech event cannot possibly take time to employ such strategies consciously, but rather must be verbally and mentally quick enough to respond immediately.

The intensity of this intellectual challenge may differ according to the kind of signifying event taking place. Gates (1984, 1988) says that signifying is not primarily transmitting content, but rather rhetorical style. I agree with Gates when the signifying event involves something like rapping or playing the dozens, for in these instances truth is not the hallmark, but rather style. However, when the signifying event is meant to be directive or persuasive, and particularly when the event involves extended dialogue, quick interpretation of meaning (having rejected the surface meaning) is mandatory and ongoing throughout each speech turn. In such signifying events, the signifiers must be astute enough to process the reconstructed meaning immediately. I argue that expert signifiers have a richly embedded network of associations represented in signifying schemata that allow them to respond immediately. This embedded network distinguishes expert signifiers (of whatever signifying category) from novices and the ordinary folk. I consider myself among ordinary folk in the world of signifying discourse in that I can recognize signifying and interpret it accurately and quickly, but I am not adept at the quick verbal retort. This richly embedded network of associations may relate to ritualized themes (such as "yo mamma," or "what's happenin' baby?") or to rhetorical techniques such as exaggeration.

A pivotal inference that participants in a signifying dialogue must make concerns the motives of the signifier. What one interprets about motives determines the category of signifying being invoked and directs the kind of response that is appropriate. The second party in the dialogue (as the first speaker initiates the signifying event or "sounds out" the second party) must infer one or some combination of the following motives:

1. A challenge to a verbal duel
2. An attempt to persuade
3. Criticism
4. Praise
5. A reversal of an existing relationship

Failure to interpret accurately the motives of the speaker may result in dire consequences. The tale of "The Signifying Monkey" demonstrates such results. The monkey speaks metaphorically as a signifier, but the lion interprets literally. Kochman (1972) and others (Baugh, 1983; Gates, 1984, 1988; Mitchell-Kernan, 1981; Smitherman, 1977) argue that these two interpretive stances reflect fundamental differences between the African American speech community and the European American English-speaking community in terms of attitudes toward language.*

Applying Strategies for Processing Irony and Related Rhetorical Tropes to Signifying Discourse

I will apply Smith's (1989) four steps in reconstructing the meaning of irony and the choices of motives to be inferred to an extended signifying dialogue reported by Mitchell-Kernan (1981, p. 319). The researcher in the dialogue is Mitchell-Kernan. The dialogue occurred while she was conducting ethnographic fieldwork for her doctoral dissertation on language practices in the Black community. All comments in brackets are my analysis of the strategies used by both parties in the exchange to identify and reconstruct ironic meanings throughout the dialogue.

The following interchange took place in a public park. Three young men in their early 20s sat down with the researcher, one of whom initiated a conversation in this way:

I: Mama, you sho is fine.

        [Initiates a signifying event]

R: That ain no way to talk to your mother.

        (laughter)

[Researcher rejects the surface meaning of the statement. She decides what is not under dispute, i.e., the young man is not trying to offend or seduce her. She signals by her use of the reference to his mother that she recognizes that a signifying speech event is underway – in this case and at this point in the dialogue a challenge to a verbal duel – and that she is willing to participate in the ritual.]

---

* I recognize that the European American English speech community is not monolithic. One European American English-speaking group demonstrating different discourse, syntax, and prosody features speaks Appalachian English. I use the term *European American English speech community* to represent what is institutionally captured in assumptions about mainstream standard English.

I: You married?

[Since this is a signifying speech event, this question sets the stage for an unexpected turn by the interlocutor, something to be expected by an expert signifier. The interpretation of this request will then be held critically in abeyance until further information is available.]

R: Um hm.

[Researcher remains uncommitted in her response. Because of her "knowledge of the world" of signifying, it is important that she hold her options for response open.]

I: Is your husband married?

[An obvious case of signifying because, to use Booth's strategy for recognizing irony, the speaker in this instance (as opposed to the author's speaker in a written text) proclaims a known error. Obviously her husband is married.]

R: Very.

[The researcher accepts the statement as signifying. She recognizes that what is not under dispute is whether her husband is married or not. Using her knowledge of the world of signifying – i.e., the interlocutor's motives may now have changed to either persuade her to do something or to reverse an existing relationship, namely, to question the fidelity of her husband – and her knowledge of the rules operating around even the surface meaning of to be married – i.e., to be sexually loyal to one another – she infers that the interlocutor is asking whether her husband operates according to the same rules of fidelity as she, and if not, perhaps she needn't operate by them either. At the same time, this exchange at the level of inferences must be understood within the context of signifying, which means that neither the interlocutor nor the researcher takes these understandings as literal attempts to seduce. This, I think, is verified by the fact that the researcher does not get offended by the question; nor does she encourage the interlocutor to continue any serious attempts at seduction. In this case, she has checked her reconstructed meaning against her knowledge of the intent of the interlocutor.]

(The conversation continues, with the same young man doing most of the talking. He questions [the researcher] about what [she is] doing, and [she tells] him about my research project. After a couple of minutes of discussing "rapping" I [interlocutor] returns to his original style.)

I: Baby, you a real scholar. I can tell you want to learn. Now if you'll just cooperate a li'l bit, I'll show you what a good teacher I am. But first we got to get into my area of expertise.

[The interlocutor is now rapping, praising himself and the researcher. However, the signal statement in this exchange is the phrase "into my area of expertise." This statement signals an act of signifying and therefore calls for an ironic interpretation.]

R: I may be wrong but seems to me we already in your area of expertise. (laughter)

[In order to interpret the interlocutor's statement as continuing to signify, the researcher using Booth's clues for identifying irony must recognize a kind of clash of style, if you will, and a known error. That is, the interlocutor is not a teacher in the traditional sense, and whatever his area of expertise is, it is not likely to be one traditionally associated (surface meaning) with the profession or art of teaching. To reconstruct the ironic meaning, then, the researcher must again reject the surface meaning. She must decide that what is not under dispute is whether he has some area of expertise, but exactly what that area of expertise is. She applies her knowledge of the world of signifying and infers his motive to be both to persuade and possibly to reverse a relationship – namely, her relationship as the researcher/teacher/scholarly expert and his as the object of study. She must also check her reconstructed meaning against her knowledge of the interlocutor. He has proven himself to be good at flirting and at signifying. She then reconstructs the ironic or signifying meaning as a kind of double entendre, deciding that his area of expertise is in fact both. However, as an expert signifier herself, the researcher redirects the double entendre and redefines his area of expertise simply as signifying.]

I: You ain' so bad yourself, girl. I ain't heard you stutter yet. You a li'l fixated on your subject though. I want to help a sweet thang like you all I can. I figure all that book learning you got must mean you been neglecting other areas of your education.

[In the first two sentences, the interlocutor praises the researcher because she has played the game well. These sentences are meant to be interpreted literally as content, but within the play of the verbal game, they act as a setup for his redirection of her last verbal volley. In other words, he recognizes that he has been signified upon.]

II: Talk that talk! (Gloss: Ole)

[This is the response of a third party to the interchange. He is now *tes-tifying*, a form of signifying in which a respondent praises and reinforces the verbal skill of the signifier. This response is a further indication by all parties involved that everyone recognizes this speech event as an act of signifying.]

R: Why don't you let me point out where I can best use your help.

[The researcher has accurately interpreted his redirection and has redirected his intent again. In order to recognize the interlocutor's last statement as continued signification, the researcher realizes that within his statement there is both a clash of styles and exaggeration. From what she surmises of the interlocutor from the circumstances of their meeting and from her real-world knowledge that middle-class Black scholars don't ordinarily carry on extended signifying with people they meet in the park, she concludes that there is some discrepancy between his concern about book learning and other areas of her education. This discrepancy, along with the recognition that this entire speech event so far has been an act of signifying, would lead her to recognize the statements as signifying and therefore ironic. In order to reconstruct the meaning of his last statements, the researcher decides that what is not under dispute is whether she studies the linguistics of signifying too much. She uses her knowledge of the world of signifying and infers his motives as a challenge to continue the verbal duel, possibly to persuade her still, and to reverse the relationship of teacher and object of study. She checks her reconstructed meaning against her knowledge of the past exchanges with the interlocutor, namely, his sly, gamish attempts to flirt with her and his prior rapping to establish himself as a lover – but only in the context of the verbal game of signifying. She thus interprets the other areas of her education with which he can help her as an intended double entendre, involving the area of love making and flirting, along with her formal education in linguistics. By making the response she does, the researcher redirects his verbal volley once again. At the same time, the researcher signals her willingness to continue the game because she maintains the metaphor established by the interlocutor.]

I: Are you sure you in the best position to know?

[The interlocutor accepts the challenge and volleys back. The elaborate metaphor has been maintained and redirected by each signifying participant.]

        (laughter)

I: I'mo leave you alone, girl. Ask me what you want to know. Tempus fugit, baby.

[This response is very important in the interchange because it signals the end of the signifying event.] Mitchell-Kernan (1981) comments that "the interchange is laced with innuendo – signifying because it alludes to and implies things which are never made explicit" (p. 319). Mitchell-Kernan's analysis of the preceding speech event is quite informative and has influenced the analysis offered by this author to each turn in the exchange.

Having attempted to establish in some sense the parallel uses of strategy in identifying and reconstructing meaning in both signifying speech events and irony and other rhetorical tropes in literature, I can reasonably argue that signifying represents the special kind of concept that fits nicely into the possibilities of transfer suggested by Vygotsky's notion of the interchange of spontaneous and scientific concepts within a ZPD. That is, both concepts have enough common attributes to provide unique bridging possibilities for using knowledge in one arena to scaffold formal knowledge in the second arena. Because the two concepts require comparable mental processing, I argue that Vygotsky's construct of higher mental functions operates in both signifying and the interpretation of literary tropes.

Signifying and African American Literature

Besides sharing formal qualities with the literary constructs of irony, metaphor, symbolism, and point of view, signifying also serves well in a Vygotskian ZPD because it is widely used within African American literature. This context is important for several reasons. First, Booth (1974) and Smith (1987) both argue that knowledge of literary genres plays an important role in the act of recognizing and reconstructing ironic meanings in literature. Although the use of oral language traditions such as signifying and the use of AAVE are factors that help constitute African

American literature as a unique literary tradition, African American literature also is constituted through traditional and postmodern Western literary genres. Thus in the context of literature, to bring the shared strategies of identifying and reconstructing ironic, metaphoric, and symbolic meanings in oral signifying and in literature to a metacognitive level of explicit awareness is to strengthen the shared lessons of the two experiences. The advantage that African American literature potentially gives young, novice, African American readers is through their prior knowledge of the social milieu, values, and issues addressed in such texts, as well as their familiarity, in many cases, with the language style and its import for meaning. Hynds (1989) has acknowledged the role of social knowledge in constructing meaning from literary texts. She accurately points out that knowledge of the social world is too seldom used to assist students in constructing meaning from literary texts, an observation that she believes intensifies student alienation from literature. These observations, however, are not meant to imply that all African American literary texts offer such a privileged position to African American students, nor that there is a straightforward advantage that African American literary texts offer African American students. I have argued elsewhere that a close analysis of the interpretive demands of the text is required to understand how to prepare students to tackle such problems independently. In one sense, Vygotsky's conception of capacity as the relationship between what the novice can do alone and what the novice can do with the support of a more knowledgeable other (i.e., the ZPD) applies. A central premise of the conceptual framework on which this chapter is based is that when the capacities of underachieving African American students in terms of literary analysis in signifying dialogues are recognized, honored, and addressed in the design of supports for learning, the independent capacities of these students are powerful. What that support looks like is addressed in the next section of this chapter.

Gates (1984, 1988), Ishmael Reed (1974), and Zora Neale Hurston (1935) all talk about the talking book, the oral book. Such texts within the African American literary tradition give voice and tenor to the speech of ordinary Black folk. In a culture in which the African American has historically been viewed as the *Invisible Man*, in a Western literary tradition in which the Black voice is not heard, the speakerly text, as Gates calls it, resonates the choir's *Talkin' and Testifyin'* from the fields, the bedrooms, the parlors, and the bar rooms, from the church pulpits and the street corners. The Black talking book represents the oral tradition of the African American community. Jones (1991), Gates (1988), Baker (1984), and Smitherman (1977), among others, recount significant literary texts in which the oral tradition, and specifically signifying play important roles. Signifying, then, is not limited to the context of oral conversation, but is catapulted into the realm of rhetorical technique within the tradition of African American literature.

Signifying in a ZPD: Classroom Application

This section moves from a theoretical discussion of signifying as a bridge between spontaneous and scientific concepts to examine how the mediation occurs within classrooms. Because issues of culture and ethnicity are central to the argument of this chapter, I will illustrate how the culturally rooted prior knowledge of these African American students was used by the teacher to apprentice these students into a particular community of practice.

Scribner (1984) and Leont'ev (1981) argued that activity as a unit of analysis offers a useful way to understand thinking in context. I will describe the enactment of this instructional unit wherein spontaneous concepts guide the development of scientific concepts played out in a Vygotskian ZPD. The process of semiotic mediation is enacted between teacher and student, as well as among students with evolving levels of expertise. This semiotic mediation is rooted in a cultural foundation, just as the premise of signifying as a spontaneous concept linked structurally to literary tropes is cultural. This semiotic mediation also unfolds over time. Understanding its changes over time, changes in the reasoning processes of both students and the teacher, is important. The process of semiotic mediation demands a classroom culture in which the salient elements of the practice are assumed over time by the novice and monitored by more expert-like others. In the case of this class, this means students not only learning to see connections about what they know about signifying and how to attack problems of literary analysis, but also learning how to raise appropriate questions, how to attend to salient parts of the text, how to generate arguments using both textual and real-world knowledge, and how to monitor this understanding.

I have previously (1991, 1993, 1994, 1995a, 1995b, 1997) implemented an instructional intervention based on the conceptual framework described in this chapter. I have labeled this conceptual framework *Cultural Modeling* (Lee, 1994). In Cultural Modeling, explicit strategies for attacking problems of irony, symbolism, and point of view are modeled as students make public the strategies they invoke in interpreting such problems in signifying dialogues and other cultural data sets. Extending the analysis of signifying as a conceptual tool, such cultural data sets include not only signifying dialogues but also lyrics to rap songs, as well as rap and popular music videos. In order to illustrate the effects of this theoretical framework, I will draw from transcripts of several days of instruction in one classroom in which a unit based on Cultural Modeling is being carried out. Results of gain from pre- to posttesting provide evidence that the quality of reading and reasoning evident in the transcripts is not confined to these examples (Lee, 1993). Rather, the transcripts are used to provide a detailed view of the nature of expert-like practice into which these students had been apprenticed.

The student population included African American underachieving seniors in two urban high schools. A quasi-experimental design was implemented involving four experimental classes studying the short story "My Man Bovanne" by Toni Cade Bambara (1972) and two novels, Zora Neale Hurston's *Their Eyes Were Watching God* (1937/1990) and Alice Walker's *The Color Purple* (1982). I taught two of the experimental classes. The students in the experimental classes studied samples of signifying dialogue taken from Mitchell-Kernan (1981) and extrapolated the rules they intuitively used to generate the intended meaning for each turn of talk. They then applied those strategies to the interpretation of complex inferential questions based on the two novels. One control class in each high school studied its usual curriculum for world literature. The experimental group achieved a statistically significant gain from pre- to posttesting over the control classes (Lee, 1993, 1995a, 1995b).

In these transcripts students demonstrate the mental qualities of reasoning about literary problems, the same habits of mind that Vygotsky argued are required by scientific concepts: deliberate attention, comparison and contrast, and abstraction. Although not explicitly stated, Vygotsky implies that an understanding and use of scientific concepts involves expert-like activity in a community of practice. An analysis of how the ZPD plays out in this instructional unit involves a focus on the definition of what is to be learned, what the learner knows and what the teacher or more expert-like other wants the novice to learn, what the teacher understands about the task, and what the learner initially understands that is related to the task. Of interest in this instantiation of a ZPD is how the novice's knowledge of signifying is transformed over time. The observed transformation is from a spontaneous concept that is applicable in the students' minds only to the oral contexts of signifying talk to a more scientific representation of literary tropes, sometimes embedded in signifying examples in literary texts. The exploration of the links between

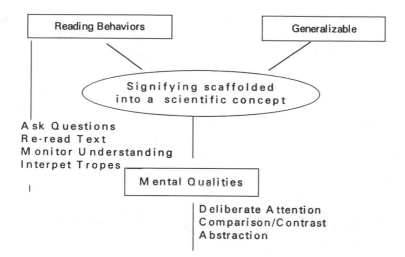

Figure 9.2 Reading strategies and habits of mind linking signifying to scientific concepts.

the spontaneous concept of signifying and its scientific counterparts leads to a shared sense of the following: (1) what to value in literary texts and (2) what tools to use deliberately to construct the kinds of generaliza tions about works of fiction that are characteristic of more expert-like practice. Figure 9.2 provides a graphic representation of the features of reasoning about scientific concepts in the Vygotskian sense that come to be associated with signifying. In this framework, signifying is used as a mediational construct through which to apprentice these students into ways of reasoning about literary texts.

A pattern of classroom culture (Green & Dixon, 1994; Gutiérrez & Stone, Putney et al., this volume) provided a structure through which semiotic mediation took place:

1. Posing questions that require students to make inferences that draw on evidence from across the text.
2. Modeling through practice the reasoning processes required to approach such questions.
3. Constantly probing students to question their assumptions and to prove their claims, not only by evidence from the text but also by articulating the warrants based on values and beliefs that would make one accept the evidence as applicable.
4. Modeling and asking students what one point in a line of argumentation has to do with another point.

The unit began with analyses of signifying dialogues and then applied strategies gleaned from the signifying to analysis of "My Man Bovanne" (Bambara, 1972) and then *Their Eyes Were Watching God* (Hurston, 1990). By the time the class reached the second novel, *The Color Purple* by Alice Walker (1982), it had become clear that the intellectual culture of the class had drastically changed. In the Bakhtinian (1981) sense, the utterances of students were dialogically responsive to the prior conversations that had occurred in the class. One can begin to hear the earlier voice of the teacher resonating through the voices of the students. Bakhtin's question "Who is doing the talking?" is of interest here. A response to that question may provide insight into the importance of the role of the teacher as one who explicitly models, guides, and supports not only what students do but also how they think. In addition, there is a historical and cultural antecedent to the shared norms or intersubjectivity evident in these discussions. The content on which questions and reasoning processes were based consisted of linguistic knowledge and practices with which this group of students was very familiar.

The content of many of the discussions that occurred over the next 2 weeks focused on questions generated by the students. However, because the students and the teacher had come to think alike – in essence valuing and becoming interested in the same questions – the questions posed by the students were some of the same questions the teacher had been thinking about. Earlier discussions were very teacher directed, in part indicating the distance between the conception of the task held by the teacher and the conceptions held by the students.

Achieving Intersubjectivity: Engaging in Expert-Like Practice

In the transcript examples that follow, students demonstrate their participation as members of a community of practice. They exemplify some of the habits of mind that expert-like readers bring to the challenge of interpreting complex works of fiction. They consciously use metacognitive strategies like text reinspection. They make explicit statements that articulate what counts as questions worth asking, engage in analysis of point of view based on issues they have raised, and respond to questions by constructing mini-arguments with positions, evidence, and warrants.

In the first instructional episode, the teacher gathers questions from the students about *The Color Purple*. This lesson differs substantially from earlier ones because the entire lesson and many that follow are driven by student-initiated questions. The level of involvement in the intellectual issues of the unit is exemplified in the following exchange:

S: Mrs. Lee, before we get started . . . remember last Friday you told us that we were going to finish why we think God

T: We were going to do that at the very end of the period. Maybe we will stop by 2:30 so that you could finish that question on why *Their Eyes Were Watching God* is called that. . . .

The teacher passes out index cards on which the students can write their individual questions. One student says, "I need about thirty of them." Re-iterating the kinds of questions that students should generate, the teacher says:

T: But it ought to be a question that you don't know the answer to, and preferably they should not be questions like how old was Celie or those kinds of questions. They should be things that you really worry about. For example, a question that

S: Why is Mister referred to as Mr.

T: Right. That was a good question that Calvin came up with last week.

This exchange suggests that a focus on this quality of question has become part of the norms of the class, because Calvin doesn't wait for the teacher to provide an example but interrupts and provides his own, one that he came up with the week before. It is common for the teacher to respond to students' questions, rather than to questions the teacher herself poses, and for students to interrupt the teacher's talk. In the midst of fielding students' questions, one student initiates a micro-episode by posing a question of interest to her:

1 S: Mrs. Lee, look at this. This letter is typed to Nettie, right?

2 T: Yes.

3 S: So why does she refer to Nettie like she ain't writing to Nettie? It is like she ain't writing to Nettie.

4 It is like she is writing to somebody else. Then I look back to one of Nettie's letters (unintelligible).

5 T: Because she hadn't sent it. She didn't know where Nettie is.

6 S: She do. She had been reading Nettie's letters.

7 T: When Nettie and Celie write the letters do they ever

8 S: She, Nettie never got none of Celie's letters, but Celie got all of, well not all of them at first. She

9   got half of them and then Harpo made his father give her the rest
             later.

In lines 3–4, the student's question is asking implicitly about point of
view. The student in line 4 uses a metacognitive reading comprehension
strategy by selectively reinspecting an earlier letter sent by Nettie. After
the teacher, who in the beginning lessons had been the primary source
of authority, responds, the student in line 7 contradicts the teacher. In
the next line (8), the teacher attempts to pose a probe question, but the
student interrupts with evidence from the text. This micro-episode re-
volving around a student's question continues for 20 turns and ends with
the teacher asking a student to explain a question the student had, when
the student responds, "You know how my questions could be." This student seems to recognize something about her own learning style and
thinking habits as they relate to the quality of the questions she asks. The
responsibility for directing this intellectual activity has shifted to include
much more student initiative. In response to a student's question, "It says
that she had two kids, right?" the students exchanged 14 rounds of talk,
working through the text to answer a question asked by a member of the
group. After hearing the questions generated by the students, the teacher
revoiced them:

Let me share the questions that you all can come up with. And they are very good
questions. Why did she start each letter off with dear God and then later on change
it to dear Nettie? Don't try to answer, I'm just going to share with you what the
questions are. We are going to take a few of these each day. Why didn't Nettie tell
Corine and her husband the truth about being Olivia and Adam's aunt at first or in
the beginning? Who told Celie they had sex with her and if is her husband, why
would they say that to her? This was relative to a particular page. We will find that
page. Why did Shug marry Brady if she loved Celie? Good question. Why does
Celie act the way she does when it comes to sex? . . . What was Mister's reason for
not giving Ms. Celie Nettie's letters? Why did it take Celie so long to leave Mister?
Why does Mister love Shug so? Interesting question . . . Why is Mister referred to as
Mr. blank? Why did Celie stop writing to God? Why did Celie start bad mouthing
God? Why do Celie and Shug always play with each other?

None of the questions posed by the students is limited to a single answer,
and none of the answers can be isolated to a single page or paragraph in the
text. The questions are authentic, complex, and intriguing. They formally
initiate a new phase in the instruction that is truly dialogic. The role of
the teacher is no less pivotal, but it is less directive. The second episode
that follows on this day of instruction is in response to a student-initiated
question.

In this second episode, the teacher decided that in order to respond adequately to the question of why Celie addresses her letters to God, a reader must infer some essential qualities of Celie's personality early on. For that reason, the teacher turned attention to the first letter that Celie writes. Not only were the class discussions marked by student-initiated questions, long turns of student–student interchange, and debate, but also the quality of students' responses to questions changed since the beginning of instruction. Students were more likely to offer responses that were longer and structured as mini-arguments with claims, evidence, and occasionally warrants. The question arose as to whether Celie recognizes that she has been raped and is pregnant. One student responded:

Cause she was crying. Most people, when it comes down to sex and stuff, they don't cry and do certain things. And then again when he started choking her and said she better get used to it and stuff. That in a sense makes me think that she don't know what she is doing.

The implicit claim is that Celie doesn't understand. The evidence is based on text, namely, that she was crying. The warrant is that most people don't cry when enjoying sex. The second source of evidence from the text is Celie's stepfather's choking her and telling her to get used to it. The warrant for that evidence is in the last two lines. The warrants are based on prior social knowledge.

In the continuing dialogue around the micro-question of whether Celie truly understood what was happening to her, another student introduces as evidence:

Because this never happened to her before. Cause he said that "you better get use to it" and then it later says "but I don't never get use to it and now I feel sick every time I be the one to cook."

This response was also a mini-argument with a claim, evidence, and a warrant. The exchange that followed introduced briefly a new literary concept and an interesting mini-debate of students over warrants. Several students introduced the fact that Celie says she gets sick at the smell of food as an indication that she is pregnant.

T: Alright, you are saying that when she says she feels sick every time she cooks that is an indication that she is pregnant. But does she know that? Does she say that I'm pregnant?

S¹: No

T: So who is letting us know that she is pregnant?

S^2:	The letter.
S^3:	Nobody yet.
S^4:	We don't know she is pregnant.
S^5:	We know she is pregnant, but she don't.
S^6:	Because of the symptoms, the way she is feeling.

Implicit in the question of the teacher in line 4 is the concept of authorial voice. Although the focus was brief and abbreviated, the responses of Students 2 and 5 distinguished the point of view of Celie from that of the author implicit in the language Alice Walker chose to place in the letter. Several turns later, the discussion focused on a mini-debate among students over the warrants offered to support the claim that Celie was pregnant because she became sick at the smell of food:

S^1:	If you knew the symptoms of a woman being pregnant, certain smells make her sick.
S^2:	What if you were a man and didn't know nothing like that?
S^1:	If you are a man you should know that.
S^3:	It might be like that cause of the (inaudible) of the word. She might not be pregnant.
T:	At least you know that it is a possibility.
S^3:	When I smell chitterlings, I get sick. That don't mean that I'm pregnant.

According to Toulmin, Rieke, & Janik (1984), the use of warrants in argumentation marks sophisticated forms of reasoning.

Signifying as a Scientific Construct: Generalizing Across Texts

In the transcript that follows, students demonstrate how they use their knowledge of signifying as a formal construct, as a heuristic through which to analyze formal properties across several texts. The participants in this transcript distinguish signifying in texts according to how the signifying functions. They distinguish its informal use just as a form of oral talk from its use in the texts as representational, symbolic of major shifts in the internal states of characters. They make these comparisons across the two novels and in this way use the concept as a generalizable construct. They work intentionally and deliberately to resolve the questions at hand.

Another final characteristic of the changes in student interpretive strategies and reasoning processes is exemplified in the following segment, where students demonstrate a cumulative understanding of relationships across the texts in the unit. The teacher initially revoices conclusions the students have generated about why Celie writes letters to God and then asks a probing question:

1	*T:*	Because when she writes them her writing is another way of her speaking and expressing herself in things that she can't do. This is an idea to keep in mind because talk does become important in this book, doesn't it? 'Cause does Celie begin to change along the dimensions of talking?
2	S^1:	Yes.
3	*T:*	Where?
4	S^1:	She starts signifying. There is a lot of signifying in this book.
5	*T:*	Was that important?
6	S^1:	What? The signifying? That depends on where it is at. In some places they were just sitting around joking. In other places, they were serious, like when he told her, you ugly, you can't cook and all of that, and she came back and crack on him.
7	*T:*	Does the signifying in that instance have anything to do with the signifying in *Their Eyes Were Watching God*?
8	S^2:	Nope.
9	S^3:	Yes it do. Because when they were in the store when Jody told Janie that she was ugly and that she was getting old and stuff. That is the same thing that he is telling her.
10	S^4:	No, he was just trying to front her.
11	S^5:	You know how Jody never did want her to say anything. He didn't want her to speak. In a way, Mister was the same way with Celie. She couldn't do nothing but what he told her. And she couldn't say nothing but what he told her to say. So in a sense, it is like the same.
12	S^6:	I think there is a little bit of similarity to it. They both are trying to front each other.
13	S^7:	Jody was trying to keep that control back. He was starting to lose it. Just like Mister was trying to get in this book.
14	S^6:	That is what I'm talking about.
15	S^8:	Jody lost his control until he snapped. He wasn't going around beating her like he is.
16	S^6:	Yes, it did.

17 S^9 :   This broad gets beat everyday.

18 S^{10}:   Why she got to be a broad?

19 S^{11}:   No she not.

20 S^9 :   Why he got to be a Mister?

21 S^{10}:   Don't use the name broad.

In line 6, the student reasoned conditionally, indicating that the significance of the signifying in the novel depends on the context. Students applied their linguistic knowledge to an interpretation of the two novels. When the teacher asked the students to consider links between the two novels in the unit, a debate began among them. Their level of engagement was evident in the interchange from lines 17–21, where a male student and a female student argued over the points of view implicit in the terms *broad* and *Mister* and demonstrated a personal identification with the characters.

In the final sections of this day's dialogue, the teacher stated that she would not be in class the next day. The students would work in groups the next day on questions they had generated. Because what was going on in this instructional intervention was so contrary to the culture of the school, the students recognized the difficulty they would have in conducting their own intellectual inquiry with a substitute teacher.

1   S: Could you leave a note because. . . .

2   T: I am going to leave a note.

3   S: Calvin is going to try to run the class.

Implicit in line 1 is that the teacher's authority will be necessary to allow the students to work independently the next day.

Conclusion

I have attempted to argue in this chapter that signifying as a form of social discourse within the African American community has attributes in common with the strategies used to identify and reconstruct the intended meaning of literary tropes, including irony, metaphor, symbolism, and point of view in literature. I argue that the strategies used in signifying made explicit and applied to examples within the African American literary tradition serve as a propaedeutic guide to the refinement and sophistication of knowledge in both the oral and literary arenas. Such an interaction of concepts in the oral and literary domains exemplifies

Vygotsky's (1986) general genetic law of cultural development. That is, concept formation evolves from the social/interpsychological level to the individual/intrapsychological level. This evolution from the social to the individual occurred in this instance within a classroom culture that honored the prior knowledge brought by these African American adolescents while carefully designing cognitive and social supports for their apprenticeship. The instructional framework based on cultural modeling (Lee, 1993, 1995a, 1995b) draws on the interanimation of spontaneous and scientific concepts, as described by Vygotsky. The assumptions about a ZPD implicit in the instructional design take seriously the relevant prior knowledge that these African American students brought to the English class. The level of problem solving toward which the instruction aimed bridged the informal knowledge that students employed independently in circumscribed settings and formal literary constructs that were applicable across multiple settings. Studies of cultural modeling begin to address Vygotsky's claim that "Future studies should include concepts from various fields of school instruction, each set matched against a set of everyday concepts drawn from a similar area of expertise" (p. 20).

References

Abrahams, R. D. (1970). *Deep down in the jungle: Negro narrative folklore from the streets of Philadelphia*. Chicago: Aldine.

Andrews, M., & Owens, P. (1973). *Black language*. Los Angeles: Seymour-Smith.

Baker, H. (1984) *Blues, ideology and Afro-American literature: A vernacular theory*. Chicago: University of Chicago Press.

Bakhtin, M. M. (1981). *The dialogic imagination: Four essays by M. M. Bakhtin* (M. Holquist, Ed.; C. Emerson & M. Holquist, Trans.). Austin: University of Texas Press.

Bambara, T. C. (1972). My man Bovanne. In T. C. Bambera (Ed.), *Gorilla, my love* (pp. 1–10). New York: Random House.

Baugh, J. (1983). *Black street speech: Its history, structure and survival*. Austin: University of Texas Press.

Booth, W. (1974). *A rhetoric of irony*. Chicago: University of Chicago Press.

Brown, R. (1969). *Die nigger die!* New York: Dial Press.

Cazden, C. (1988). *Classroom discourse*. Portsmouth, NH: Heinemann.

Cook-Gumperz, J. (Ed.). (1986). *The social construction of literacy*. New York: Cambridge University Press.

Cooke, M. (1984). *Afro-American literature in the twentieth century: The achievement of intimacy*. New Haven, CT: Yale University Press.

Delpit, L. (1990). Language diversity and learning. In S. Hynds & D. L. Rubin (Eds.), *Perspectives on talk and learning* (pp. 247–266). Urbana, IL: National Council of Teachers of English.

Ellison, R. (1964). *Shadow and act*. New York: Random House.

Gates, H. L. (1984). The blackness of blackness: A critique of the sign and the signifying monkey. In H. L. Gates (Ed.), *Black literature and literary theory* (pp. 285–322). New York: Methuen.

Gates, H. L. (1988). *The signifying monkey: A theory of Afro-American literary criticism.* New York: Oxford University Press.

Goodlad, J. I. (1984). *A place called school: Prospects for the future.* St. Louis: McGraw-Hill.

Green, J., & Dixon, C. (1994). Talking knowledge into being: Discursive and social practices in classrooms. *Linguistics and Education*, 5, 231–239.

Heath, S. B. (1989). Oral and literate traditions among Black Americans living in poverty. *American Psychologist*, 44, 367–373.

Hurston, Z. N. (1935). *Mules and men*. New York: Harper & Row.

Hurston, Z. N. (1937/1990). *Their eyes were watching God*. New York: Harper and Row.

Hynds, S. (1989). Bringing life to literature and literature to life: Social constructs and contexts of four adolescent readers. *Research in the Teaching of English*, 23, 30–61.

Jones, G. (1991). *Liberating voices: Oral tradition in African American literature*. New York: Penguin.

Kochman, T. (Ed.). (1972). *Rappin' and stylin' out: Communication in urban Black America*. Urbana: University of Illnois Press.

La Rocha, O. D. L. (1985). The reorganization of the arithmetic practice in the kitchen. *Anthropology and Education*, 16, 193–198.

Lave, J. (1977). Cognitive consequences of traditional apprenticeship training in West Africa. *Anthropology and Education Quarterly*, 7, 177–180.

Lee, C. D. (1991, April). *Signifying as a scaffold to literary interpretation: The pedagogical implications of a form of African-American discourse*. Paper presented at the annual meeting of the American Educational Research Association, Chicago.

Lee, C. D. (1993). *Signifying as a scaffold for literary interpretation: The pedagogical implications of an African American discourse genre*. Urbana, IL: National Council of Teachers of English.

Lee, C. D. (1994). Cultural modeling in reading comprehension. Proposal submitted to the McDonnell Foundation, Cognitive Studies in Educational Practice.

Lee, C. D. (1995a). A culturally based cognitive apprenticeship: Teaching African American high school students skills in literary interpretation. *Reading Research Quarterly*, 30, 608–631.

Lee, C. D. (1995b). Signifying as a scaffold for literary interpretation. *Journal of Black Psychology*, 21(4), 357–381.

Lee, C. D. (1997). Bridging home and school literacies: Models for culturally responsive teaching: A case for African American English. In J. Flood, S. B. Heath, & D. Lapp (Eds.), *A handbook for literacy educators: Research on teaching the communicative and visual arts* (pp. 330–341). New York: Macmillan.

Leont'ev, A. N. (1981). *Problems of the development of mind*. Moscow: Progress Publishers.

Major, C. (1970) *Dictionary of Afro-American slang*. New York: International.

Michaels, S. (1986). Narrative presentations: An oral preparation for literacy with first graders. In J. Cook-Gumperz (Ed.), *The social construction of literacy* (pp. 94–116). New York: Cambridge University Press.

Mitchell-Kernan, C. (1981). Signifying, loud-talking and marking. In A. Dundes (Ed.), *Mother wit from the laughing barrel* (pp. 310–328). Englewood Cliffs, NJ: Prentice-Hall.

Nunes, T., Schliemann, A. D., & Carraher, D. W. (1993). *Street mathematics and school mathematics.* New York: Cambridge University Press.

Philips, S. U. (1985). Indian children in Anglo classrooms. In N. Wolfson & J. Manes (Eds.), *Language of inequality* (pp. 311–323). Berlin: Mouton.

Rabinowitz, P. (1987). *Before reading: Narrative conventions and the politics of interpretation.* Ithaca, NY: Cornell University Press.

Reed, H., & Lave, J. (1981). Arithmetic as a tool for investigating relations between culture and cognition. In R. Casson (Ed.), *Language, culture, and cognition: Anthropological perspectives* (pp. 437–455). New York: Macmillan.

Reed, I. (1974, June). Ishmael Reed: A self interview. *Black World*, 20–34.

Rogoff, B. (1990). *Apprenticeship in thinking.* New York: Oxford University Press.

Saville-Troike, M. (1989). *The ethnography of communication, an introduction.* New York: Basil Blackwell.

Saxe, G. B. (1988). The mathematics of child street vendors. *Child Development, 59,* 1415–1425.

Scribner, S. (1984). Studying working intelligence. In B. Rogoff & J. Lave (Eds.), *Everyday cognition: Its development in social context* (pp. 9–40). Cambridge, MA: Harvard University Press.

Smith, M. W. (1987). *Reading and teaching irony in poetry; Giving short people a reason to live.* Unpublished doctoral dissertation, University of Chicago.

Smith, M. W. (1989). Teaching the interpretation of irony in poetry. *Research in the Teaching of English, 23*(3), 254–272.

Smitherman, G. (1977). *Talkin and testifyin.* Boston: Houghton Mifflin.

Toulmin, S., Rieke, R., & Janik, A. (1984). *An introduction to reasoning.* New York: Macmillan.

Vygotsky, L. S. (1978). *Mind in society: The development of higher psychological processes* (M. Cole, V. John-Steiner, S. Scribner, & E. Souberman, Eds.). Cambridge, MA: Harvard University Press.

Vygotsky, L. S. (1986). *Thought and language* (A. Kozulin, Ed. & Trans.). Cambridge, MA: MIT Press.

Walker, A. (1982). *The color purple.* New York: Simon and Schuster.

Wertsch, J. V. (1984). The zone of proximal development: Some conceptual issues. In B. Rogoff & J. V. Wertsch (Eds.), *Children's learning in the zone of proximal development* (pp. 7–18). San Francisco: Jossey-Bass.

Wertsch, J. V., Minick, N., & Arns, F. J. (1984). The creation of context in joint problem-solving. In B. Rogoff & J. Lave (Eds.), *Everyday cognition: Its development in social context* (pp. 151–171). Cambridge, MA: Harvard University Press.

Winner, E. (1988). *The point of words: Children's understanding of metaphor and irony.* Cambridge MA: Harvard University Press.

Wright, R. (1963). *Lawd today.* New York: Walker.

10 Teachers' Developing Philosophies on Literacy and Their Use in Urban Schools

A Vygotskian Perspective on Internal Activity and Teacher Change

Arnetha F. Ball

Wertsch and Stone (1985) argue that one way to construct an integrated account of internalization is to examine an individual's emerging control of external signs. They conclude that "Vygotsky laid the groundwork for our argument, but he left many aspects of it largely undeveloped. We would argue that future work in this area would contribute significantly to our understanding of the nature and origins of internal activity" (p. 177). The purpose of this chapter is to revisit prior work on internalization and to report on recent research that contributes to our understanding of the nature and origin of internal activity. My interest in this topic applies particularly to teachers' developing perspectives on the strategic use of literacies to enhance the teaching and learning of students in urban schools (cf. Ball, 1992, 1995a, 1995b, 1999; Dyson, Gutiérrez & Stone, Lee, this volume).

In the first section of this chapter, I draw primarily on the work of Vygotsky (1981), Leont'ev (1981), Bakhtin (1981), and Wertsch (1985) to develop a model of what internalization might look like as a process and to consider the role this process might play in the preparation of teachers who are interested in teaching in urban schools. In the second section, I describe my method for studying the ways in which a set of four preservice teachers internalized new conceptions of literacy and the implications of these conceptions for teaching inner-city students. In the third section, I use the literacy histories and reflective writings of individual preservice and practicing teachers to support the development of my model. These literacy histories and reflective writings reveal the origin and nature of internal activity, providing glimpses into the worlds of these teachers' early literacy experiences and their evolving thoughts on how literacy can be used to educate their students. In the final section, I return to Vygotskian theory and explore how it helps account for internalization in the teachers' developing personal voices and their plans of action that reflect their developing commitment.

A Model of Internalization in Teacher Education Programs

The Need to Prepare Teachers to Work in Urban Schools

American public schools have had relatively little success in educating students who are poor, members of racially or ethnically marginalized groups, and speakers of first languages other than mainstream or academic English. According to Banks (1991), those individuals who have traditionally been considered minorities in this country are now becoming the majority population in many of the nation's largest cities. Although only 17% of European American students living in these larger metropolitan areas attend local public inner-city schools, more than 50% of the Latino students and 68% of the African American students living in the largest metropolitan areas attend public schools (Orfield & Reardon, 1993). When comparing these urban schools with suburban schools, Orfield and Reardon found profound differences in the quality of educational opportunity and the teaching staff, with urban schools functioning at a grossly inferior level. Given these differences, it was not surprising that Orfield and Reardon also found that students in disadvantaged schools have lower scores on standardized achievement tests and higher dropout rates than those in advantaged suburban schools. After looking closely at the nature and extent of the differences, they reached the following conclusion:

If the [urban] schools lack certified teachers, offer few academically challenging courses, and track disadvantaged students disproportionately into low-level courses; if the community is economically depressed, with few libraries, museums, and other non-school educational opportunities; and if a large number of adults with high school diplomas are unable to find adequate employment; then we cannot in good conscience claim that many disadvantaged students have simply failed to do what it takes to succeed in school. Rather, our society has failed to give them the opportunity to succeed. These students have not failed school; society has failed them. (p. 29)

Despite the considerable rhetoric about school restructuring that has emerged in the past few decades, recent research continues to indicate that African American, Latino, Native American, and some Asian

American students are faring very poorly in inner-city schools (Carnegie Council on Adolescent Development, 1989; Quality Education for Minority Project, 1990). Thus, the challenge remains for schools and other institutions to find ways to maximize the development of one of America's greatest and most underused resources: its urban youth.

The preparation of teachers to teach diverse populations in urban schools stands out as a critical area for improvement in teacher education. Orfield and Reardon's (1993) description of the current teaching force in urban schools draws attention to the need to prepare more excellent teachers who are committed to improving education for all students and the education of urban students in particular. On the one hand, suburban schools, particularly those in communities that are predominantly wealthy and White, report few teacher vacancies. On the other hand, 37% of the principals in poor inner-city schools report difficulties finding qualified teachers. Orfield and Reardon report that young teachers in these schools find fewer rewards and often consider leaving teaching, and so "schools serving poor and minority children often hire less-qualified teachers than advantaged schools.... [M]inority and low-income students tend to be in schools and school districts with ... less well prepared teachers and counselors [who have] larger class sizes" (p. 24). As these inequitable situations become more widely known and less tolerated, educational reformers are challenging teacher preparation programs to enable student teachers to work effectively with students who are culturally and linguistically diverse and who attend urban schools (Carnegie Council on Adolescent Development, 1989; Darling-Hammond, 1986; Hartshorne, 1992; Quality Education for Minority Project, 1990; Rosenholtz, 1986). In order to address this challenge and to impact the learning experiences of students attending urban schools in significant ways, it is necessary to investigate the mechanisms through which developing teachers become interested in considering the option of teaching diverse students in urban schools.

The work of Ladson-Billings (1994), Foster (1987), and others reveals that there are exemplary teachers who possess the skill and the desire to work effectively with diverse student populations. Their numbers, however, are too few. In American teacher education programs there is "presently an undisputed mismatch in the race, social-class, and language backgrounds of teachers and students in the United States" (Gomez, 1993, p. 460). Grant and Secada (1990) report that members of the predominant teaching force – young, White, middle-class females – are often assigned to classrooms and schools serving diverse student populations where their more experienced colleagues do not wish to teach. Thus, these teachers often find themselves working with students they had no intention of teaching and teaching in situations where they are least prepared to teach. More important, Grant and Secada and others have pointed out that the perspectives of many U.S. teachers can be a major barrier to the effective instruction of many students.

Pang and Sablan (1995) state that one perspective of many novice teachers that acts as a major barrier to effective instruction is the belief that many students of color are not capable of learning. This belief has an impact on teacher efficacy, an important construct in student achievement. Teacher efficacy concerns what teachers believe about their ability to teach children from various cultural and linguistic backgrounds and about their power to produce an effect on students. Pang and Sablan note that teachers with high efficacy believe that all students can be motivated, and that it is their responsibility to explore with students the tasks that will hold their attention in the learning process. In teaching literacy to diverse students in urban schools, the question becomes, how do teachers come to understand and internalize this world view on efficacy?

One way to investigate this question is to conduct research in specialized teacher education programs that focus specifically on preparing teachers to teach diverse populations. But a majority of the American teaching force will not come from these types of specialized programs because the number of these programs is few. Thus, teacher educators must give serious consideration to theoretical frameworks that can help them better prepare teachers to work effectively with diverse and urban student populations. Vygotsky's (1981) discussions on internalization account for how teachers' developing philosophies on literacy can be seen as internal activities that can become observable through the change in teachers' discourse practices over time. As developing teachers engage with theories and pedagogical approaches in teacher education programs, their considerations about teaching diverse student populations arise out of external, practical activities such as assigned readings on theory, interactive discussions, writing assignments, and practical teaching experiences.

Vygotsky argued that there is an inherent relationship between external and internal activity, but that it is a *developmental* relationship in which the major issue is how external processes are *transformed* to *create* internal processes. *Internalization* is the process through which developing teachers move beyond positions of cognitive internalization of theory and practices toward transformative positions of reflective commitment needed to guide them in their generative development as urban classroom teachers. In Leont'ev's (1981) words: "the process of internalization is not the *transferal* of an external activity to a preexisting, internal 'plane of consciousness': it is the process in which this plane is formed" (p. 57; emphasis in original). According to Vygotsky, developmental functions move from the social to the psychological plane: "First it appears between people as an interpsychological category, and then within the [adult or] child as an intrapsychological category. This is equally true with regard to voluntary attention, logical memory, the formation of concepts, and the development of volition" (p. 163). Vygotsky's notion of internalization contributes to a sociocultural theoretical perspective in that it focuses on the mechanisms that account for how literacy perspectives move from the interpsychological to the intrapsychological plane to become catalysts for generative, meaningful activity on the part of the developing teacher. I draw primarily on the work of Vygotsky, Leont'ev (1981), Bakhtin (1981), and Wertsch (1985) to build a theoretical model that can help explain teachers' developing perspectives on literacy as they consider the option of teaching in urban schools in a course designed to facilitate this consideration.

The overarching theoretical frame for this work is that of *social constructivism*, a theory about knowledge and learning that describes what knowing is and how one comes to know. Knowledge is temporary, developmental, internally constructed, and socially and culturally mediated. From this perspective, learning is a self-regulatory process of struggling with the conflict between existing personal models of the world and discrepant new insights, constructing new representations and models of reality as a human meaning-making venture with culturally developed tools and symbols, and further negotiating such meaning through social activity and discourse. According to Fosnot (1996), a constructivist approach

gives learners the opportunity for concrete, contextually meaningful experience through which they can search for patterns, raise their own questions, and construct their own models, concepts, and strategies. The classroom in this model is seen as a minisociety, a community of learners engaged in activity, discourse, and reflection. The traditional hierarchy of teacher as the autocratic knower and learner as the unknowing, controlled subject studying to learn what the teacher knows begins to dissipate as teachers assume more of a facilitator's role and learners take on more ownership of the ideas. Indeed, autonomy, mutual reciprocity of social relations, and empowerment become the goals. (p. ix)

Within this broader frame, I draw on the work of Bakhtin (1981, 1986) to consider ways in which semiotic systems in general, and language (both written and oral) in particular, can serve as a means for mediating human activity (see also Wells, this volume). I also draw on the work of Leont'ev

(1981), who discusses activity – such as the activities that took place in my classroom – as setting where the processes that people use to form real connections with the world evolve. Leont'ev asserts that

human psychology is concerned with the activity of concrete individuals, which takes place either collectively – i.e., jointly with other people – or in a situation in which the subject deals directly with the surrounding world of objects – e.g., at the potter's wheel or the writer's desk.... [I]f we remove human activity from the system of social relationships and social life, it would not exist.... [T]he human individual's activity is the system of social relations. It does not exist without these relations. (pp. 46–47)

Leont'ev emphasized the fact that intellectual activity, such as engagement with theory in teacher education programs, is not isolated from practical activity, which includes ordinary daily activity as well as activities that are generally counted as intellectual. This notion is particularly germane to considerations of literacy socialization on the part of developing teachers. As preservice and practicing teachers come into teacher education programs with their own literacy histories, they discuss ideas interactively; challenge preexisting assumptions; teach, write, and read new information; and reflect on theories and practice within the learning context. Thus, their learning is activity based. This activity occurs with the support of instructors as more knowledgeable others, with exemplary teachers, and with peers.

According to Wertsch (1985), three themes underlie a Vygotskian social constructivist theoretical perspective. First, individual internal activity can be understood as it is situated in a broader social, historical, and evolutionary context. This notion seems especially important when considering the development of individual philosphies concerning literacy. This development occurs within particular social, historical, and evolutionary contexts that influence how individual philosophies concerning literacy will be shaped and enacted.

Second, learning is facilitated through the assistance of more knowledgeable members of the community and culture. For Vygotsky (1978) the zone of proximal development is the distance between the actual level of development and the level of potential development as determined through problem solving under the influence or guidance of a more knowledgeable other. This problem-solving guidance can come in the form of advanced theoretical considerations that are presented within a teacher education program. By extension, the development of teachers' philosophies on literacy can be altered by contact with more knowledgeable perspectives presented to them within their zone of proximal

development in the form of inputs from teacher educators, from theoretical readings, or from discussions and interactions with colleagues
in teacher education programs when negotiated within the context of
reflective journal writing and discussions that extend teachers' zones of
proximal development. Forman and Cazden (1985) examine the cognitive value of peer interaction and conclude that not only is work with
more knowledgeable others important, but also that peer relationships
can function as intermediate transforming contexts between social and
external interactions and the individual's developing inner voice.

Third, human action is mediated by signs and tools – primarily psychological tools such as language. The facilitation of language use within
a sociocultural environment, then, is the predominant means by which
people make sense or meaning. In my research, teachers' written reflections and oral discussions served this function as preservice and practicing
teachers used these methods to consider their developing philosophies
about literacy in their own lives and in the teaching of others.

I also focus on Bakhtin's (1981, 1986) writings that relate to meaning-
making through language use. Three key concepts underscore Bakhtin's
notions about semiotic mediation: dialogicality, utterance, and voice
(Wertsch, 1991). *Dialogicality* refers to "the ways in which one speaker's
concrete utterances come into contact with . . . the utterances of another"
(Wertsch, 1991, p. 54). *Utterance* refers to Bakhtin's notion that meaning
does not reside in words; rather, it resides in the ways in which words are
used in particular contexts. A key notion for Bakhtin is that "any true understanding is dialogic in nature" (Wertsch, 1991, p. 54). In essence, then,
for Bakhtin, true understanding occurs when speakers can effectively orient themselves with respect to one another in the broader context of a
conversational exchange (see Dyson, this volume). *Voice* pertains to the
role of language in constructing meaning. Voice applies to written as well
as spoken language and relates to point of view: "it is concerned with
the broader issues of a speaking subject's perspective, conceptual horizon,
intention and world view" (Wertsch, 1991, p. 51).

As preservice and practicing teachers come into teacher education programs with their own literacy histories, they discuss, read, write, reflect on
theories and practice, and challenge preconceived notions about literacy
within the learning context. Within such an environment where it is safe
to take risks, their utterances come into contact with the theoretical and
practical utterances of others. Understanding begins to occur when these
teachers begin to orient themselves with respect to the theory and practical
ideas that are presented. Bakhtin's assertions about voice have significant

implications for working with preservice and practicing teachers' developing philosophies on literacy. This work suggests that merely attempting to impart literacy skill-and-drill strategies to teachers is not sufficient to develop true understanding or commitment. When preservice and practicing teachers take on the meaning of theoretical and practical concepts at an intrapsychological level, Bakhtin argues, true understanding will be dialogic in nature, such as being constructed in collaboration with instructors, students, texts, and other developing professionals. Teachers' developing philosophies concerning literacy are shaped to a great extent not by what professional educators attempt to impart to them but by what educators understand about their thinking, and how they mutually (or dialogically) shape their interactions around the theory, concepts, and ideas that they focus on inside and outside class. Oral language in the form of the interactive discussions that take place in class and written language in the form of reflective written texts play key roles in this process of internalization.

Classroom socialization is an important part of this teacher development process. As preservice and practicing teachers participate in planned activities and events, they construct meanings about the tasks, responsibilities, and commitments that are required of a successful teacher. Throughout this process language plays an important role, not only in teachers' learning about the real-world meanings and social functions of language forms, but also in the development of their philosophies concerning literacy and its use in their future classrooms (Freeman, 1992; Minami & Ovando, 1995; Tardif, 1991). Based on the processes of socialization that occurred in my classroom, I noted that three profiles of developing teachers emerged: (1) teachers who started the course with a commitment to the issue of diversity and whose commitment seemed to become more evident throughout the semester; (2) transitioning teachers who started the course without a commitment to the issue of diversity and who displayed evidence that such a commitment was developing; and (3) teachers who started the course without a commitment to the issue of diversity and whose attitude did not appear to change over the course of the semester. After an initial analysis of my data, I decided to focus specifically on the transitioning teachers because they were being taught within their zone of proximal development. According to Vygotsky, the best instruction occurs when it proceeds ahead of development, when it awakens and rouses to life those functions that are in the process of maturing. In this way, instruction plays an extremely important role in development. This phenomenon was most evident in the transitioning teachers.

One primary goal of my research was to create a model that helped explain how teachers' developing philosophies on literacy serve as internal activities in which teachers move toward transformative positions of reflective commitment needed to guide them in their generative development as urban classroom teachers. Through studies of the transitioning teachers' change in discourse practices over time, I was able to observe their considerations about literacy as they engaged with theories and pedagogical approaches to teaching diverse students. The model depicted in Figure 10.1 was developed to show the transitioning discourse practices that characterize the oral and written language of those teachers who were considering how to use literacy strategically to teach more effectively in urban schools. My goal here is to provide a model for considering how the evolving language practices of teachers who are involved in teacher education programs reflect their internal movement beyond cognitive internalization of theory to become reflective, thoughtful, committed action agents with a personal voice to direct their generative development as urban teachers.

Within their zones of proximal development, these teachers showed a willingness and a readiness to engage in the activities that I designed to facilitate the consideration of issues relevant to using literacy effectively to teach urban students. As shown in the *legend insert* of Figure 10.1, the classroom activities that I designed (including the generation of narratives of their own literacy experiences, questioning and challenging their prior perspectives on literacy, reflective writing in response to the theory that was introduced, teacher research projects, and planning and implementing teaching strategies) were the driving forces that led students to engage in some progressively complex cognitive activities (e.g., raised levels of metacognitive awareness, increased personal involvement with issues of urban education, greater consideration of becoming agents of change in urban schools, and new theorizing about what can and should take place within these schools). Risk taking increased in these classrooms as students felt freer to seek out verification and validation of their ideas and beliefs from the theory, from the instructor, and from their peers. As illustrated in the legend insert in Figure 10.1, the cognitive activity that was taking place was revealed in the teachers' discourse practices (including their increased use of reflection, introspection, and critique and an emerging personal voice on important issues raised in class). According to the legend insert in Figure 10.1, future classroom activities were influenced by the increased use of these types of discourse practices within the learning environment.

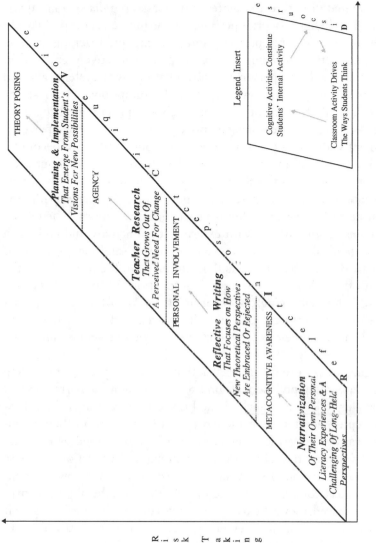

Figure 10.1 The process of internalization that takes place within the zone of proximal development.

As illustrated in Figure 10.1, interactive classroom discussions, questioning and challenging of prior perspectives on literacy, reflective writing activities, teacher research projects, and planning and teaching projects all constitute activity systems that participants collectively engaged in initially at external interpersonal levels. These activity systems allowed teachers to challenge their own beliefs and assumptions. These activities acted as catalysts to facilitate increasingly complex internal cognitive activities – including raised metacognitive awareness, increased personal involvement with issues of urban education, consideration of becoming agents of change within urban schools, and theory posing about their visions for new possibilities for education within urban schools. Thus, internalization is viewed as part of a larger picture concerned with how consciousness emerges out of human social life and activity. The overall development scheme begins with external social activity and ends with internal individual activity. Vygotsky's account of semiotic mechanisms provides the bridge that connects the external with the internal and the social with the individual. Thus, my investigations of the teachers' language use – their emerging discourse practices – provides a bridge that allows us to connect the external with the internal and the social with the individual and, to some extent, to observe it through discourse analysis.

Building on the works of the theorists discussed earlier, my research was designed to explore the internal activity of preservice and practicing teachers' developing philosophies on literacy through the narratives and texts that they created – which yielded powerful disclosures about how they conceptualize literacy in their personal worlds and in their teaching. The various texts that they created over time served as evidence of their developing thoughts, providing thoughtful reflections as these teachers moved beyond interpsychological external activity toward an intrapsychological commitment to action. As these teachers' perspectives on literacy evolved, they articulated reflective comments concerning their experiences and the theory they encountered, giving narrative form to their experiences – to shape them as they critiqued them, transformed them, and applied them to the teaching and learning of students in urban schools.

How Teachers' Reflective Writing Supported the Development of the Model

Among educators in the United States, literacy histories and the reflective writings of individual learners, whether the normal course of formal education or in informal or adult education programs, have become extremely popular (Brodkey, 1994; Evans, 1993; Florio-Ruane, 1994; Knowles & Cole, 1994; Ritchie, 1993; Soliday, 1994). These autobiographical and narrative sketches often indicate the ways in which individuals developed their perspectives on literacy and their interest in reading or writing, as well as the ways in which they did not develop either habit with much enthusiasm or skill. In this chapter such histories are juxtaposed with (1) teachers' reflective writing about their evolving perspectives on literacy to portray how teachers demonstrated the process of internalization and (2) teachers' shared reflections on readings they encountered during the course of a semester that helped to alter their philosophies on literacy. These teachers shared reports on how encounters with theoretical readings (or with more experienced others) were used to help them consider the challenges of teaching different types of students. These writings reveal the mechanisms that stimulate internal activity as preservice and practicing teachers considered their developing perspectives on teaching in urban schools. These data are shared with the assumption that teachers' self-reports can be used to help capture the processes of internalization that they experienced.

Numerous studies have suggested that ideologies as well as practices associated with literacy experiences help to shape an individual's attitudes and emotions with long-lasting impact. Research documents how early formal educational experiences with literacy have seemed to shut down learning in ways that came to light only years later, during periods of duress or at times of critical need. For example, Walker (1981) documents the case of Native Americans whose early literacy learning experiences within schools and within some family contexts caused many Cherokees to refuse literacy in English. Later in life, however, these students shared reports of developing a range of literacy abilities in a "sudden revelation" (p. 172) that was linked back to learning that took place during their early literacy experiences. Similarly, some studies document positive emotions linked to literacy learning that continue to be associated with positive feelings toward literacy during later periods of life (Brodkey, 1994; Thomas, 1996).

Other studies document the fixed negative associations that come with literacy views. Studies on college students enrolled in introductory composition, reading, and study strategies courses tell about their negative memories of literacy learning and the influences those memories have on their current attitudes and behaviors toward literacy (Clery & Pikrone, 1991; Fox, 1992). Many other individuals have what amounts to positive, negative, or neutral perceptions concerning the merits or pleasures of reading and writing.

In this chapter I draw on the literacy histories and journal entries of individual participants in teacher education programs in three settings to investigate the changes these teachers went through as they internalized theory and then moved beyond internalization to positions of commitment to using that theory as change agents. These writings were used to open up the teachers' previously held views on literacy and its use when teaching. In three settings – two in South Africa and one in the United States, highly varied on many dimensions – I carried out research to investigate my developing ideas on internalization, with the belief that teachers' interpersonal encounters with theory, coupled with opportunities for interactive discussions, deep reflection, and strategic sharing, can result in intrapersonal transformations in these teachers' perspectives on literacy and its use when working in urban schools.

Method

Setting

This study draws on my research with teachers in the United States and South Africa, two countries with similarities and differences that make them well suited for this study. Both countries are seeking ways to educate more effectively large numbers of urban students who are culturally and linguistically different from the dominant culture, from their teachers, and from the students for whom the majority of instructional materials and school expectations are tailored. With similar histories of social, economic, and educational inequalities in the education of marginalized populations, both countries now perceive the state of education for diverse populations in poverty areas to be in crisis. With an end to official forms of segregation and a need for massive reconstruction of their education systems, both countries have the potential to demonstrate an expanded vision of the possibilities for change in poor and urban schools.

The United States in particular has the potential to learn a great deal from a close examination of the teacher education programs in South Africa, which has a population of over 30 million people who have historically been undereducated. With a recent end to apartheid and an emerging crisis that now exists in the education system in general and in teacher education programs specifically, South Africa is seeking innovative ways to facilitate the development of teachers who are committed to teaching diverse populations. As South African classrooms become increasingly diverse, educators are challenged daily to use literacies in strategic and thoughtful ways to implement instructional programs for culturally and linguistically diverse students. In many cases there are mismatches between the economic, social, cultural, and linguistic backgrounds of the students and their teachers. So drastic have been the changes in the education system in South Africa that some preservice teachers in my classes have decided to abandon teaching as a career because of poor preservice preparation for emerging teaching challenges and because the job provides too few rewards in relation to its responsibilities. Those who elect to persist with careers in education often voice an enthusiasm for confronting the challenges of multilingualism and multiculturalism that face them. They express a commitment not only to working with diverse student populations, but also to drawing on their students' cultural and linguistic resources to bring about school success for all students.

The data were collected from students who participated in three teacher education programs. One secondary teacher education program was offered at a major university located in the midwestern region of the United States. This program enrolled approximately 500 students each year, the majority of whom came from White working-class and middle-class homes. Of the students enrolled in my course that year, 58% were female and 42% were male. Approximately 86% of these students came from nearby cities within the state, and 14% came from other states throughout the country. Approximately 74% of the students came from European American backgrounds, 15% were minorities, and 11% were unidentified.

The second teacher education program was offered at a major college of teacher education located in the Guatang province of South Africa. This program was designed to prepare teachers to teach in primary and secondary schools. It enrolled approximately 200 students annually, the majority of whom came from White working-class and middle-class homes. Over 90% of the students came from nearby cities and townships within the province. Fewer than 10% came from other locations throughout the country. Approximately 84% of the students came from English and Afrikaans backgrounds, and approximately 16% were from other cultural and linguistic groups.

The third teacher education program was offered at a major university located in the Western Cape province of South Africa. Although the university offered a traditional teacher education program, the students enrolled in this course were current teachers who were seeking further certification in a Further Diploma in Education program. This teacher education program was designed specifically to prepare teachers to teach in multilingual and multicultural schools. This new program enrolled 36 students during its first term. Over 85% of the students came from nearby townships within the province and came from Black African language speaking backgrounds. Fewer than 15% came from locations throughout the city that had been designated as living areas for "coloureds" during the former system of apartheid. These students had English- and Afrikaans-speaking backgrounds.

For many students in both the United States and South Africa, the college campus environment was their first experience with a racially heterogeneous population. Students often complete their elementary and secondary education without having attended a school enrolling sizable numbers of students of other races and without living in a neighborhood where other races are well represented. A majority of White students traveled from racially homogeneous neighborhoods and schools to college campuses where they were unprepared for the racial diversity they encountered. Most students of color had grown up in equally homogeneous neighborhoods. Upon entering my teacher education course, students were asked to describe the population of students they envisioned teaching. Most replied that they would like to teach students who were very similar to themselves. A small percentage wished to teach students who were very different from themselves in racial, ethnic, academic, or socioeconomic status.

Course Structure

Over the course of 3 years, 50 U.S. teachers and 50 South African teachers agreed to participate in my study. The course in which the study took place focused on theoretical considerations and practical strategies for using literacy in the content areas to teach all students more effectively, including students from poor, urban, and diverse backgrounds. In each course, I introduced the teachers to a sociocultural theoretical perspective (Vygotsky, 1978; Wertsch, 1985) in addition to a wide range of other readings. The course drew heavily on discussions of Vygotsky's concept of internalization.

Each week, preservice and practicing teachers integrated their own teaching and learning experiences with discussions and writings about linking theory and practice when teaching poor, urban, and diverse student populations. Both before and after their engagement with readings, discussions, teaching, and teacher research assignments, teachers wrote reflective narrative essays. The topics that these essays focused on included the students' personal experience with literacy, their developing definitions of literacy, their reactions to theoretical readings, and their developing philosophies about the use of literacy in their current and future classrooms. Throughout the course, these teachers kept journals reflecting on the readings and their teaching practices. Additionally, we made audiotapes of dialogues about their actual and planned application of theory in their classrooms.

Data Sources

The data collected from the students in all three programs included narrative essays of their own literacy autobiographies, transcripts of classroom and small group discussions, and journal entries and reflections written in response to class readings, including Vygotsky's (1978) writings on internalization.

Results

In the next section I report on the case studies of four students: two South African and two American preservice and practicing teachers. All four were from the group I labeled *transitioning teachers*, that is, those who started the course without a firm commitment to issues of diversity and who then showed evidence that such a commitment was developing. The two South African students are Edward, a 20-year-old male of English descent, and Dingani, a 25-year-old male who spoke a Black African language. The two American students are Mieko, a 26-year-old Asian American female, and Jim, a 23-year-old European American male. I will trace their transformation by looking at their views of literacy in their early literacy experiences, their reflections on the course readings, and their definitions of literacy at the end of the course. These three data points illustrate the way in which the teachers internalized new understandings of literacy and the implications of these conceptions for teaching diverse populations of students.

Autobiographies of Early Literacy Experiences

Preservice and practicing teachers began the course by sharing their personal literacy experiences. As shown in my model, this was done in an effort to bring to conscious awareness various experiences that influenced the development of their views concerning literacy. These experiences varied from student to student, yet the process of reflection enabled each of them to identify key events in their personal histories that affected their feelings about reading and writing.

Edward came from a family that emphasized sports rather than reading. His school experiences also did not encourage him to embrace literacy: "Within school my desire to share my writing was disregarded, as the time limit was placed before my personal wants. As school literature went, I despised reading the texts placed in front of me by most of my teachers. Up until now, I still hate reading short stories and I am frightened off by South African authors such as Alan Paton who was introduced to us in Standard Five [the equivalent of the U.S. fourth grade]." His high school experiences were little more encouraging, save for one teacher who recommended books for him to read and who encouraged him to write poetry.

Dingani had similar experiences, coming from a home with few books and experiencing reading as tedious in the primary years because of the instructional emphasis on memorization and choral reading. However, he said, in high school he developed an interest in reading because he realized that "reading could help me to develop my spoken English. I started reading African literature, especially the books written by Ngungi wa Twona, Chinua Achebe, etcetera. I also read books on the South African situation, though it was a risk because some of these books were banned. I read much and as a result I can assume that my language has developed." Despite the fact that Dingani had poor experiences with reading in his primary years, he nevertheless developed an interest in reading at the secondary school level that has supported him in his language and literacy development.

Mieko, in contrast, was an avid reader as a child:

I remember the little fantasies I would immerse myself in as I'd read about the adventures of those wonderful characters in the land of Oz. One of the worst disasters I was to experience in my childhood descended upon me the day I read the ninth and *last* volume of these great stories. I was devastated to find that my excursions with the Strawman and Tinman were over – I had lost my friends. Such was my dedication to my books in those early years.

This interest flagged briefly in high school, then was rekindled in college and was sustained in the years thereafter.

Jim was an equally enthusiastic reader as a child, but he preferred comic book heroes such as Alley Oop and Spiderman to literary characters. His first literary hero was a rural boy like himself, Pinch, whose cleverness helped him prosper in spite of his initial poverty. Jim's school experiences, however, did not build on this appreciation for reading:

The fourth grade was a rough year for me. I strongly disliked my teacher. In my eyes she was sarcastic and discriminatory and lacked compassion. I composed a poem about her one day. In the bathroom I shared it with all the boys in my class. It was vile; the most damaging line contained "she has no brain and has no heart." This was mailed home to my parents. A week later disquisition ensued in the family room during prime time TV hours. This was always a sign of serious trouble. My punishment was to memorize two poems a week from *The Best Loved Poems of the American People*. . . . It was a long time after reading Pinch before I read another book in its entirety. On a family vacation during the sixth grade I read *A Wrinkle in Time*. The messages about conformity and inner-voice were cached in my memory for nearly two decades. Recently during a mid-morning coffee break in Silicon Valley, images of the monolithic society described in that children's novel poured into my head. The horror of it paralleled my life completely. What I had read has helped in the difficult decision about a career change.

Jim's autobiography recounts early life experiences that were filled with literacy-related activities that took place at his father's knee. Growing up in rural America, Jim recounted the joys of reading books about characters who were much like himself and the sadness of a literacy-related punishment for using his literacy skills to speak out against a disliked teacher. All these rich literacy experiences helped to sustain Jim as he was called upon to make some difficult career discussions later in life.

Each participant in my course engaged in this activity of reflection in an autobiography of literacy in order to bring to a metacognitive level those experiences that influenced their own literacy attitudes and to allow them an opportunity to question and challenge some of their own long-held perspectives that they may not have been consciously aware of. This activity served as a readiness exercise to prepare these students to consider new and different perspectives, attitudes, and visions for literacy and its uses.

Reflective Thoughts on Vygotsky and Other Course Readings

After sharing their personal literacy histories and other reflections, the teachers were exposed to assigned readings that were selected to broaden their views on literacy. One topic that we considered in great detail was Vygotsky's notion of internalization as it applies to teachers' developing philosophies about the strategic use of literacy to enhance the learning of students in poor and urban schools. The teachers came to realize that the process of internalization is concerned with internal activity that can result in transformations in which theory moves from being an *external activity* (primarily concerned with social processes between teacher and learner) to an *internal activity* (in which knowledge becomes one's own). Exposure to Vygotskian theory; other carefully selected readings, practical strategies, and reflective writing; and interactive discussions that allowed them to question and challenge their perspectives served as the catalysts for transformative internal activity. According to the students, the reflective writing played a significant role in this process. Their responses imply thoughtful consideration and keen understanding of the concept as it applied to their own teaching and learning and the learning of their students. Edward wote:

Vygotsky taught me that the pupils' mental abilities are important and that they can be extended. Learning begins outside of school and is a continuous cycle that must not become static. Too often, this [becoming static] is what I see happening to many gifted pupils as they are kept behind and restricted by the age levels and development of other pupils. It is also important to note the individual pupils' potential. In our readings, collaboration is seen as an asset as opposed to a liability. This is so true. This idea seems to permeate throughout all of the articles.

Dingani reflected on his reading of Vygotsky along with other theorists from the course:

When you bring Vygotsky (1981) and Cummins (1994) together, they highlight a very crucial issue which has been neglected in Department of Education and Training (DET) schools: that critical literacy and knowledge are attained as a result of interaction between adults and students and that this interaction is very important for the development of literacy. I also found Hudelson's (1994) article incredible in its proposed strategies for second language literacy development. I have learned that teachers must create environments that are conducive to learning and that educators must create a literate classroom environment that will instill confidence in the pupils. Also I have learned that a new role can be played by collaboration in the learning process. This could be especially helpful in the former Department of Education and Training (DET) schools, which were meant for blacks. This collaborative learning can help bring about real learning in these schools. For example, in DET schools teachers are seen as the only people who possess knowledge and the peer groups are seen as blank slates. Collaborative learning could change this. Hudelson (1994) suggests how this might be practically implemented through the strategy of utilizing dialog writing.

Mieko shared the following reflective comments concerning her readings of Vygotsky and others:

When I think about this notion of internalization and combine it with our reading of Nieto's article on bilingual education, I inevitably reflected on the nature of my own early education, and was shocked to realize that my own learning had been an internalization process and an "immersion" experience. Living in Panama, I knew only Spanish when I began second grade at St. Catherine's, an American school where most of my classmates and all of my teachers were native English speakers with little or no knowledge of Spanish. I eventually learned to communicate in English, as young minds are apt to do. But had this internalizing and the process of becoming proficient in English taken place at the expense of failing to develop a voice? Like the Chinese girl in "The Woman Warrior," I likened speaking or reading to an audience to running through a gauntlet of painful and unrelenting words. I was ashamed of my voice and my heavily accented English, and so I spoke only under duress. I wholeheartedly agree with Nieto (1992) and her research. Children need to feel comfortable and to make the most of the language they already know before they are exposed to instruction in a foreign language. Their development is otherwise invariably stunted as they struggle to suppress those differences that set them apart from their peers.

Jim shared the following insights in his reflections on his readings of Vygotsky and others:

I would like to focus on internalizing two specific theories in literacy which will directly influence decision making in my instruction. The first will be striving to give voice to the voiceless (Bakhtin, 1986; McElroy-Johnson, 1993) through building the confidence and self-esteem of every student. And the second will be to help students to bridge societal gaps to be able to communicate effectively in the vernacular of the poorer structure of our society (Gee, 1989).... I hope to move beyond the instructional model which I observed all through high-school and college. I plan to view my students as a whole and not just as a learner of math.

These reflections reveal that all of these teachers were affected by Vygotsky in equally profound yet different ways. Edward was impressed with the idea that "learning begins outside of school and is a continuous cycle that must not become static." Dingani was struck with the notion that teachers must have strong personal relationships with their students. In a personal communication he extended this statement, adding that this relationship building is necessary for teachers to be able to plan appropriate literacy activities for their students. Dingani was also deeply impressed with the concepts of critical literacy and collaboration as useful mechanisms for improving the educational plight of students of color who are educated in the former DET schools, which were meant for Blacks. Mieko came to realize that her own early educational experiences were a process of internalization and an "immersion" experience. This realization solidified her commitment to the notion that children need to feel comfortable and to make the most of the language they already know before they are exposed to instruction in a foreign language. And finally, Jim was impressed with the simple idea that internalization is making a body of information an integral part of an individual – whether that individual is a teacher or a student. This realization solidified his commitment to move beyond the instructional model that he observed throughout his years as a high school and college student. He planned to view his students as whole individuals and not merely as students who come to his classroom for instruction in mathematics.

Changes That Occurred in the Students' Philosophies and Definitions of Literacy

As a result of being exposed to the readings of Vygotsky and others, and of having opportunities to reflect on them, discuss them, complete teacher research projects on topics that interested them, and apply the principles to their teaching and learning, these teachers began to internalize useful knowledge; as a result, their perspectives on literacy began to broaden. In addition, these teachers began to develop their own voices that reflected their evolving perspectives. One critical result of this internalization process was that they no longer simply parroted back the information that they had read. Instead, after internalizing the information, these teachers began to express their own developing definitions of literacy and their emerging philosophies about its use. They also began to share other important insights that they were gaining of their own. Edward told of the changes that were taking place in his philosophy on literacy. He then went on to share his changing perspectives on other language-related issues, like the notion of one language being superior to another, which he no longer considered a viable option:

My definition of literacy has changed. My definition of a literate person within the South African context now is not only someone who can read and write, but someone who can read and write and communicate in English and in one's mother tongue in order to be able to contribute to society in an educated manner and to improve one's individual quality of life.... My philosophy about using literacy in my classroom has also changed. Now I am more interested in using my pupils and their environment as my resources, making literacy relevant and functional as well as interesting.

Dingani shared his changing perspectives on critical literacy, which requires an individual to apply his or her literacy learning in meaningful ways outside schools:

In my view, literacy now means the ability for one to read purposefully and with understanding in his or her language of learning. Again, in order for him/her to be called literate he/she has to read the text and read between the lines. This will enable the learner to exploit the resources around him in an attempt to formulate constructive alternatives.

My philosophy on the use of literacy is that it has to produce critical thinkers and creative citizens. This, in a way, entails that literacy must be offering something to people that is worthwhile.... Literacy is something that needs to be shared to help others develop personally, socially, intellectually, and otherwise.

Mieko's definition of literacy originally referred to the ability to read and understand the ideas that the author is trying to get across and be able to express one's ideas in writing. It changed, however, to accommodate literate thinking in math, her specialty area:

I now realize that literacy is not only the ability to express one's mathematical reasoning in writing, it is the way in which writing helps students understand what they're thinking as well as the limitations in their knowledge on a topic. More importantly, perhaps, literacy, for me, now involves students' group discussions on an assigned problem. If students are able to work in groups, discussing strategies, comparing different solutions, explaining concepts to each other as each one understands it. This, I believe, is one of the best and more effective ways to learn math.

Jim's definition of literacy originally included being able to read graphs, find meaning, and interpretation. By the end of the course, it also included teaching beyond application to reach for understanding and the development of a personal voice on the part of his students:

After the readings, I am coming to realize that to be literate in mathematical situations, one must be able to interpret the materials as well, including graphs, charts, and tables. One must also be able to construct informative reports which call for the interpretation of this mathematical data. This requires making meaning or internalization on the part of the student.... [T]he goal in our schools must be to teach beyond application and reach for understanding. To be able to read a graph to find meaning and then write an interpretation of what is being represented, this is the sort of skill that will be useful again and again.... Only a small fraction of my students will work with complex mathematics to construct informational graphs and tables as part of their adult lives. But the majority will be at an advantage when they have the ability to read and interpret mathematical information: when they are able to question what is being presented and derive their own meaning.

In each case, internalization on the part of these preservice and practicing teachers involved the development of a personal voice on issues related to the teaching and learning of literacy. Based on what I have seen in the data thus far, I propose that when internalization is taking place, then and only then will the innovative and personal voices of teachers begin to emerge: voices that are their own. As these teachers begin to move beyond quoting the words of theorists to populate the words of others with their own intentions, when they can appropriate the words and adapt them to their own purposes, then we have evidence that internalization is occurring.

This development of a personal voice is evidence that internal activity is taking place within the teachers themselves. Before this point in our course, the words existed in other people's mouths, in other people's contexts, serving other people's intentions (Bakhtin, 1986). These teachers were taking the theories and suggested practice of others and making them their own – combining the utterances of others with their own utterances. Students in teacher education programs must move beyond simply parroting information to teachers to achieve what Wertsch (1991) refers to as *appropriation*, a process dependent on how one can take something that belongs to others and make it one's own. From this perspective, internalization involves an interaction among thought, speech, and action in which ideas and activities become, at least in part, one's own: "The word in language is half someone else's. It becomes 'one's own' only when the speaker populates it with his own intention, his own accent, when he appropriates the word, adapting it to his own semantic and expressive intentions" (Bakhtin, 1981, p. 293). Internalization as appropriation is thus a property of action in which developing teachers populate theory and suggested practices with their own intentions as they develop a voice of their own and move from this point to generate meaningful activity based on their convictions.

Personal Voice That Emerges in Students' Final Reflections

After spending many classroom hours discussing sociocultural theory and writing reflectively on their developing ideas, students began to bridge their old perspectives and new information. The four teachers in this study provided final reflections on the links that they forged, on their continuing commitment to teaching, and on their emerging thoughts about literacy and its use in diverse classrooms. Although he had questioned the notion from time to time, Edward linked old experiences with new deliberations and concluded that he still wanted to teach:

Yes, I still want to be a teacher. I must admit that through the years [that] I have been [in this teacher education program], I have sometimes questioned my reasons for being here. That reason began when I was in Grade One and I had a teacher who was interested in me and created and instilled a love of learning within me. I must say I've been lucky in having had the pick of the crop teacher-wise. Another reason I have gone into teaching is because I have always been the quiet underdog in the classroom without much say or power in the classroom. I want to change that. I want to make a difference and help pupils like me to break the shackles imposed on me by a conservative African society. I am . . . more determined because I plan to use all that I have learned to stand-up for my beliefs, as they can only help the pupils and help me to not get stuck in a traditional classroom rut.

Dingani reflected on this class as a worthwhile educational experience and linked it to his emerging philosophy on literacy:

At first I felt literacy was the ability to read and write. That definition broadened to include the ability to exploit the resources around people in order to make them understandable. . . . Now my philosophical views are that literacy must in all respects equip people with all the skills that will enable them to cope with the challenges of the 21st century. For one to be literate, one must be in a position to exploit all possible means to interpret or approach any given task. Once the person can use those techniques every time, that, in my view point, reflects literacy.

Mieko linked her reading experiences in this class with her continuing search for ways to encourage thinking on the part of her students:

Andrea Fishman's *Amish Literacy* supports my developing voice on my rejection of direct instruction. I agree with her assertion that the mode of instruction presently prevalent in America's high schools is outdated. Direct instruction works for Amish students, and it worked for mainstream society half a century ago. But it is inappropriate for today's schools. Students in my classroom do not know how to *think*, and this "lack of thinking" is fostered in direct instructional classrooms. I have a good feeling for what does not work and in what direction I must proceed to encourage my students to think, but I'm not sure how I will apply this. I've tried to include a lot of group work in my class, but I have a feeling there's a lot more structure I must supply in their group problem sessions. I'm just not sure how.

Jim forged links between his own developing experiences and his desires to encourage development on the part of his students:

I suppose that my earlier view of literacy was very narrow when beginning this class. My definition of literature was "the ability to read and write well enough to function in society at the socio-economic level one desires." Now I still believe being literate is to be able to communicate as our daily functioning requires. But I have expanded my concept of literacy. . . . People must also learn to construct these tools of communication. These skills did not occur to me before as a part of literacy. But the readings for this class, and particularly the ethnography "Growing Up Literate" has made it clear to me that people are required to complete standardized forms and use tables and charts in order to meet many of the logistical demands of society. There are forms at social services offices, bus tables to read, etc., which were essential to the survival of the very poor.

Of course, I'd like to think that I am not educating students to merely function at the lower socio-economic levels of our society. That is why probably the most significant insight which I have gained about literacy in this course is the idea that a certain style of teaching can give "voice to the voiceless." Acquired literacy can give a learner the confidence and skills to verbalize their own thoughts and beliefs. This is a level of empowerment for the individual which I had not considered being teachable. I guess I was taught as a child to question, and to read analytically, but I wasn't aware of an effort to educate people in a way which encourages liberation of the inner-voice. I imagine my educators were much more interested in controlling than liberating me.

I now realize that a people without voice is the definition of oppression. Perhaps the most valuable thing we can do as new educators is make a career long commitment to developing skills which encourage our students to express inner voice. If disadvantaged sectors of our society are to raise themselves from situations of economic, social, and educational poverty, they will require a voice.

Discussion

When preservice and practicing teachers first enter my course, most of them freely admit that they have given very little conscious consideration to (1) their own philosophies about literacy and the impact it has had on their personal lives, (2) the role that their past literacy histories play in their developing philosophies about literacy, and (3) their current commitment to considering ways to use literacy strategically to effectively teach students from poor, urban, and diverse populations. On entering my course, students are invited to consider the challenge of teaching students from different backgrounds. They engage with important issues through interpersonal and socially mediated forums, including individual and shared reflections on these issues, written engagement with carefully designed prompts on the topics, and discussions that cause them to consider these issues and to question and challenge their prior perspectives. Exposure to theoretical readings and practical activities take place during the course to engage students in dialogic conversations that can impact their thoughts on issues of teaching and diversity.

As a result of these engagements, information that was once represented on an external level (the theories and teaching strategies of others) begins to take on personal meaning for the students and interacts with students' prior perspectives to create new perspectives. As Leont'ev (1981) said, "the process of internalization is not the transferal of an external activity to a preexisting, internal 'plane of consciousness': it is the process in which this plane is formed" (p. 57). Internalization is the process of coming to understand something independently of someone else's thoughts or understandings. It is the understanding of something in one's own mind. When an individual has internalized an idea or activity, she has truly grasped the concept and is able to explain it clearly. When someone has internalized something, he can go beyond the initial idea or activity and beyond his own previous levels of functioning to expand on the concept, relate it to new situations, and act on this understanding with personal conviction.

The study reported in this chapter reveals that in many cases it is possible to observe aspects of internalization through students' developing oral and written discourse practices over time and through the reflections they share as learners. In the case of the teachers who participated in my study, at least two forms of evidence suggest that internalization was indeed taking place: teachers' movement toward the development of a personal voice and teachers' movement beyond the ideas and activities presented to them in class to generate plans of action that reflect their developing commitment. In his final reflection, Edward voiced his commitment to "make a difference and help pupils like me to break the shackles imposed on me by a conservative African society." Based on this commitment, he generated a plan of action: "I plan to use all that I have learned to stand-up for my beliefs, as they can only help the pupils and help me to not get stuck in a traditional classroom rut." Dingani voiced the belief that literacy must "equip people with all the skills that will enable them to cope with the challenges of the 21st century." He then proposed that as a literate individual "one must be in a position to exploit all possible means to interpret or approach any given task." Throughout the course, Dingani articulated a plan of action that entailed offering people "something that was worthwhile" in the form of skills that can be applied beyond the school walls and a perspective that was "not self-centered." As discussed in his prior reflection, Dingani's plan involved promoting a vision of literacy as "something that needs to be shared to help others develop personally, socially, intellectually, and otherwise." Mieko spoke of her own "developing voice" and her emerging "rejection of direct instruction." Even as she wrote this reflection, her plans of action were evolving. She had "a good feeling for what does not work" and definite thoughts about the direction she must proceed in to encourage her students to think. Although she was not exactly sure how she would apply all that she had learned, she knew she planned to include a lot of group work and group problem-solving sessions in her classroom. Mieko was encouraged by reminders from her fellow classmates that "learning is an ongoing process" for teachers and learners of all ages. And finally, Jim's own voice emerged as he said, "Of course, I'd like to think that I am not educating students to merely function at the lower socio-economic levels of our society. That is why probably the most significant insight which I have gained about literacy in this course is the idea that a certain style of teaching can give 'voice to the voiceless.'" He then began to articulate a plan of action in which he intended to help students gain "the confidence and skills to verbalize their own thoughts and beliefs." This was a critical plan because it was based on his realization "that a people without voice is the definition of oppression." Jim voiced his very strong belief that "[P]erhaps the most valuable thing we can do as new educators is make a career long commitment to developing skills which encourage our students to express inner-voice. If disadvantaged sectors of our society are to raise themselves from situations of economic, social, and educational poverty, they will require a voice."

Conclusions

The work of Malcolm (1991) on literacy socialization within a multicultural society confirms the need for language teacher education that is socially relevant in light of the current emphasis on diversity and multiculturalism in education (see Moll, this volume, for an argument supporting inservice efforts dedicated to understanding diversity). Malcolm further discusses the ramifications of perspectives and policies that promote multiculturalism versus assimilation, nationalism, or instrumentalism. To address such issues, teacher educators must take into account teachers' own experiences, their self-perceptions of being literate, and their perceptions concerning how literacy can be used to enhance teaching and learning.

I have presented the voices of these teachers to illustrate some of the internal activity that went on as their literacy perspectives developed. I have shared their thoughts as interdependent forces that came into play in the process of learning, a process that occurs only within social contexts. I have also presented a model of what the process of internalization looked like for the preservice and practicing teachers who participated in the activities presented in my course to facilitate change in perspectives on literacy. Drawing on a Vygotskian sociocultural perspective of internalization, this research considers how particular experiences within a social context can encourage thoughtful reflection and growth over time that alters teachers' developing philosophies concerning literacy and its strategic use when teaching poor, urban, and diverse students. This information can be helpful in designing teacher education programs that prepare excellent teachers for all student populations.

There is a growing need to prepare teachers specifically for work in poor and urban areas (see Lee, this volume). In most teacher education programs, however, there are few theories on how to accomplish this goal. Through this research, I have demonstrated how interpersonal encounters with advanced theory and principles that undergrid effective literacy teaching can lead to intrapersonal transformations in how prospective teachers envision, plan, and perhaps eventually implement teaching strategies for students from diverse cultural and linguistic backgrounds. I have also provided a model to illustrate the process. Continued work in this area can provide improved conceptualizations that will enable teacher educators, administrators, and policy makers to better understand and subsequently support the development of urban teachers. This support will be based on a better understanding of the processes by which preservice and practicing teachers can use theory and reflective experiences to transform their notions about using literacy to better serve diverse types of students in poor and urban settings.

References

Bakhtin, M. M. (1981). *The dialogic imagination: Four essays by M. M. Bakhtin.* (M. Holquist, Ed.; C. Emerson & M. Holquist, Trans.). Austin: University of Texas Press.

Bakhtin, M. M. (1986). *Speech genres and other late essays* (C. Emerson & M. Holquist, Ed.; V. W. McGee, Trans.). Austin: University of Texas Press.

Ball, A. F. (1992). Cultural preference and the expository writing of African-American adolescents. *Written Communication, 9,* 501–532.

Ball, A. F. (1995a). Text design patterns in the writing of urban African-American students: Teaching to the strengths of students in multicultural settings. *Urban Education, 30,* 253–289.

Ball, A. F. (1995b). Community-based learning in urban settings as a model for educational reform. *Applied Behavioral Science Review, 3,* 127–146.

Ball, A. F. (1999). Evaluating the writing of culturally and linguistically diverse students – The case of the African American English speaker. In C. R. Cooper & L. Odell (Eds.), *Evaluating writing* (pp. 225–248). Urbana, IL: National Council of Teachers of English.

Banks, J. A. (1991). Multicultural literacy and curriculum reform. *Educational Horizons, 69,* 135–140.

Brodkey, L. (1994). Writing on the bias. *College English, 56,* 527–547.

Carnegie Council on Adolescent Development. (1989). *Turning point: Preparing American youth for the 21st century.* New York: Carnegie Corporation.

Clery, C., & Pikrone, G. A. (1991). *Reading autobiographies written by special admission college freshmen.* ERIC Document, microfiche no. ED341029.

254   *A. F. Ball*

Cummins, J. (1994). Knowledge, power, and identity in teaching English as a second language. In F. Genesee (Ed.), *Educating second language children: The whole child, the whole curriculum, the whole community* (pp. 33–58). New York: Cambridge University Press.

Darling-Hammond, L. (1986). A proposal for evaluation in the teaching profession. *Elementary School Journal, 86*, 531–551.

Evans, R. (1993). Learning "school literacy": The literate life histories of mainstream student readers and writers. *Discourse Processes, 16*, 317–340.

Florio-Ruane, S. (1994). The future teachers' autobiography club: Preparing educators to support literacy learning in culturally diverse classrooms. *English Education, 26*(1), 52–66.

Forman, E. A., & Cazden, C. B. (1985) Exploring Vygotskian perspectives in education: The cognitive value of peer interaction. In J. V. Wertsch (Ed.), *Culture, communication, and cognition: Vygotskian perspectives* (pp. 323–347). New York: Cambridge University Press.

Fosnot, C. T. (1996). *Constructivism: Theory, perspectives, and practice.* New York: Teachers College Press.

Foster, M. (1987). *It's cookin now: An ethnographic study of the teaching style of a successful Black teacher in a White community college.* Unpublished doctoral dissertation, Harvard University.

Fox, S. L. (1992). *Memories of play, dreams of success: Literacy autobiographies of 101 students.* ERIC Document, microfiche no. ED348681.

Freeman, D. (1992). To make the tacit explicit: Teacher education, emerging discourse, and conceptions of teaching. *Teaching and Teacher Education, 7*, 439–454.

Gee, J. P. (1989). What is literacy? *Journal of Education, 171*, 18–25.

Gomez, M. L. (1993). Prospective teachers' perspectives on teaching diverse children: A review with implications for teacher education and practice. *Journal of Negro Education, 62*, 459–474.

Grant, C. A., & Secada, W. G. (1990). Preparing teachers for diversity. In W. R. Houston (Ed.), *Handbook of research on teacher education* (pp. 403–422). New York: Macmillan.

Hartshorne, K. (1992). *Crisis and challenge: Black education 1910–1990.* Cape Town, South Africa: Oxford University Press.

Hudelson, S. (1994). Literacy development of second language children. In F. Genesee (Ed.), *Educating second language children: The whole child, the whole curriculum, the whole community* (pp. 129–158). New York: Cambridge University Press.

Knowles, J. G., & Cole, A. L. (1994). *Through preservice teachers' eyes: Exploring field experiences through narrative inquiry.* New York: Merrill (an imprint of Macmillan College Publishing Company).

Ladson-Billings, G. (1994). *The dreamkeepers: Successful teachers of African American children.* San Francisco: Jossey-Bass.

Leont'ev, A. N. (1981). The problem of activity in psychology. In J. Wertsch (Ed.), *The concept of activity in Soviet psychology* (pp. 37–71). Armonk, NY: M. E. Sharpe.

Malcolm, I. G. (1991). *Language teacher education for social cohesion.* ERIC Document, microfiche.

McElroy-Johnson, B. (1993). Teaching and practice: Giving voice to the voiceless. *Harvard Educational Review, 63*, 85–104.

Minami, M., & Ovando, C. J. (1995). Language issues in multicultural contexts. In J. A. Banks & C. A. M. Banks (Eds.), *Handbook of research on multicultural education* (pp. 427–444). Seattle: Macmillan.

Nieto, S. (1992). Linguistic diversity in multicultural classrooms. In S. Nieto (Ed.), *Affirming diversity: The sociopolitical context of multicultural education* (pp. 153–188). New York: Longman.

Orfield, G., & Reardon, S. F. (1993). Race, poverty and inequality. In G. Orfield, S. Schley, & S. Reardon (Eds.), *The growth of segregation in American schools* (pp. 17–32). Alexandria, VA: National School Boards Association.

Pang, V. O., & Sablan, V. (1995, April). *Teacher efficacy: Do teachers believe they can be effective with African American students?* Paper presented at the annual meeting of the American Educational Research Association, San Francisco.

Quality Education for Minority Project. (1990). *Education that works: An action plan for the education of minorities.* Cambridge, MA: MIT Press.

Ritchie, J. (1993). Turning telling into knowing: Teacher and student literacy stories. *Quarterly of the National Writing Project and the Center for the Study of Writing and Literacy, 15*(4), 10–16.

Rosenholtz, S. J. (1986). Career ladders and merit pay: Capricious fads or fundamental reforms? *Elementary School Journal, 86*, 513–529.

Soliday, M. (1994). Translating self and difference through literacy narratives. *College English, 56*, 511–526.

Tardif, T. (1991, December). *Language acquisition and language socialization.* Paper presented at the Annual Convention of Experimental and General Psychology, Jinan, China.

Thomas, L. (1996). Knowledge as power: Frederick Douglass and the roots of literacy. *Teachers & Writers, 27*(3), 9–11.

Vygotsky, L. S. (1978). *Mind in society: The development of higher psychological processes* (M. Cole, V. John-Steiner, S. Scribner, & E. Souberman, Eds.). Cambridge, MA: Harvard University Press.

Vygotsky, L. S. (1981). The genesis of higher mental functions. In J. V. Wertsch (Ed.), *The concept of activity in Soviet psychology* (pp. 144–188). Armonk, NY: M. E. Sharpe.

Walker, W. (1981). Native American writing systems. In C. A. Ferguson & S. B. Heath (Eds.), *Language in the U.S.A.* (pp. 145–174). New York: Cambridge University Press.

Wertsch, J. V. (Ed.). (1985). *Culture, communication, and cognition: Vygotskian perspectives.* New York: Cambridge University Press.

Wertsch, J. V. (1991). *Voices of the mind: A sociocultural approach to mediated action.* Cambridge, MA: Harvard University Press.

Wertsch, J. V., & Stone, C. A. (1985). The concept of internalization in Vygotsky's account of the genesis of higher mental functions. In J. V. Wertsch (Ed.), *Culture, communication, and cognition: Vygotskian perspectives* (pp. 162–182). New York: Cambridge University Press.

11   Inspired by Vygotsky

Ethnographic Experiments in Education

Luis C. Moll

For the past 15 years or so, in collaboration with several colleagues, I have been conducting studies in education that have as a central theme the cultural mediation of educational practice. The theme of cultural mediation has been inspired, as should be obvious, by Vygotsky's writings. I should mention, however, that our research approach, what I call *ethnographic experiments* (presented later), is patterned after the work of Michael Cole, especially his combination of ethnographic observations and experimental tasks in studies of the situational variability of thinking (e.g., Cole, 1996; see also Laboratory of Comparative Human Cognition, 1983, 1986; Scribner & Cole, 1981). In this chapter I want to explain why we think the cultural mediation of educational practice is such a significant topic, not only for elaborating alternative pedagogical practices but also for understanding and formulating a contemporary cultural-historical or Vygotskian theoretical approach. I will concentrate on one particular aspect: the understanding of culture within a contemporary cultural-historical or Vygotskian approach. I propose moving away from normative notions of culture, prominent still in the field of education and psychology, toward more dynamic, processual, or practice interpretations, what we call in Spanish *la cultura vivida*, how people live culturally.

Let me start, however, by summarizing what I think is the essence of Vygotsky. Scribner (1990a) has written about it in the following way:

Vygotsky's special genius was in grasping the significance of the social in things as well as people. The world in which we live is humanized, full of material and symbolic objects (signs, knowledge systems) that are culturally constructed, historical in origin and social in content. Since all human actions, including acts of thought, involve the *mediation* of such objects ("tools and signs") they are, on this score alone, social in essence. This is the case whether acts are initiated by single agents or a collective and whether they are performed individually or with others. (p. 92; emphasis added)

As Scribner emphasizes, the concept of mediation is central to Vygotsky's theorizing, perhaps its defining characteristic. To put it simply, human beings interact with their worlds primarily through mediational means; and these mediational means, the use of cultural artifacts, tools, and symbols, including language, play crucial roles in the formation of human intellectual capacities (see Scribner, 1990b; Wells, this volume).

Although Vygotsky emphasized semiotic mediation through tools and symbols – artifacts – his concept of mediation was constantly evolving, including considerations of broader social and cultural processes, as found in activity systems such as schools or, as in our work, in other "built environments" such as households. Stetsenko (1993), for example, has pointed out that what was important for Vygotsky was not only culture in its broadest forms, as that variable across which nations and populations differ, but also culture as the social "milieu in which the life of the people is embedded," culture understood as an "accumulation of the social experiences of humanity in the concrete form of means and modes, schemes and patterns of human behaviour, cognition and communication" (p. 40). Culture, therefore, understood in its concrete forms, as practice, as a system of accumulated human social, material, and ideological experiences (Putney et al., this volume).

In our applied work in education, we have supplemented our understanding of culture and of mediation by turning to theory and methods borrowed from social and cultural anthropology. For present purposes, I want to mention how we are rethinking the normative notions of culture that, as mentioned, are quite prominent in education but perhaps becoming obsolete in anthropology (see, e.g., González, 1995; Ingold, 1993, 1994). We usually think of culture as neatly bounded traditions that help differentiate groups of people, as when we say "Mexicans do this; Anglos do that." These statements imply a concept of culture as well-integrated, cohesive entities whose values are shared by all members of a particular group; an example would be Ogbu's (1993) theory, in which minorities are differentiated neatly into voluntary and involuntary (caste-like) immigrant groups, each with its own predictable folk theory and values, socialization patterns, and academic outcomes.

In contrast, we are moving toward a more dynamic, processual notion: that cultural life consists of multiple voices, of unity as well as discord, including an imperfect sharing of knowledge; of intergenerational misunderstanding as well as common understandings; of developing both adaptive and maladaptive practices while discarding others – in short, of human actions that are always creative in the face of changing circumstances. That is, *we seek culture in human practices*, situated in people's involvement with (and creation of) the multiple contexts that constitute their social worlds. As Ingold (1994) has put it, it might be more realistic to say "that people *live culturally* rather than they *live in cultures*" (p. 330; emphases in original).

Accordingly, we must study those lived experiences dynamically, so we have also borrowed our methods of study from anthropology, primarily qualitative methods that place us *in situ*, engaged with instead of detached from human beings and sociocultural dynamics, whether in classrooms, households, or other settings. This engagement is particularly true, as I describe later, in our collaborations with teachers. Therefore, from our sociocultural perspective, schools and households, as well as all other built environments, no matter how natural they may seem, are always artificial settings in the sense that they are, as Scribner (1990a) put it, culturally constructed, historical in origin, and social in content.

Ethnographic Experiments

Our most recent educational research has as a central activity the ethnographic analysis of households by classroom teachers. The purpose is for teachers to develop both theory and methods to identify and document the cultural resources found in the immediate school community, as represented by the children's households, that could be used for teaching (see Dyson, Gutiérrez & Stone, Lee, Putney et al., this volume). This applied project, then, contains two elements that are essential within a Vygotskian theoretical formulation: It seeks to understand culture as practice and to harness its resources to transform social (educational) reality.

We have concentrated, among other things, on documenting the productive activities of the household, including its involvement in the formal and informal economies, as well as its domestic labor, and the maintenance of social networks that tie the household to other households (and other settings) in the community and facilitate the exchange of resources (especially labor and knowledge). What we refer to as *funds of knowledge* are the bodies of knowledge that underlie household activities. Their documentation makes obvious the wealth of resources available within any single household or its social network, resources that may not be obvious to teachers or students. A sample is included in Table 11.1 (adapted from Moll, 1994).

One important consequence of the work is to shape the definition or social representations of community that teachers and researchers have

Table 11.1. *Examples of household funds of knowledge*

AGRICULTURE	ECONOMICS
Ranching and farming	Renting and selling
Gardening	Loans
Hunting, tracking, dressing	Accounting
Animal husbandry	Trade/finance
CONSTRUCTION	REPAIR
Labor laws/construction codes	Automobiles
Carpentry	Airplanes
Roofing	Household appliances
Masonry	Tractors
Design and architecture	Fences
ARTS	RELIGION
Music	Bible studies
Lyrics	Catechism
Painting	Sunday school
Sculpture	Liturgy

by reorienting theoretically and empirically through active engagement with the school's surroundings. In so doing, we are hoping that teachers attend not to perceived *limitations*, as is emphasized in the educational literature, but to the *possibilities* represented in the funds of knowledge found in the community. We claim that these funds of knowledge eventually become, through the teachers' own research efforts, the accepted cognitive background of teachers' community perceptions, where competence is simply and routinely assumed and expected (Lee, this volume).

But there are other important consequences to engaging families in order to learn from them. One is the creation of new social relationships between teachers and families. It has been our experience that in conducting conversations and interviews with household members, teachers develop the beginnings of a trusting relationship with the family, what we refer to as *confianza*. This is the sort of relationship with a *persona de respeto* that allows for easy exchange of information and trust, the expectation that this information will be used to help the students or the teachers in some way. These are the types of relations that create what Coleman (1988) referred to as *social capital*, those collective actions and resources that support schooling.

We have also documented instructional innovations as teachers attempt to move from the documentation of household activities and knowledge to instructional practice. These teaching experiments, based on the ethnographic understandings of households, have taken several forms, most commonly the development of theme units or cycles that involve the students actively in their own learning and that build directly on knowledge or practices found in local homes (see, e.g., González, et al., 1995; Moll, Amanti, Neff, & González, 1992; Moll, González, & Civil, 1995). To be sure, I am making this move from field research to practice seem unproblematic; it is far from that. We are asking teachers to use information or insights gained in one social context, households, to modify the sorts of activities and routines available within classrooms, to create a completely different social context with its own dynamics and constraints, and for these new activities and routines to make a difference in students' learning. This sort of transfer and transformation, from household knowledge to classroom practice, is a very challenging theoretical and practical task. We usually suggest that teachers create *household analogs*, where the goal is not to replicate the household in the classroom, but to re-create strategically those aspects of household life (e.g., social networks, funds of knowledge) that may lead to productive academic activities within the classroom. The task, in a sense, is to bring together both contexts and their resources through the academic work of the students. Needless to say, this is no easy task, although we have documented several cases of success (Moll et al., 1995).

To facilitate this process, we have developed study groups to meet with teachers and jointly attempt to figure out what we are doing. We refer to these study groups as *mediating structures*; these are settings purposely created to help us think together about households and classrooms and give intellectual direction to the work. Practically every teacher we have worked with has mentioned that these study groups were central to his or her development during the course of the study. They were also central to the development and definition of the relationship between researchers and teachers, a constant issue in our work (see Wells, this volume). In brief, the study group is the place where we try to make sense of what we are doing in the households, what we should attempt to do in the classrooms, and whether our work is worthwhile for the teachers and students. These settings became new *cultural devices* for thinking and learning, to use Vygotskian terms. The formation of new settings of all kinds, with a potential impact on learning and development, is a constant cultural activity (Sarason, 1972). However, it is a phenomenon that we rarely study in terms of its psychological implications for its participants or for others influenced by their social relations.

It is these mediated moves from household ethnography to study group to classroom practice (and sometimes back), and the theoretical implications of these moves, that I refer to as *ethnographic experiments*.

Three Mediating Concepts

"Theories," Scribner (1990a) wrote, "including sociohistorical and activity theory which seek to understand social practice, do not contain within themselves 'prescriptions' for changing these practices" (p. 91). She continued as follows:

What a theory "means" for practice cannot be read off from texts of the theory. Notions such as "translating theory into practice" or "applying theory to practice" are based on the contrary assumption. They imply, erroneously in my opinion, that grand theoretical propositions can be directly converted into methods for transforming established practices in the contingent here-and-now. (p. 91)

Scribner believed that we had to do considerable theorizing, including developing model systems, both in the sense of an analytic-investigative device and as visions of desired states of affairs, to mediate between an interpretation of theory and the development of practice. It is in this spirit that I offer these three notions, which have influenced our work, as somewhat rough mediating concepts between Vygotskian theory and practice. Each of these notions will now be briefly reviewed.

Re-presenting Culture

We started with the idea that the normative concept of culture, as usually thought about in education and psychology, is not only of little utility for teaching but may have little to do with the everyday lives of children or their families. Here is how we expressed it in an earlier article (Moll et al., 1992):

Our concept of funds of knowledge is innovative, we believe, in its special relevance to teaching, and contrasts with the more general term "culture," or with the concept of a "culture-sensitive curriculum," and the latter's reliance on folkloric displays, such as storytelling, arts, crafts, and dance performance. Although the term "funds of knowledge" is not meant to replace the anthropological concept of culture, it is more precise for our purposes because of its emphasis on strategic knowledge and related activities essential in household functioning, development, and well-being. It is the specific funds of knowledge pertaining to the social, economic, and productive activities of people in a local region, not "culture" in its broader anthropological sense, that we seek to incorporate strategically into classrooms. (p. 139)

The emphasis, then, is on connecting our ideas of culture with empirically grounded knowledge, not handed to the teachers by academics but developed firsthand through their own inquiry about a group of people and their lived experiences, about what their everyday life is all about (cf. Ingold, 1994, p. xvii). We have learned that normative models capture little of the diversity of life, especially how families strategize to deal with the concrete and changing conditions they face.

We have also started to address an essential area using a Vygotskian approach: how humans organize life for new generations to rediscover and appropriate mediating artifacts – how, through the process of enculturation, older persons arrange for younger ones to acquire the accumulated artifacts of the group or culture. Here the notion of the *zone of proximal development* comes to mind, understood not only in terms of more capable others assisting less capable ones but, more broadly, in terms of how human beings use social processes and cultural resources of all kinds in helping children to construct their futures (Scribner, 1990a, p. 92). Accordingly, we have extended our household inquiry to address issues of the children's social worlds (see Andrade, 1994; Andrade & Moll, 1993). We have come to realize, at least within our specific sociohistorical circumstances, that the cultural life of children rarely replicates or reproduces that of their parents, for they are themselves fully creative beings (Andrade, 1994). Therefore, documenting the life experiences of adults and their funds of knowledge may tell us a lot about household dynamics and social contexts that may include children, but that in many circumstances it may not necessarily tell us anything important about children. Children create their own social worlds with their own material and ideational artifacts that are distinct yet mediate (and are mediated by) their relationships with adults and adult institutions, most prominently schools (Dyson, this volume). Teachers and researchers, as adults, are usually privy to a small slice of children's social worlds, but our pedagogy and our psychology must make contact with it if it is to acquire any lasting significance.

It is also noteworthy that, ethnographically speaking, we could say, the most important artifact created by children is themselves, the formation of their personalities. This is an aspect that some Cuban psychologists are currently developing (e.g., González Rey, 1995), the subject of the individual within a cultural-historical approach, influenced not only by Vygotsky, but especially by the ideas of Bozhovich (1976), Vygotsky's student, emphasizing the affective components of the active, thinking individual. Consider the following passage:

The relation between the cognitive and affective domains constitutes a central issue in understanding personality development, something which, in its permanent form, becomes formed in the synthesis of both processes, and also in the activation of one or the other through the intentionality of the thinking individual.... The latter is characterized as an essential aspect of the individual's active nature, as a thinking and conscious entity, therefore the individual or psychological subject will reflect and construct information through those areas or problems in which the more intense experiences (and also via the very intensity of those life experiences) will be mediated by thinking. However, his thinking activity in these cases will never be neutral, objective, in the sense of following the logic of the object at the subjective level; it will be thought organized over a system of senses, where the world and its subjective configuration will form a complex unit through which the thinking individual will act. (González Rey, 1995, pp. 55–56)*

It is common in qualitative inquiry to consider the researcher as the most important research instrument. This notion is similar to what I am trying to convey: that the most important cultural mediating creation in the child's development is the child – not the child's personality created in the abstract, but rather one that is inseparable from the social and cultural context of its development and the social relations that constitute these contexts. To develop further this theoretical insight, we need to consider culture not as a normative model but as practice, as activity, and not with all of its practice equally significant for the mediation of the individual's development but with a significance mediated by the individual's actions and thinking as well.

Re-presenting Community

A central aspect of our work is how we have come to redefine the concept of school community. Most of us hold what we can term an imagined notion of community (a term borrowed from Anderson, 1991). That is, we imagine, based on what we have heard or read, or based on personal experiences, a general normative notion of what a school's community may be like. It is imagined because it is not based or grounded in personal relationships, or on intimate knowledge about community members, most of whom we will never meet or know anything about. This kind of projection is probably true of all communities: They are imagined,

---

* This passage was translated by Pedro Portes.

we create or fabricate them, and we attribute imagined characteristics to them or let others define them for us. So when poor people are defined as the underclass, that usually influences how we imagine other poor communities or large portions of them, even if the concept of *underclass* is formally and theoretically inapplicable to a particular school community (Vélez-Ibáñez, 1993).

Many of the teachers we have worked with do not live or at least initially know anybody within the communities in which they teach. These teachers may be the most susceptible to limiting, normative notions about the working-class school's community, such as "They don't care about education in this community." Even teachers who do know the community, such as former residents, may define the community based solely on their memories or experiences, or as these have been redefined for them through their many years of schooling, with little insight into how to define the community educationally or pedagogically in terms that help their teaching.

That all communities will remain to a large extent imagined communities is probably unavoidable, but educators can help to deliberately, intentionally determine how they are defined or imagined. A lot of our work has concentrated on creating a different imagined community of the working-class neighborhoods in which the schools are located. We (teachers and researchers) have set out to develop intentional educational communities: a new imagined school or classroom community, grounded in social relationships with families, and intentionally defined by the knowledge and resources found in local households. Note that the school's community remains to a large extent an imagined one, for teachers cannot conduct household analysis with all their students, but deliberate inquiry into funds of knowledge helps define how a community is imagined and how it will be imagined in the future, with new generations of students.

Developing imagined communities, as a theoretical concept, forms part of what del Río and Alvarez (1994) call *los mitos que nos hacen vivir* (the myths that help us live). These myths, including our imagined communities, are important cultural artifacts because they are created by human beings and are used to mediate in important ways our actions and thinking.

Re-inventing Literacy Practices

One of the most provocative ideas to come out of sociocultural psychology is that of *distributed cognition*. Stated briefly, thinking is usually considered as taking place solely within the mind of the individual, what some psychologists refer to as *solo* or *in-the-head cognition*. Schools accept this notion, testing students to determine their presumed individual ability or intelligence, which is considered an immutable, fixed attribute or trait of the individual. Conclusions about children's abilities (reflected in the tests) are reached readily by many educators, and these conclusions are usually connected to the children's social class background, if we are to judge by the sort of schooling different social class groups receive. To put it bluntly, rich children are considered smart, or at least given the benefit of the doubt; poor children are considered stupid unless they can prove otherwise, and the nature of the instruction they receive reflects these assumptions.

Conceptions of human activity, including intellectual activity, as culturally mediated bring about a radically different idea about thinking. The key point is that human beings and their social and cultural worlds are inseparable; they are embedded in each other. Thus, human thinking is not reducible to individual properties or traits. Instead, it is always mediated, distributed among persons, artifacts, activities, and settings. People think in conjunction with the artifacts of the culture, including, most prominently, the verbal and written interactions with other human beings.

Accordingly, we have paid considerable attention, as have many others, to understanding the intellectual consequences of literacy, especially in relation to how literacy forms part of particular social groups and their cultural practices (Scribner & Cole, 1981). We have attempted to extend the gist of this cultural practice analysis to an understanding of biliteracy: how children become simultaneously literate in two language systems and the consequences of such actions. This biliteracy is a phenomenon, we should point out, that takes place in the United States primarily, if not exclusively, among working-class language minority students. Concurrent biliteracy (not solely bilingualism) is not required or expected of any other children in this country, with the possible exception of Cuban children in Florida (see García & Otheguy, 1985). And when it occurs, it is constrained by the limiting characteristics of working-class schooling, which reduce to basic elementary functions what the children can do with literacy. Furthermore, Latino children in the United States are schooled within a neocolonial education system that always seeks to fulfill other people's purposes and interests, not theirs; but that is a topic beyond the scope of the present chapter (see Moll, 1992).

Given our theoretical orientation, we have come to emphasize two aspects of this biliteracy. One is how it can help students and teachers access the cultural resources of the immediate community, thus enhancing the personal significance of the academic work. The second is how it can amplify access to knowledge through literature in Spanish and English, supplementing and expanding the resources available within the immediate community; for example, we could transport ourselves to Latin America and the Spanish-speaking world, even as we remain within relatively insular communities in this country, and the children can always find themselves in the text or at least in some texts, an experience that is now rare for Latino students in the United States. In this respect, the intellectual power of biliteracy resides in being able to read a text in one language and discuss it in the other. In this sense, biliteracy mediates and amplifies the cultural experiences of learners in ways not possible in one language alone (Moll & Dworin, 1996).

A third aspect, most relevant for present purposes, that we have now begun to explore is how literacy (especially writing) may serve its most important mediating intellectual function, not by facilitating communication or obtaining information but by helping students create new worlds; these are imagined but profoundly social and cultural worlds. I like the way Smith (1983) explains this power of writing:

The power of writing is not initially lost upon many children. A child writes "The dog died" is astounded at what has been accomplished. The child has put a dog into the world that did not exist before – created a world that would not otherwise have existed – and then has killed the dog. None of this can be done in any other way. And if the boy is contrite, a stroke of the pen is all that is required to bring the dog to life, something else again that would be difficult to accomplish in any other way. (p. 129)

This is an aspect of literacy, the creation of imaginary worlds, that has been mostly neglected in the sociohistorical psychological literature, but it has enormous implications for the development of thinking (but see John-Steiner & Meehan, this volume; Vigotskii, 1982). Also consider that for biliterate children, these worlds may reflect their bilingual communities in that they can be created in Spanish, in English, or in both; and we could argue, these worlds in Spanish bring with them cultural experiences that can never be fully replicated in the other language, rather, they are unique. Biliteracy, then, mediates the intellect not only by providing access to the real world of the community and by offering the expanded possibilities of broader or different experiences of the literate world, but also by creating new worlds that have not existed before. In this sense, thinking is distributed by the child creating diverse worlds that become part of the varied cultural contexts within which thinking develops.

Conclusion

From a sociocultural perspective, living together in a society is the foundation for all mental and personal development. We have turned to cultural-historical psychology and anthropological theory and methods to obtain a more dynamic understanding of living together, especially those cultural practices that constitute settings that are called classrooms and households, within specific social and historical conditions. We argue that these settings (classrooms and households) can be conceptualized as culturally mediated activity systems. Theoretically, we have moved away from notions of culture that appeal to observable surface markers of folklore and assume that all members of a particular group share a normative, bounded, and integrated view of their own culture. This concept of culture emphasizes how shared norms shape individual behavior; the assumption is of a monolithic, harmonious vision of culture with standardized rules for behaving. Instead, we argue for a focus on the processes of how people live culturally. There is no clearly defined culture out there in the world; these static notions do not take into account the everyday lived experiences of children and their families, which may or may not coincide with normative cultural behavior.

Studying the diversity of life in households, drawing on multiple cultural systems and using these systems as strategic resources, has provided us with an alternative view of how we can come to mediate educational practices in schools in ways that connect to lived and imagined experiences while addressing the academic development of the students.

References

Anderson, B. (1991). *Imagined communities* (Rev. ed.). New York: Verso.

Andrade, R. A. C. (1994). *Children's constructive social worlds: Existential lives in the balance*. Unpublished doctoral dissertation, University of Arizona.

Andrade, R. A. C., & Moll, L. C. (1993). The social worlds of children: An emic view. *Journal of the Society for Accelerative Learning and Teaching, 18*(1, 2), 81–125.

Bozhovich, L. I. (1976). *La personalidad y su formación en la edad infantil*. La Habana, Cuba: Editorial Pueblo y Educación.

Cole, M. (1996). *Cultural psychology*. Cambridge, MA: Harvard University Press.

Coleman, J. (1988). Social capital in the creation of human capital. *American Journal of Sociology Supplement, 94*, 95–120.

del Río, P., & Alvarez, A. (1994). Introducción: La educación como construcción cultural en un mundo cambiante. In A. Alvarez & P. del Río (Eds.), *Education as cultural construction* (pp. 230–251). Madrid: Fundación Infancia y Aprendizaje.

García, O., & Otheguy, R. (1985). The masters of survival send their children to school: Bilingual education in the ethnic schools of Miami. *Bilingual Review/Revista Bilingüe, 12*(1, 2), 3–19.

González, N. (1995). Processual approaches to multicultural education. *Journal of Applied Behavioral Sciences, 31*(2), 234–244.

González, N., Moll, L. C., Floyd-Tenery, M., Rivera, A., Rendón, P., Gonzales, R., & Amanti, C. (1995). Funds of knowledge for teaching in Latino households. *Urban Education, 29*(4), 443–470.

González Rey, F. (1995). *Communicación. personalidad y desarollo.* La Habana: Editorial Pueblo y Educación.

Ingold, T. (1993). A social anthropological view. *Behavioral and Brain Sciences, 16,* 84–85.

Ingold, T. (1994). Introduction to culture. In T. Ingold (Ed.), *Companion encyclopedia of anthropology: Humanity, culture and social life* (pp. 329–349). London: Routledge.

Laboratory of Comparative Human Cognition. (1983). Culture and cognitive development. In W. Kessen (Ed.), *Mussen's handbook of child psychology* (Vol. 1, pp. 295–355). New York: Wiley.

Laboratory of Comparative Human Cognition. (1986). Contributions of cross-cultural research to educational practice. *American Psychologist, 41,* 1049–1058.

Moll, L. C. (1992). Bilingual classroom studies and community analysis: Some recent trends. *Educational Researcher, 21*(3), 20–24.

Moll, L. C., Amanti, C., Neff, D., & González, N. (1992). Funds of knowledge for teaching: Using a qualitative approach to connect homes and classrooms. *Theory into Practice, 31,* 132–141.

Moll, L. C., & Dworin, J. (1996). Biliteracy in classrooms: Social dynamics and cultural possibilities. In D. Hicks (Ed.), *Child discourse and social learning* (pp. 221–246). New York: Cambridge University Press.

Moll, L. C., González, N., & Civil, M. (Eds.). (1995). *Funds of knowledge for teaching.* Final report submitted to the National Center for Research on Cultural Diversity and Second Language Learning. Tucson, AZ: College of Education and Bureau of Applied Research in Anthropology, University of Arizona.

Ogbu, J. (1993). Variability in minority school performance: A problem in search of an explanation. In E. Jacob & C. Jordan (Eds.), *Minority education: Anthropological perspectives* (pp. 83–111). Norwood, NJ: Ablex.

Sarason, S. (1972). *The creation of settings and the future societies.* San Francisco: Jossey-Bass.

Scribner, S. (1990a). Reflections on a model. *The Quarterly Newsletter of the Laboratory of Comparative Human Cognition, 12,* 90–94.

Scribner, S. (1990b). A sociocultural approach to the study of mind. In C. Greenberg & E. Tobach (Eds.), *Theories of the evolution of knowing* (pp. 107–120). Hillsdale, NJ: Erlbaum.

Scribner, S., & Cole, M. (1981). *The psychology of literacy.* Cambridge, MA: Harvard University Press.

Smith, F. (1983). A metaphor for literacy: Creating words or shunting information. In F. Smith, *Essays into literacy* (pp. 117–134). Exeter, NH: Heinemann.

Stetsenko, A. (1993). Vygotsky: Reflections on the reception and further development of his thought. *Multidisciplinary Newsletter for Activity Theory, 13/14,* 38–45.

Vélez-Ibáñez, C. (1993). U.S. Mexicans in the borderlands: Being poor without the underclass. In J. Moore & R. Pinderhughes (Eds.), *In the barrios: Latinos and the underclass debate* (pp. 195–220). New York: Russell Sage Foundation.

Vigotskii, L. S. (1982). *La imaginación y el arte en la infancia.* Madrid: Akal.

Author Index

Abrahams, R. D., 196, 197, 198, *223*
Akhutina, T. V., 75, *79*
Alton-Lee, A., 114, *122*
Alvarez, A., 1, *15*, 264, *267*
Alvarez, H., 152, *163*
Amabile, T. M., 31, *46*
Amanti, C., 260, *268*
Anderson, B., 263, *267*
Andrade, R. A. C., 262, *267*
Andrews, M., 196, *223*
Applebee, A. N., 77, *83*, 165, *187*
Arns, F. J., 195, *225*
Atkinson, J. M., 158, *162*
Atwell, N., 182, *187*

Bailey, F. M., 92, *122*
Baker, H., 212, *223*
Bakhtin, M. M., 2, 6, 13, *13*, 72, *82*, 91, 92, 93, 105, *122*, 129, *148*, 152, *162*, 216, *223*, 226, 230, 232, 245, 248, *253*
Ball, A. F., 226, *253*
Bambara, T. C., 214, 216, *223*
Banks, J. A., 227, *253*
Baquedano-Lopez, P., 152, 157, *163*
Baugh, J., 207, *223*
Belenky, M. F., 45, *46*
Bennett, W. J., 167, *187*
Bentley, A., 151, *162*
Bereiter, C., 63, 67, 71, 72, 74, 77, *82*, *84*
Bettencourt, A., 64, *82*
Birdwhistell, R., 90, *122*
Block, G., 43, *46*
Bloome, D., 92, 94, *122*
Bogdan, D., 167, *187*

Booth, W. C., 136, *148*, 201, 202, 205, 211, *223*
Bourdieu, P., 142, *148*, 152, 156, *162*
Bozhovich, L. I., 262, *267*
Bradley, M., 110, *124*
Brilliant-Mills, H., 95, *122*
Brodkey, L., 237, *253*
Brown, A. L., 63, *82*
Brown, N., 63, *84*
Brown, R., 196, 198, *223*
Brown, R. G., 165, 167, *188*
Bruner, J. S., 2, 3, 4, *13*, 51, 53, *82*, 128, *148*
Buckingham, D., 130, *148*

Campione, J. C., 63, *82*
Carnegie Council on Adolescent Development, 228, *253*
Carr, W., 66, *83*
Carraher, D. W., 196, *225*
Cassirer, E., 24, *29*
Cazden, C. B., 6, *13*, 151, *162*, 165, *188*, 195, *223*, 232, *254*
Ceci, S. J., 2, *14*
Chaiklin, S., 1, *14*
Chang-Wells, G. L., 81, *83*, 86, 121, *125*
Christie, F., 110, *122*
Civil, M., 260, *268*
Clery, C., 237, *253*
Clinchy, B. M., 45, *46*
Cobb, P., 33, 34, *46*
Cochran, J., 86, *122*
Cohen, D. K., 63, *83*

269

Subject Index

abstraction
  in concept formation, 20–22
  designative approach, 27
  and imagination, creativity role, 44
  and signifying, 214–215
  in word meaning development, 21
activity system, 151–153
activity theory
  cultural applications, 1
  education application, 58–62
  and human development, 54–56
  identity formation link, 55
  and literacy learning, 158–160
activity unit, 195
aesthetic knowing, 68
affiliation
  in children's stories, 131, 134
  definition, 145
African American Vernacular English (AAVE), 11, 191–223
  definition, 197–198
  irony link, 199–211
  processing strategies, 207–211
  as rhetorical stance, 197
  semiotic mediation function of, 194
  signifying genre, 191–223
anthropological methods, 258; *see also* ethnographic approach
apprenticeship
  and childhood, 144
  and contemporary educational practices, 59–60
  in creative process, 36–40
  and internalization, 35
  in literacy learning, 160

appropriation
  in creativity, 36–40, 42–44
  in human development, 55
  and internalization, 33
  and mentoring, 2
  teacher development, 248
artifacts
  educational application, 60–61
  in human development, 54
  mediating role of, 2, 257, 262–263
attitudes toward literacy, 237–238
autobiographical writing, *see* narrative generation

backward mapping, 96
Bakhtin, M. M.
  dialogic perspective, classroom community, 129
  meaning making writings, 232–233
biliteracy, 265–266
body biography, 10
  definition, 167
  Hamlet interpretation, 170, 174–187
  methodology, 186–187

capacity, underachieving students, 212
child prodigies, 39–40
classroom collective
  development, 104–110
  ethnographic approach to, 90–122
  identity formation link, 120
  in learning process, 87–89
  small group interactions, 111–115

274